SPIRIT SPEAKS

SPIRIT SPEAKS

Death & Rebirth on the Wings of Angels

by
KATHLEEN K'EARNS

SUNSTONE PRESS

SANTA FE

Cover design by Sue Denniston
Cover art by Kathleen K'earns
Triad picture by Julie Butler

Sunstone books may be purchased for educational, business, or sales promotional use. For information please write: Special Markets Department, Sunstone Press, P.O. Box 2321, Santa Fe, New Mexico 87504-2321.

Library of Congress Cataloging-in-Publication Data:

K'earns, Kathleen.
    Spirit speaks: death & rebirth on the wings of angels / by Kathleen K'earns.
    p. cm.
ISBN: 0-86534-390-X
1. K'earns, Kathleen. 2. Sprittual biography—United States. I. Title.
BL73.K43 A3 2004
133.9'092—dc22

                         2003026820

Published in SUNSTONE PRESS
POST OFFICE BOX 2321
SANTA FE, NM 87504-2321 / USA
(505) 988-4418 / *ORDERS ONLY* (800) 243-5644
FAX (505) 988-1025
WWW.SUNSTONEPRESS.COM

This book is dedicated to my Mother.

I graciously appreciate all of the gifts she's given me:
the love, tenderness, and devotion.
My heart overflows with intense gratitude for the way
she is serving me now in Spirit.
Not only is this book about her death and my resultant
Spiritual transformation,
It would never be possible without her continued guidance and support.

"I'm listening, Mom . . . I love how your Spirit Speaks to mine!"

≈≈≈

"Thank you, honey . . . I'm so proud of you . . . and I love you, always!"

I gratefully acknowledge the following Earth-Angels
who assisted me from their Spiritual hearts
during the journey of creating this book:

Andrea Berg
Julie Butler
Della Louise Carter
Penny Coleman
Sonia Choquette
Sue Denniston
Jane Francis
Patricia Henderson
Sara Hosier
Theresa McGoff
Samone Michaels
Liz Myers
Rose Osorio
Richard Robinson
Barb Sanderson
Doreen Virtue
Vicki White

I would also like to express my deepest gratitude for the many other individuals
who "believed in me" and held my dreams in High regard. These include many
of the people mentioned in my book, especially my family, as well as others
from the various Spiritual circles throughout which I have been weaving. You
know who you are and how much you mean to me! Yes, you too Oren!

CONTENTS

PROLOGUE

THE SOUNDS OF INTENSE YELLING
AND FEELINGS OF REJECTION
ECHO INSIDE THE AMNIOTIC FLUID
FLOWING IN THROUGH WAVES OF FEAR
AND ETCHING, SCRATCH BY SCRATCH,
THE VERY BASIC FIBER OF MY BEING
RECORDING NEGATIVITY AND PAIN
AT THE CELLULAR LEVEL OF MY BODY
AND I REMAIN, A GROWING FETUS
FORMING MY FIRST GUT INSTINCTS
AND IMPRESSIONS OF THIS HUMAN FORM
THAT I AM TO BECOME IN THIS LIFETIME
~welcome back to the world~

From the moment my Soul entered my body, I began feeling "unwanted" waves of energy penetrating through me. Then I felt this during a reoccurring nightmare, and later as an ingrained pattern spiraling with repetition throughout my life. I have always felt "different"—not quite belonging and not easy to accept or like. I never understood why nor thought I knew how to change it. . . .

The recent death of my Mother has given wings to my heart! I rose from the ashes of my past, miraculously with a new will to live, while learning to listen to how Spirit Speaks. I am now beginning to rejoice in my uniqueness, revel in my creativity, and radiate my sensitivity within a whole new perspective.

I still do not know why God exists, and our Souls with their thirst for growth, yet I do know I am supposed to be here or I would not be alive. As well I know I have much more to experience and a Voice needing to be heard.

I believe my words expressed in this book will in some way touch the core of your Being; and in so doing, I hope that we may tune in to that invisible cord Divinely connecting us. And maybe we will finally realize, we are not so different after all!

<u>Note</u>:

The use of *italicized print* in this book indicates the critical voices of ego—
Those judgmental, negative thoughts and expressions, which elicit fear, worry
and discord; Whereas, the use of **bold print** demonstrates the Voice of Intuition—
Those Divine messages of Higher-Self guidance, and "love-notes" sent from
God, the Creator and Great Spirit.

FOREWORD

Prepare to cry, laugh, cringe, and relate as you fly with the author, Kathleen K'earns on the wings of angels. Who are the angels, you might ask? They are Kathleen, her mother, her dogs, and the angels that you normally think of—the ones that the five major world religions have in common. The latter type of angels is present in our every day activities from soft whispers in our ears to assisting us during the most traumatic of circumstances. They frequently guide us, whether we are aware of them or not. Often they make themselves known with a soft brush on the cheek . . . changes in the pressure of a room . . . a gentle breeze out of nowhere . . . a pleasant fragrance hanging in the air . . . or unexplained beautiful glowing white light orbs. Have you experienced them?

Yet angels are only one aspect of Kathleen's spiritual growth experiences. Ms. K'earns moves you to love her, dislike her, and admire her! Her honesty in describing her journey is important to enable you to see that there is a natural course many of us take to grow spiritually. As you read, it is possible to grow with her and notice many experiences that you may have already encountered. This is a strong message in itself. Imagine that one woman can write about her experiences involving the death of a parent and describing her growing spiritual awareness and have it touch every reader in some way. Now that's a powerful message!

What does that tell me? It suggests that there are inherent messages regarding the death of a loved one with the outcome being spiritual growth. Granted, we are on different levels of spiritual awareness at different times, and that is appropriate. For this reason, the manner in which "Spirit Speaks, Death and Rebirth on the Wings of Angels" is written does a wonderful job of opening a view into each level of understanding regarding the death process, self-discovery, trials and tribulations about various discriminations, and ultimately the only true voice we should listen to—Spirit.

Kathleen's account of her mother's death is emotionally infused as expected. My own father's death ten years ago brought about a strong sense in me to seek answers, and eventually led to a tremendous awakening to who I am as a Spiritual Being. While reading "Spirit Speaks . . ." I was able to easily re-live those moments with my dad. Some were happy moments. Some made me cry. And all of these "moments" are honored and appropriate, as yours will be. Further, the various levels of understanding about spirituality that are interwoven throughout the book allowed me to see myself in Kathleen. The author reflects her truth so that you can see yours.

In addition, her approach to revealing the ego voice is so honest that at times you are embarrassed for her and with her because you know that you, too, have that haunting voice. Ego, as demonstrated in this story is an essential element to our physical existence. However, the more we become aware of our Spirit Voice, and the fact that it comes from us, is evidence of us moving toward the raising of global consciousness. The expression, "Me, Myself and I" also suggests that all there is to life is within us.

So acknowledge that ego voice! Thank it for all of its hard work over the years. Then, listen to your own Spirit speak. Allow it to be your guide. And when you do, you will become your own angel.

Love & Light,

Samone Michaels
Author, *Messages Within* and
Speak Your Truth, See No...Hear No...Speak No UFOs!

ALONE ON BEACH

1

"On My Way"

~present day~
February—March 2001

I can't believe my Charley is dying. To look at her you would think she was a beautiful, normal six-year-old golden retriever. Every day she still has moments of playing with her stuffed animals ("babies"), begging for treats at the usual times, chasing around my other little guy (a mixed breed named Jamey), and of course following me around. That's her purpose here in my life: to constantly be at my side. Although at times in my floundering past, I would lash my irritability and impatience onto her. It seemed no matter what I did, she was always under foot, practically tripping me! She was also high-strung and used to jump all over people. When I was in a hyperactive mind-set, striving to accomplish many tasks around the house yet deep inside upset with various aspects of my life, she would often get in my way or not do what I commanded. It would instantly cause me stress. Since I express anger through voice and movement, I often yelled any frustrations with myself at her. *"Damn-it Charley, get out of my way! Go on! Get out of here! Go lie down! God, you drive me crazy sometimes!" I would burst out without thinking.*

Bless her heart—hanging in here with me these past six years! Actually, both my dogs have played a very important part of my healing and growing. In fact, this has been during the same time frame as my Spiritual awakening, although I have been slowly gathering the information my whole life. It was in 1995 when I seriously began studying and applying metaphysics and Spiritual laws; this also was the year of their puppy-hood. We've been through two relationships, three residencies, and a three-month excursion to Illinois to help my Mom "pass-over." They are my support.

For the last three years, it's been just these canine-Angels and me in my wonderful home, which I "manifested" and fixed-up. These two loving, good-to-the-bone, furry animals have cuddled me through many downs, plus provided me with endless hours of joy in watching them live and play. Charley especially, has been both **an amazing mirror for me, and a great teacher.** And now in light of the fact that she is dying of kidney failure, **she is a living miracle.** She's had deformed kidneys her whole life, yet I didn't awake to this fact until six months ago when she collapsed on me. I thought she was dead. I carried her limp body (80 pounds) to my car, and took her to the emergency clinic. I actually suspect she died and came back to life when I was carrying her. Many extensive tests later, they still are not sure why she passed out, perhaps holding her bowels/ bladder too long. However, because of this blessing in disguise, her ultrasound and fluid tests showed only 25% kidney function. A human would be dead, or on dialysis. Yet she showed no extreme toxicity in her system.

I am immensely grateful for her miraculous life. She has such a strong will to live, and intense love for Jamey and I, that her body has learned other ways to compensate for her kidneys. For example, she has always drunken an enormous amount of water, and panted almost constantly. I assumed this was just her nature, however it has been her way of flushing and sweating the toxic wastes which her kidneys would usually process. I feel blessed to have time now to practice always loving her, softly and gently, making up for the times I couldn't. I feel honored to be chosen to receive this gift, and to have the knowledge now to specially feed her for her condition. I know that if she had just died, *I'd have added much more guilt to that bag of crap with which I beat myself.* **Instead, I believe her Spirit is giving me an opportunity to heal, and to see more clearly into those patterns in my life that are not working for my Higher Good.**

I know I have been a very good mom, too. Some would say ridiculously so; "Hey, Kath, they're just dogs!" Regardless, I now have the chance to practice being a more awakened "Light-worker." I am learning to **tune in and feel energy, then move that energy as intuitively guided.** For instance, Charley's hip areas and forehead get very hot several times a day and I believe that this is pain needing to be released. So, I put my left hand over these hot spots, close my eyes and connect with Spirit, concentrating on my intention to lovingly help heal her. I then see the pain move up my left arm. I can actually feel this as a quick tingly tension, and I will frequently pull my arm away to shake it out. After several times of doing this, it really seems to remove the heat and I know she feels better. It's definitely another way of visualizing that toxins are being removed from her body. Additionally I place my right hand over her and send her waves of love from my heart. I use this particular "handy" approach knowing the philosophy that the left side of our bodies is "feminine-receiving," and the right side is "masculine-giving." Therefore, my left hand easily absorbs energy and the right allows it to be released. This is an example of "hands-on healing."

My inner guidance teaches me how not to absorb this energy. It also reminds me to always affirm that everything is perfect and healthy in Spirit, and love is all that matters. Plus, I receive messages saying, "Everything that is created and manifested, is actually illusory." So, the biggest lesson I'm learning lately is that of reflection—and in more ways than one! **Everything in my life mirrors my illusive side, my Being. All that I visually see around me is the result of my Soul growth issues, or those lessons to be learned, plus my expectations.** Whatever I may feel is happening to me in my life, is really the way I interpret the events, and what I need to pay attention to. I am just now, at this time in my life, committing to doing God's will in an ever-more awakening state. I am constantly affirming to follow my heart, do that which brings me joy, and help others in the process.

This month truly marks the beginning of my freedom. Here I am, almost forty years old, newly unemployed by choice to explore my creative talents and passions, and totally on my own with limited responsibility (i.e. no children). **I feel newly open to Divine guidance to direct my life—trusting . . . believing the Universe will provide . . . knowing I'm "on my way."** To learn all this has certainly come with a price, and its value is reflected in my work. The steps that led me to this place were extremely difficult, and not all of these concepts were easy for me to incorporate into my life as will be evident as my story unfolds.

Over the last several years, I had plenty of time alone to reflect on my life and face the shadows. I found myself moving away from people, fading from all past friends in varying degrees, and being as introverted as my personality could possibly be. After a lifetime of being socially active, both personally and professionally, *I suddenly felt unable to relate to other adult human beings most of the time. Inside I desperately yearned for more Spiritually minded, understanding friends with whom I could relate—people who had become honest enough with themselves to let me be honest about who I was . . . and it was all okay! However, everywhere I seemed to look, nobody's energy mixed very well with mine. In fact, many people were down right verbally and emotionally abusive to me.* Internally, my ego would question, *"What could I have possibly done to deserve this? I am not like that to others so why am I seeing this disrespect? What do I need to do to release, to change, or to stop this pattern?"* It frequently *felt like God would not clearly answer me.*

Talk about reflections. Wow! It is very difficult to get away from those mirrors. It's like being in a not-so-fun fun house: running around in a maze trying to find the right exit; searching for a clearer image; praying for a beautiful, joyous, glowing-with-love reflection. *"After all,"* I'd tell myself, *"I don't deserve these distorted images! I'm really trying here. I'm on my way, somewhere, if I could just figure out which turn to take. At least I keep moving. But, I can't deal with all that I see around me. It just doesn't make sense!"* That feeling of being trapped yet moving—like a rat on a spinning wheel—is extremely discomforting. And to think I allowed myself to feel this way for the last decade of my life, during the bulk of my "professional" experiences. The lies I told myself, the concepts I reluctantly adopted, the tricks I played to keep learning the same lessons over and over again disguised under a myriad of packages, all are amazing to consider now. Yet I am grateful for the added intensity this build-up produced. It seems that **the more you have to go through, the more positive energy you can then potentially have towards creating a work from your heart that has an exponential healing factor.**

Take my Charley for example, here she is with future days lessening and reminding me even more of the stages of dying and grief. I must have faith that her dying is emphasizing just how important it is for me to better understand "passing-over." The timing can seem unjust when you consider that my Mother died just five months ago—she was an integral force in my life and I deeply miss her . . . Now, it could appear that I'm losing major support systems in my life. I could really fall apart. Yet, **I'm clearly seeing that my faith is being challenged in a non-threatening way, as my inner strength and Spiritual sensitivity are ever growing. My Guardian Angels are helping me to see only God as my support system in life, and all else is falling into place.** I know that living with Charley through this time is adding even more passion to my creative endeavors. I no longer wish to get stuck in patterns of self-reproach and verbal abuse, like some of what she used to mirror. Rather, I have an opportunity both to practice being more loving, which she now reflects, plus process death and dying in creative, artistic ways. Even after only one month away from "Corporate America," I can feel my life moving and shifting in many exciting ways. *Of course fears and worries creep in,* but I'm learning to catch negative ego thoughts quicker and cancel them by **affirming my dreams and my pure potential**.

Many great teachers have touched my path to enlightenment, whether through one-on-one contact, workshops, healing circles, books or audio programs. A main principle they have all emphasized, one which is finally sinking in to my head, is the power of our mental body. The potential our words have, and the impact our thoughts are capable of creating are significant. This is so crucial for me to get. I half-heartedly began doing intermittent affirmations years ago, operating under the philosophy "act as if until you are," assuming I had nothing to lose, and figuring I should practice what I preach. I have always worked with children and helped them to think about their self-talk, what messages they routinely tell themselves, and how to change that. However, I couldn't see just how out of sync I was with controlling my own mind chatter.

My head—my thinking and my ego—has been and is the biggest enemy I'll ever fight. I know this sounds strong, but I didn't realize just how common my negative, critical, self-defeating thought patterns were. A lifetime of deep-seated messages had been so automatic. It was often difficult to decipher everyday interactions because my ego tried to play tricks on me to keep me safe in what I "knew." In other words, when something happened in my life that I didn't expect or understand, *my thoughts interpreted the situation through old familiar paths— usually negatively, and always concluding there* was *something wrong with me. Then, a defensive voice that I misinterpreted as my self-worth, would always take over in my head, and also make everyone else involved wrong. This interpretation would quickly trigger feelings of hurt, and the perpetrators would go in the bag of "all who have done me wrong."* Another voice of the ego would mislead me by saying, *"Hey, I'm doing my best here, or trying my hardest and being so nice that others just don't get it!" This thinking got to the point where I started believing that no one else could really understand me. "After all, if they did, they'd see how good I really am and would treat me with more respect, damn-it!"* I know that this way of processing the world was modeled and taught to me and did seem to be a fairly common phenomena; however, this system is ineffective and detrimental to one's health!

What a cyclone! Again, I was walking around in the house of mirrors. Hmmm, which reflection do you get honest with first? One of my teachers,

Mackenzie Jordan "Bodhi," used to say to me, "Can you see the truth in it? What is God trying to tell you?" This would drive me crazy because I just wanted to discuss how inappropriate other people were being towards me. I also wanted to learn how to change these uncomfortable communication patterns. I thought I was being Spiritual about it because I would pray for these people, as well as try to give them what I thought they needed. I thought I was being mature and realistic about it, because I would think it out trying to take everything into account; I take pride in knowing I can usually see the bigger picture. I thought I was showing good commitment and/or work ethic by staying part of the "team" and/or friendship. I thought I had to keep going through whatever was happening because God wanted me to learn something. Voices told me: *stay and fight for what you believe in, keep trying different ways to handle things, strive to affect change—it will stop once you get it.* (Whew! I thought too much!) So, whenever I suddenly found myself with someone who was mad at me over something, and communicating to me in a rude or abusive manner—I would go into that defensive, protective, wounded mode. I would tell myself that I just needed to see their Spirit, pray for them, and try again to explain what happened or how they misinterpreted it. *"No, that's not what I meant! I was just . . ."* I frequently found myself pleading.

It took nearly forty years of this patterning until I awoke and decided, **"I'm not going to take it anymore!"** How simple, yet seemingly difficult because of habits, it is just to say that and walk away! **"Yes!" my inner Spirit shouted, "What power, in a positive light! What a demonstration of self-respect on the way to self-love!"** Where would I be right now if I had always just politely removed myself anytime I felt uncomfortable in a situation? Not the uncomfortable feeling that is sometimes a precursor to learning and growth, *but that feeling of being out-of-place, not welcomed, or not worthy—to the point where defenses naturally pop up to try to belong, to be involved, and to have value.* I'm learning that it should not be this way. **I have a rightful place where I am always welcomed because I am always worthy. The new process for our loving selves is to tune in to that intuition that tells you when it's time to move on to keep finding those "rightful places."**

My first real influential teacher of metaphysics with whom I studied for several years, Jane Fendelman, used the humorous analogy: "Do you have to get hit on the head with a two-by-four in order to learn your lessons?!" She opened my eyes to this concept, and would always pray, "Please, God, let me learn my lessons in a gentle way. Let me be conscious enough to feel your prompts for me and act accordingly so I will no longer need to experience major dramas as a wakeup call to move on!" I've learned that **God guides us through our intuition**. If a channel is unclear, messages of where to be in life aren't readily heard. If the Universe wants you to be somewhere else, messages will be repeatedly sent to you, ever-increasing in intensity, until you hear them. You can either wait for life to force you, which causes restriction and pain, or you can choose to listen to the "gentle prodding" and move more joyously with the flow. So often, when a tragedy or life-changing event happens, people often say that there were signs leading up to it, or "if I would only have listened to my gut sooner . . . "

For the last seven years, my job was working with the Agency for Incarcerated Juveniles running therapeutic recreation programs for teens: six years as Recreation/PE Director at a boys institution, then one year as Grant Coordinator for girls in various stages of release from "Corrections." Although for the last 25 years I have always led various programs for children of all ages and abilities in many diverse settings, this last job was quite unique! It involved working for a large institution, with adjudicated youth, and with staff who were "not on the same page" as I. This environment, albeit a valuable learning experience, was overcast with so many shadows, that it made shining my light very difficult. Nonetheless, it was due to the very nature of this job that I told myself, *"I need to be one of the few and do God's work here."* The sacrifice I allowed this to play-out on my Spirit was very damaging.

Over the duration of my time in "juvie jail," the number of staff I supervised plus various supervisory staff who were being *totally inappropriate, verbally abusive, and/or downright disrespectful towards me was astonishing. Not only were some of the youth difficult, but sadly many adults were too. Every time I thought that I had to compromise my values to follow proper protocol, every time I allowed someone to talk rudely to me, every time I felt I had to look the other way to keep peace,* **the Universe was prompting me to move.** I'm still recovering from the "2x4 abrasions." I know now that during these difficult communication patterns, **I was not aligned with my Truth and therefore off my Divine path,** no matter how much my ego told me, *"This is God's will for you: learn to get along with others."* I also heard Spirit softly add, **"You need to practice better self-love and forgiveness."** I was just *desperate* then to figure out what to do to make us a quality team to better help the kids. This was by far one of my hardest learning experiences. In retrospect, I am now grateful to use this build-up of passion to help heal these institutions and our troubled teens in another capacity, one that is directed by Spirit at a much higher level.

~~~

It is very cloudy outside this morning, totally overcast, which is pretty unusual for Phoenix. I'm so used to saying good morning to the sun that it seems hard to feel sunny on the inside when the clouds are like a blanket of gray. Sadness rolls over my Being as it dawns on me that this is the five-month anniversary of my Mother's death. Not wanting to dwell on the clouds just yet, I try to stay present and do my little gratitude prayers. I love to wakeup by sitting outside in my wonderful backyard watching my dogs do their usual routines while I sip on my coffee. Finally, after three years the grass has spread beautifully, the lawn is level and my amateur landscaping job makes me smile with admiration. My precious baby sage, pink toddler rose, and teenage bougainvillea bushes absolutely flourish in their spaces in the yard. This is my dogs' yard, of course, and they love it almost as much as I enjoy watching them sniff out every inch and run around talking to any noise they hear.

Even though I am so proud of this house, what it represents to me and how much I love living in it, I know that after twelve years of living here in this Valley it is time to move. **I am tuning in to that God-pull in my life and it is exciting.** I do not know where I'll eventually live, except that it will be wherever I need to be next **to follow God's will for me in my life**. It is a blessing to feel totally open to going with the flow. There are no ties—family, friends or otherwise—to pull me towards any particular area. If I feel any inclination, I know Hawaii—where I just happen to be going for the first time this July— keeps coming up in my life. **Ahhh, the ocean is calling me again!** San Diego was my last trip almost two years ago. **It's amazing the peace and clarity I can feel quietly sitting on the beach watching the waves. I can close my eyes anytime and be with those rhythmic waves—breathing and pulsing with the world. . . .**

"Are you thirsty, Honey?" I ask, waking from my daydream as Charley lays her head heavily on my thigh. I chuckle as her eyes dance around sending many messages—all about love. It is so strange how only a year ago her nose turned from black to a fleshy pink color, and the golden hair on her face keeps turning whiter every day reminding me she's getting older fast. After petting her soft blonde forehead and kissing her third eye, I let her back inside. I don't want her to see the tears welling in my eyes again. God, I love her so much! I sigh knowing I have to coax her now to drink more water. I can tell she moves much slower, sleeps longer and deeper, and is not as excited with mealtimes, but mimics the habitual behaviors that Jamey exhibits. She also has started to regularly lay her head in my lap, sometimes to the point of trying to nuzzle into me like she wishes she were a lapdog. Knowing her days are few, I am grateful that I can spend more time with her. Plus, I need to let her outside as often as possible because retaining urine can do additional damage to the kidneys. Thus, the timing with me quitting my job was perfect, in more ways than one!

It is an awesome feeling to finally be free like this. I'm free to do what I want, and to engage in activities that bring me joy. I'm free to see what really stands in the way of my True Self. I'm free to follow my heart, my gut, and my intuitions. In fact, **my Guardian Angels are now helping me tune in to that voice of my Soul, and I am learning to listen.** *I know I won't always be in this special situation. Actually, I need to make sure I'm taking the steps to eventually bring in more income.* However, having an opportunity like this also challenges me to **toss worry and fear to the side and practice the Spiritual principles,** which I've been so adamantly studying all these years. I know that someday I'll look back on this period of limited responsibility, good health, youthfulness, and having everything I need—as a great time in my life, so I don't want to ruin it with negative emotions. Instead, **I'm concentrating on the goal and the gold!**

This is also the time for me to release the past. I'm saying goodbye to all the people of my past: Mom in physical form, family as I knew it, old friends who have faded away, as well as ex-coworkers. **I feel gratitude for all that I've learned from them,** as well as *sadness for not relating to many of them anymore,* yet I know **it's time to move on. The biggest part of letting go has involved forgiveness.** Especially because of my Soul growth issues concerning abandonment, I tended to play a victim and repeatedly attracted people to reinforce these false self-concepts. Now, I am finally seeing that I not only need to forgive all those who have *"done me wrong"* but also **recognize each as a shadow of my own personality actually needing to be owned and embraced.** One of my favorite authors/speakers, "Angel Lady" Doreen Virtue, teaches a wonderful forgiveness technique, which I recently followed for my life. Through all these various exercises, I truly let go a lifetime of victimization and hurt, and thus am now free to more clearly follow my heart.

I further prepared for my newfound freedom through goal development and daily structures. The first major project on which I embarked was creating a special office for me in my home—one that truly reflects my talents and inspires my creativity. So, a month ago I bought a big L-shaped desk with a few additional amenities that I felt would work best for me. I then spent two weeks in semi-hard labor, by myself, putting together all the pieces of furniture. As well I was purging and reorganizing already existing "stuff" I had stored in two of my spare bedrooms. The new office now has a relevant structure, which provides a feeling of great comfort and motivation to best suit my personality and passions. I incorporated many principles of Feng Shui (ancient Chinese system of placement and mapping to promote good energy flow). I even arranged the desk so that I'm facing the doorway (opposite of how L-desks are usually placed) because this position allows for more abundance of prosperity to come forward in life.

A stunning eye-grabber as you walk into the room is the huge tapestry on the wall of an Angel carrying a young child and a bouquet of flowers. This was a tear-inducing Christmas gift from my younger bother's family after Mom died. According to a Feng Shui map, it is hanging in the "helpful people" and "creativity" sections of the room, which is very appropriate symbolically. Plus, it is in a direct-line with my forward vision, behind the angled computer screen. I also arranged items that honor me in a display format in the areas of the room known to represent "reputation" and "prosperity." These included cards, gifts, and awards I received from both children and adults over my lifetime that touch my heart, as well as samples of art and creative projects I completed. Beyond this corner, I'm constructing family picture collages to hang in the "family" section, as well as a huge mural of magazine pictures and words that represent my heart's desires, in the "career" area. In between, I built shelves on which to place all of my favorite books and resources, not-surprisingly-so, in the area known for "knowledge and self-cultivation."

Another important step for my "new life," I made an outline of a schedule for myself, and thus far I've been good at following it. First, for exercise, I started swimming laps again. This is something I've done off and on my whole life. Growing up, I was on the swim team for years. I have such fond memories of my Mom driving me all over Illinois to attend swim meets. I hold close to my heart those feelings of such special times with just her and me—staying in hotels and listening to classical music all night. I'll never forget the time I stayed in a suite that child actress, Alyssa Jones ("Buffy" from "Family Affair") was staying in the next night. I left her a note in the room and she mailed me a letter in reply. What a high moment for this nine-year-old! Nonetheless, I am a swimmer at heart. I feel at home in the water, any water. In fact, lately it seems like I can't get enough of it. I crave long hot baths almost daily and feel addicted to sitting in the steam room to meditate before and after I swim laps. I also enjoy full-moon women's sweat lodges—a healing ceremony I've sporadically attended since 1995. Something crucial in my life right now, I guess water just helps center and balance my fiery Sagittarian personality.

Furthermore, I started taking yoga classes that I enjoy, and will soon take an art/painting class as well as do more hiking. Nature is calling me back home. I miss the years of outdoor recreation activities I used to do both personally and for youth groups. This past decade slowly removed me from Mother Earth and it is time to reconnect. This is the same with friends. I need to be open to receive them, and get out more to meet them. I promised myself that if anyone invites me to anything lately, I will say "yes" (unless my gut really says otherwise) because I need people in my life with whom to grow and to share. *I'm tired of feeling so different and difficult to tolerate and understand.* My ego has separated me from love long enough! **I deserve to feel connected to loving, joyful friends**. Baby steps . . . oh, how awkward they feel as the unhealthy ego dies and self-confidence builds! My goal is to schedule at least one social event a week, even if just a luncheon. I never thought this would be something I'd have to work at.

The bulk of my new schedule is the time I need to develop all my various creative talents. This includes my Spiritual development, writing many books, exploring arts and crafts, playing guitar, singing and dancing, and finishing all the home improvement projects that I began. Although I've remodeled much of this house, I still have many finishing touches to do, as well as a couple of larger non-crucial jobs. It would feel satisfying to complete these. Therefore, this is the time, especially if I want to sell this house in a year or so. This is also the time to start researching potential graduate schools where I could get a doctorate, as well as exploring the job market across the country just to see where my life may lead. Further, I am praying to team up with other like-minded adults who have a similar vision: **to heal children and the institutions that serve them by bringing Spirit, creativity and femininity into balance.** Wow, what an exciting endeavor! I want to keep all options open as I dance with the Divine energy in my new life.

~~~

"Hey! This is Kath's ego sneaking in here while she's off meditating or whatever it is she thinks she's doing. I'm pretty pissed right now, you know? She pushes me aside and won't listen to me as much anymore—she just doesn't realize how much she needs me. I have been the one protecting her all these years. I have kept her strong in so many situations where she would have broken apart and gotten slammed even worse by other people! She is very sensitive, you know, more so than other people and as soon as they sense it, they're ready to strike at her!

"All those times I've pointed out to her about the hurtful comments another has said when she never used to notice, and now she thinks she'd rather listen to an obscure Spiritual message instead of my well-developed obvious voice?! Plus, I always helped her to see that those people were not good for her, and got her to stay away from them. You wouldn't believe how many 'so-called' friends never really liked her because she talks too much and has so much energy it drives others crazy. And the older she gets, the less people want to be around that kind of personality. Most adults get uncomfortable with someone who talks from the heart and shares emotions. And I keep telling her no one will be her friend if she keeps showing those emotions because they eventually turn people off. Every single friend, even the most Spiritual, and even her counselors, always end up telling her what I've been saying for years: 'quit bouncing off the walls, taking things personally, showing emotions, talking so much, and asking for what you need' . . . because nobody else cares. She has seen this over and over and over again in her life, especially in the last few years. Who has stood by her during the process of her mother's death? Who was there for her at work after seven years? Who has never criticized her especially after she shared a heart-felt concern? Ok, maybe one or two. But, when the majority of the people—with whom she feels close, initiates contact, and opens up to—do not return phone calls, or stand her up, or cut her down—she needs to stop being so trusting and honest. No matter how evolved they may seem, I'm telling you they will eventually make a negative or sarcastic comment about her personality or life choices.

"Of course, I always encourage her to find new friends because the people she keeps gravitating towards have no concept just how special she is. All that stuff about love, peace, and honoring your True Self is fine sometimes with the right people, but it doesn't work here in the real world! And until she finds the right people she better be careful about being so candid and open because she

will get torn apart worse than ever before! This techno-mechanical-structured-masculine-materialistic-world has little room for an Angelic-creative-sensitive-emotional-high-energetic-type of person like her. I wish she'd listen to me. She just never learns."

~~~

Oh, God . . . Oh, God! Help me please! I miss my Mom so much! I can hardly do anything around my house without seeing things that remind me of her. It's amazing how some moments it hits me like a tidal wave across my chest, sending chills of anguish throughout my body. Other times I don't even think about it, or feel much. A little while ago, all I did was pull a big slotted spoon out of the kitchen drawer to stir my linguini, and suddenly my singing along to an upbeat song in the background stopped. I cried out, and lovingly inspected the spoon. A flash of memories of growing up with this whole set of utensils came flooding into my head. I could hear Mom say with her intense conviction, "They sure don't make things like they used to!" I could actually see her hands carefully washing this particular spoon over the years alone in her condo. There seemed to be a little crud stuck along a seam where the handle connected to the stem, and I wondered what she might have last cooked with this spoon. I found myself, like so often before, holding onto the counter and gasping a few times as the tears poured forth. Yet, as quickly as this wave overtook me, I regained composure and continued cooking my lunch, still in awe at the process of grief. . . .

"What little boy? What do you want?" I ask my dog, Jamey, as he comes running into my office, then pounces back towards the door. "You know it's not time for a T-R-E-A-T," I spell-out carefully so he really doesn't know what I am saying, "and you just went outside!" He comes bounding back in carefully and playfully, whining the way he always talks. As I reach down, he rolls on his back, exposing the chest and belly he loves to have rubbed. "Mmmm, mmmm, mmm," he moans as I gently scratch all the right spots. "Ahhh, ahhh, ahh," I nasally grumble back, mimicking his groans. He's the most talkative dog I've ever known. Suddenly, he jumps up and half-howls, "Aruu ruu ruu ru ru," as I talk more and more excitedly to him. "Ok! I hear you! I see you! You just want some attention, don't you, sweetheart? Hold on—momma's coming."

Of course, Charley has by now slumped off the couch, and after stretching she walks over to sniff at Jamey. As she slowly awakes, she begins to pounce a little and round up her "babies" to play. I laugh as I start to "gentle-house" with them, and we roll around on the floor for a few minutes. "Jamey, Jamey! Help me, Jamey," I squeak in my highest voice as I lie on my stomach with my arms over my head protecting me as Charley jumps all over and Jamey tries to lick my face.

I love these dogs so much. The amount of gratitude I have in my heart for my dogs and our home is indescribable. *I feel scared sometimes when I think of how Jamey will be when Charley dies.* They are one month apart in age and have always been together, minus a couple of vet visits. Their relationship is extremely close thus *I cannot help but feel sad*, however I do try not to dwell on it. Rather, **by trusting the process of my life, I continually reaffirm that it is in God's hands.**

Actually, when those moments of grief hit me concerning my Mom, and I simultaneously think about Charley leaving me, the emptiness gets overwhelming. That is why quite frequently I am on my knees praying for my Guardian Angels and Mom to help me trust "The Plan" and turn it over to God. I thank God continually for the opportunity to live even more appreciatively knowing of Charley's condition. And when I feel the loneliness of my current life situation envelop me, **I am Divinely reminded that at least I have this beautiful dog-Angel here right now helping to reinforce my new life direction of practicing positive self-talk, loving kindness and graciousness.** Perhaps once my new ways of thinking and being become more second nature, I will be more ready to deal with her loss.

At this point, however, the timing sure seems strange. After all, it was just a little over six-months ago when I learned Charley had kidney failure. This was at the same time when we were in Illinois so that I could act as my Mother's primary caregiver during the final stages of her cancerous death. That was definitely the life-altering trip of a lifetime; it was a miraculous Angel invasion of my body from which I will never, ever be the same. . . .

~~~~

Oh, In Those Arms Of My Angels

In the arms of my Angels,
Sent down from up above,
Cradled in a peaceful light,
Surrounded all with love.

In the arms of my Angels,
I'm reminded night and day,
The toughest lessons are the best,
For spiritual strength I pray.

In the arms of my Angels,
I feel safe to stand the pain,
For knowing as I work it through,
Strength of character I gain.

Oh, in those arms of my Angels,
My purpose in life becomes clearer,
And as I serve in peace and love,
With pride I smile in the mirror!

~~~~

2

"Angel Invasion"

~back in time~
August 2000

*S*uddenly, I sit straight up in bed, heart pounding wildly and totally covered in sweat. "Oh, dear God, not again!" I sob as I realize I had that same dream again. In fact, it seems like I have been having turbulent dreams all night. *Who needs a workout routine with so much activity during their sleep?* My head is pounding, and I ache all over. I know my sleep pattern has been disturbed since my Mother was diagnosed with cancer nine months ago. I cannot remember the last time I slept through the night. I decided a long time ago that rather than get angry about not sleeping, I would take advantage of the "awareness" time and play my self-help audiocassettes until I drifted back to sleep. However, tonight is different. What are they trying to tell me?

It feels so eerily real, like Mom is right in this room with me. Since I got home two days ago from my latest visit to see her, I have not been able to shake that last look she gave me. I see it all day long! And it reaches out and grabs me in my sleep. . . .

My sister-in-law, Diana, a sweet self-conscious brunette with "over-loaded-mom" arms, had arrived at my Mother's condo to take me to the airport. Being a full-time housewife and busy mother of my two nephews, she was now using Mom's car to run errands and help out when possible. Mom had not felt like driving much since her treatments began. She especially lost all desire to drive after her unfortunate food poisoning episode three months earlier, followed a month later by a hospitalization for lung fluid build-up. Sadly, this was the first time Mom was too weak to accompany me to the airport. Nonetheless, just like

30

the last four trips out since her diagnosis, I told myself I was at peace with her, knowing this may be the last. We tried to hug goodbye as usual, our eyes brimming with tears. "It's been so good to see you again, Kathleen. I just love having you here! Thank you so much for all your help. You spoiled me!" she said in her deeply emotional voice.

"I know, Mom," I replied in my predictable response format, which always made her laugh. "Don't worry—I'll be fine and will call you the minute I get home! I love you, too!" I sincerely finished as I tried to pull away from her embrace. Only this time, she clung to me longer than before which made it much harder to be strong. "Gotta get to the airport, Mom—I love you," I stated, trying to gently leave her presence. "I love you too, Honey! It's been wonderful being with you again," she pleaded as she watched me walk out the door, across her patio and disappear around the corner. Right as I was opening the door to the car, I heard, "Kathleen?" "Yeah, Mom?" I answered as I ran back towards her front door, only to find her walking out to the middle of the porch, trying to untangle and stretch her oxygen cord as far as she could from the stationary unit inside to her nose. What a heartbreaking sight: her heavy-fragile frame in those slippers and housecoat with both of her arms outstretched towards me. The morning sun caused her new curly gray hairs to shine, and she looked glassy-eyed and pale with that tube wrapped around her straining face. She was desperate to tell me one more time, "I love you so much! Thank you for everything!" She cried as I again hugged her. "Oh, I love you too," I heart-fully said. Then sensing her fear, I added, "It's ok, Mom. I'll call you soon."

Sure enough if she didn't call me back one last time, "Give your Mother another hug," before I finally left. However, it was that last glance back towards her, which will always haunt me. It was the first time I have ever seen that look in her eyes: a passionate goodbye stare that said she knew she would never see me again. It was a penetrating message deep to my core.

Here it is, not quite 48 hours later, and my head keeps playing that last scene over and over again. Only it's like a nightmare calling to me with those desperate, reaching arms—clinging and not letting go. **"Kathleen!"** I keep hearing as it echoes. "Stop!" I yell out into the dark as my dogs quizzically sniff at me. *"What do you want me to do? I've done all I can!"* I continue begging God, *"Help me, please—make it go away!"* Yet somehow deep down this vision makes me panic with the **determination not to let that be the last time we saw each other**. The more sure-of-it Mom's eyes looked, the more obsessed I became with

not letting this be true for her. I also just had a strange dream of needing to get away from all the stress at work I'd come back to. I had put the dogs in my car to go for a drive. Only, I drove and drove until I somehow discovered myself in Illinois again. I nervously had to call my bosses to say, "Uh, I won't be able to come to work today." This was not an easy feat even for a dream because of all the time I had already taken for trips. It was during this same time period that I had started working on a new grant project for my Agency. *My work hasn't quite been what I know I am capable of and I fear I am slowly looking like a failure, unable to fully concentrate on the tasks at hand.* Now, with all these dreams and repetitive visions, I am collapsing under the stress and lack of sleep.

  I believe Spirit is guiding me. "Go back to be with her," keeps echoing in my head. I just know by the tingling in my gut, she doesn't have much time left, and the pressure to be there for her is overwhelming. I never expected to feel this way. I hear my voice of intuition stronger than ever. Tears roll down my cheeks as I softly affirm, **"She really needs me although she would never ask, and I need to be there."** *"What a scary thought,"* I realize as a louder voice pipes in, *"How can I pull this off considering the project I'm coordinating? I promised my 'bosses' from day one that I wouldn't let her dying get in the way of the job."* As I stare into the shadows of my bedroom, Spirit speaks again to me. **"Swallow your pride. Go in there tomorrow and tell everyone that you need to be with her!"** Somehow, I have to trust **it will all work out**. I have to believe **it's for the Higher Good all the way around**. Even though giving up ownership of this project is ego and heartbreaking, **I know I must do this!** Even though saying goodbye to all the girls is difficult, and burdening my over-worked partner with my job responsibilities is humbling, **I still must go! At once it felt like an Angel invaded my being!** And as soon as I surrendered to those visions, **I felt a strange sense of peace amongst the turbulence.**

  I almost couldn't wait a couple more hours to call my little brother, Edward, back home to run the plan by him: "I'll drive to Illinois with my dogs to take care of Mom until she dies!" I wasn't sure how he'd respond, but I wanted to relieve him. He has been carrying the bulk of responsibility for her care for so long, and I just saw how the strain was affecting him and his family, especially since her diagnosis. Like me, he also has had difficulty sleeping; only he works 10-12 hour days supporting his wife Diana and their two children, thirteen-year-old Ken, and 14-month-old baby, James. He talks to Mom daily, stops by several times a week (lives two miles away), tries to take her to most doctor's appointments and buys all her drugs and groceries, besides being her handyman around the condo!

When he told me, "I gotta be honest, Kathleen. If you expect me to talk you out of it—I can't. This seems selfishly based, but it would relieve me more than you'll know, to have someone there taking care of her so I won't have to worry." Although he thought I was "jumping the gun" with Mom ("Is she really that close to death?"), he welcomed the idea if I could work it out with my job. And after her doctor called me back and told me it was time to consider more advanced care for her, we decided I would be her primary caregiver so we wouldn't have to hire a nurse or send her somewhere. The doctor's words of "there's not much time left now," and "she'll benefit greatly from this," kept echoing in my head and affirming my dream visions.

Suddenly, I was on a new mission. A whole new drive had kicked in and I had so much to do. First I told Angela, my feisty-hard-working-job partner, and she said, "Go, Kathleen, do what you need to do! We'll work it out somehow." Then I spoke with the personnel coordinator who advised me to use family leave time, something I hadn't known about before. In fact, upon approval I could use up to three months under the "Family Medical Leave Act" before they could terminate me, plus I still had six weeks of personal leave time left. Knowing this helped tremendously. I now had 6 -12 weeks to spend with Mom depending on her need.

My next task was advising the "bosses." For the past year I had four different bosses, down to three now because one *(who did not like me)* quit. Nobody in this agency had thus far provided the support both this project and I truly needed to be successful, nonetheless they depended on my commitment to get it done so they could be proud of it too, when convenient. *Oh, the politics that must be played when incompetence and complacency tend to run amuck!* Because this project involved coordinating activities with the U.S. Kids Clubs for girls about to be released from incarceration, I acted as the liaison between "Corrections" and the "Clubs." This resulted in my having so many "bosses," whom incidentally were either not in agreement on most issues or had no clue how to best implement things in regards to this project. Thus, I had been the brunt of constant fall-out no matter how I tried to change it. A hard load to carry, I knew this was part of the challenge I faced to make it work.

Nicolas, my first line supervisor and in charge of the institution where girls are housed sat expressionless as I explained the whole story: the last visit, the dreams, the difficulty coming to this decision, my ideas on how to get along without me for awhile. When I was done, I sat waiting for a response. Finally, as he stared at me, I prompted, "Well?" "Well, what?" he replied innocently. *I was surprised at his lack of compassion. Had he really been listening? Did I explain too much detail? Was he just looking through me?* "Will you support me in this? Will you approve the leave time?" I asked in disbelief. "Sure," he answered monotone as usual, "just give me the completed paperwork."

Next, I spoke to Louise, the Director's "right-hand-woman" who was assigned this project to oversee from "downtown" and who was responsible for promoting me into the position. Although she was supposed to stop giving me orders or sending me on "wild goose chases," she still had a habit of calling me to remind me she was in charge and had all the power. *A nice woman overall, she was sadly in a position for which she seemed incompetent, and her insecurity came out in very inappropriate ways, often directed at me. I was nervous about her throwing my promises back in my face,* but to my surprise she responded, "Go! Take care of your Mom. That's obviously more important here. Leave tomorrow! Why are you waiting three weeks?" Slightly flabbergasted, I replied, "Well, I was just out there last week and am so far behind in all my work. I need to finish my monthly report for July. I have classes to cover while Angela takes some time off. There's the graduation party for some of the girls in the community—I promised I'd attend. We have that important meeting next Friday with the Federal Grant Administrator, plus the open house we're planning. I can't leave all that work up to my coworkers!" "So, your Mom's back home dying and you're here wanting to finish up all these things. Only, there's always more. Where do you draw the line? It may be too late, you know? You only have one Mom. The job can wait!" She went on to tell me how she had the main responsibility with her father who died of cancer a few years earlier. **Suddenly a side of her I never knew touched my heart and I thanked God, all the more affirming my decision to go.**

Yet I still had so many things to do to prepare for the drive. I had to pack for my dogs and myself for up to three months, from 115-degree weather in Phoenix in August to possible snow in Illinois in November. As well I had to prepare my house for sitting empty so long without "looking vacant," and arrange for friends to periodically water plants and check on everything. I also had to tell my plans to one more important "boss," Leonard, who was an administrator for the Kids Clubs, and assigned to this project. I was also worried about his response.

Although he was the only one who seemed genuinely interested in this project and with whom I could relate philosophically, he was a task driver who did not want to hear of any problems or excuses, only products and progress. A few months ago he had accused me of being just another "complacent institutional employee" due to his lack of understanding of my Agency's slow pace and amount of archaic red tape through which one must wind. When most people who work for this Agency propose a deadline or date for anything, you can usually add on much more time for a myriad of reasons, sometimes up to a year. Understandably, Leonard expects it to be ready on time or even in advance.

As I walked into his office to meet with him, I said one last quick prayer for him to be in a good mood and for God to guide our words. "Sit down, Kathleen, how are you? Tell me about your trip. How's your Mother doing?" he sincerely asked with an empathetic look on his face. As usual I admired his well-groomed professional yet casual attire and fell in love with his beautiful turquoise matching jewelry. I felt myself relax into the chair as I sensed his openness and good space. "Fine, well, I mean, considering everything, ya know?" I stammered. "She's not doing very well. This trip I could really see the cancer and all she's been through taking its toll on her. It was hard, very hard, to see her with that oxygen tube in her nose—it's a constant reminder of just how much she's slipping," I explained as I tried to share my feelings with him, "and to see how weak and out of breath she's become . . ." "I know, my mother went through the exact same thing just two years ago," he sympathetically replied, "the tubes, meds, hair loss, personality change—it's hard!" "Really?" I asked, not knowing the details of his mother's death. "Did you take care of her in the end?" My mind started racing, realizing our common bond. "Yep, soon as I got the call I was out of here and on a plane to the East Coast to be with her during her last days. I was lucky to have that time, you know, not everyone does. That's why it's good you've been able to go back as often as you have."

As I listened to him share his personal story, **a tremendous wave of gratitude took over me. Again, I felt the presence of an Angel inside me and beside us**. It felt wonderful to have someone like this who understood. My mind suddenly went back and remembered that Leonard was actually the first person I told about my Mother's diagnosis. I really felt appreciation for this man, although my ego was reminding me, *"Don't to be too trusting—remember the time when he snapped at you."* I knew I shouldn't care, yet *I was worried about getting on his bad side; I heard how he talked about other people at times. However, there* *were so few people in my life lately who seemed to understand me,* I deeply appreciated the connection. *Plus, I was craving for him to be both a friend and a mentor to me. On the other hand, he was depending on me with this project and I didn't want to let him down.*

Once more, the surprising message I received was one of overwhelming support. In fact, he asked me so many questions about my family and our relationship dynamics, I felt like he really cared. The tears in his eyes off and on during the hour we talked so intimately showed me his deeply sensitive side. And when he said that he wished he could have had more time with his mother, I knew **I was doing the right thing**. I fought back the urge to cry as I realized we were sharing our hearts in a way that could bring us closer together. **I kept thanking God for the positive reinforcement to follow those dreams of guidance I had been receiving.** Then, after telling me how family has to come first, he assured me that the job would be waiting for me when I returned and not to worry. As we hugged goodbye, the last thing Leonard said to me was, "Just be sure to take care of Kathleen. Do what you need to do to get through this so you can come back to us healthy and productive!"

Two other people gave me deeply motivating messages, too, about the trip home. One, my therapist, tearfully said, "Kathleen, I would give anything to have up to three more months with my mother!" Also, a part-time co-worker in the Kids Club I was running said, "When I got the message my mom didn't have much time left, I scheduled a flight out a week later so as to finish up some business, only I arrived just moments after she passed—something I'll always regret," she mournfully expressed, then added, "So, go! As soon as possible!"

After I had made all the initial plans for a trip of this magnitude, it was time to tell Mom. I had to finalize the details regarding work, my house, items to pack, and the exact travel route. Like most Mothers, she would need to be reassured of everything before I could convince her of the legitimacy of my trip. I had to be prepared to answer all her questions and counter her statements of independence. She was always so strong and stubborn and hated thinking of herself as being in need. She simultaneously could lay-on the best Catholic guilt trips about how I wasn't doing or being the best I could without quite saying it.

"Hi Mom. What are you doing?" I cheerily asked. "Oh, hello Honey! Why are you calling in the middle of day like this? Aren't you supposed to be at work? Even though it's good to hear your voice as always!" she said. "Are you sitting down, Mom?" I asked in a good mysterious way. "Well, yes. Sean and I were just getting ready to go out for a drive," she responded, "But what is it?" (Sean is my older brother from Chicago who was visiting.) "I can't talk long. I just wanted to ask you if me and the dogs could come live with you for awhile?" I announced excitedly. "What? Live-with-me?" she haltingly replied, "Well, of course, Honey. But why?" I then quickly explained my detailed plan and how I could stay 6-12 weeks! It was hard for both of us to believe: 1600 miles apart, a 30-hour drive, and exactly 7 days after leaving her, I'd be back! Along with a sense of "time warp," it seemed surreal to me how I got such an incredible amount of work done and delegated in just a few days.

∾∾∾

"This is Kath's critical ego stepping in here to say just how ridiculous this plan is! I mean, first of all, driving that far all by her self? She's asking for trouble. Even though her car is new, it could break down—and the thought of having to walk possibly in 100-degree weather with two dogs! Or someone could easily mess with her. You know, all those horror stories you hear on the news . . . she's too defenseless and trusting. Plus, leaving her house empty for so long, anything could happen!

"Even though her Mother needs extra help now, my God! She has already sacrificed so much: 6 flights out to see her within 14 months to do the 'family thing' when they don't even really accept her or let her be herself! And all the hassle and cost associated with dog-sitters. It was such a nightmare for her— jacking up the credit cards with extra gifts for 'friends' she could convince to help her along with her family. It just doesn't make sense when she's barely living paycheck to paycheck. Now, to drive out there, live with a woman she can barely stand to be around for a few days, nursing a disease she knows her Mom created as a way to leave this world after being so closed off to emotions, and giving her needy Mother attention in a way that she never received—just sounds too crazy! Not to mention that this very important grant job is one that could lead to promotional job offers if she would just put more into it. But no, instead she's letting her Mother interrupt this potential and distract her which makes her crazy with emotions at work and repels others away from her when she really needs their support!"

"Stop it! Right now!" I yell at myself as I shake my head, trying to release these crazy fearful thoughts that keep running through my head, questioning my decision. "Please, God, guide me through this," I counter-attack my ego. **"I know in my heart I love my Mom so much,** and *I'm scared*, Lord, *really scared. I hate these thoughts. I am so sick of my mixed emotions about my Mother: the love-hate relationship, the independent yet needy feeling, the understanding but confusion that looms over our relationship! She can invalidate me so fast it drives me crazy! What am I supposed to be doing or learning here? When will the intensity stop running my life? How many times must I repent for years of guilt? Why can't I forgive myself?*

"Please, hear my prayer, Lord, for I know not what I'm doing. I am humbled before you, asking for your guidance to be clear so that I may move through this incredible time with love and grace. Let me look upon this trip as an adventure, an exciting time where everything will work out the way it is supposed to. I totally surrender to you, God, for I believe you are leading me in this direction. Give me trust to squelch my fear. Give me hope of a better tomorrow for the sacrifice today. Give me patience to love my Mother through her last days in a way that I would want to be treated. Keep my thoughts on this, oh Lord, for I need you now more than ever!"

As I cry myself to sleep, this last night before my trip home, in my bed, in my house, in my sacred space that I will be leaving indefinitely, **a peaceful Divinity brushes over me. I feel the presence of an Angel holding me, reassuring me, "You are doing the right thing," and reminding my heart, "Some things just can't be understood at the time. This is where you are right now. It will make sense later."** *"But what if I use up all my leave time and she plateau's . . . and"* my overly fatigued head tries to pose more questioning. **"Shhhh,"** I feel the Angel hushing my mind. **"Just follow this feeling in your heart,"** is the sweet message I received. **The feeling is too intense yet too serene not to be a gift from God, or not to be Divine guidance from my heavenly Creator. It is directing me home to spend the last days of my earth Mother's life with her in a way about which I could never carry guilt, and with the potential to heal a lifetime of hurt. "Shhhh," I feel echoing through my Being, quieting my thoughts.** As the tears stop wetting the pillow, **"Shhh," I hear, rocking, lulling me to sleep.**

〜〜〜

Now here I am, traveling north on Interstate 17. I didn't actually leave until 5pm, however, I am on such an adrenaline rush, that I know I'll drive through the night before finding a place to sleep. My intention was to drive 8am to 6pm or so for three days, stopping two nights and cutting the trip into thirds. Yet, with all the last minute things I found myself doing, and the strong urge to get home to Mom, I decided to cut the trip in half and make only one stop.

As I break free of the congested inner-city traffic in Phoenix, the reality of the trip finally starts to set in. Driving past the high-fence-razor-wired-top-security institutions where I've worked for nearly seven years, I yell out, "Adiós Muchachos!" I then visualize a thousand faces watching me as we enter into the majestic mountainous terrain of this desert-land I call home. I always promised myself to never take this beauty for granted, and have attributed this to assisting with my sanity. Currently 112 degrees, it occurs to me that this summer has seemed hotter than usual and I will be glad to get away from it. I smile as I realize how cool it will be when I return. From the weather reports, it sounds like record heat, even in northern Arizona and all across New Mexico. It was a smarter decision to drive through the night; it'll be a lot cooler for the dogs and my car. Almost an hour now into the trip and they're still panting.

I twist around the steep grades and say "wow" to spectacular valley views as I shudder with appreciation. I see how the westerly sun amongst billowy clouds sends breath-taking hues of crimson red and burnt orange across the skyline, illuminating the tops of the stately saguaros. "Thank you, God!" I whisper with awe. "What a way to start a trip, huh, babies?" I ask offering my dogs some water. Jamey is in the passenger seat next to me and Charley is in the backseat. They have finally settled down. It's like they know we have a long trip ahead of us. They sure were acting crazy as I was loading up the car—in a way I've never seen. It's not like we've ever done this before. In fact, the longest trip they've ever been on was maybe a two-hour drive to go camping years ago. As I feed them their dinner, I realize just how hungry I am. So, I get some cherry yogurt and spicy scrambled eggs with cream cheese from the cooler in front of Jamey.

By the time I reach Flagstaff, I'm on my third CD, and dark clouds are starting to roll in as the temperature drops along with the sun. I fill up my first tank of gas, find a little grass strip off to the side and encourage the dogs to go "potty." This is no problem for my little-long-haired-wiener-lookin'-dog, Jamey; however, queen Charley only likes to go in her backyard and has trouble going on command by leash. "You better get used to this soon, Honey," I coax rather impatiently. "This is how it's going to be for awhile now!" As drops of rain start to fall on us, we quickly return to the car and continue on our "adventure."

Back on the freeway, I look up through my windowed moon roof. I see a beautiful half-moon smiling down upon us as the darkness encroaches and the rain continues dancing lightly atop the car. "Qué Buéna la Luna!" I exclaim per habit to honor this moon. Westward we drive, on I-40 towards Gallup, New Mexico, where I plan to make the next gas/bathroom stop. As I adjust to the glares of headlights flashing in my eyes, my thoughts scan over various memories of my childhood. Here I am, 38 years old, and it hits me that Mom was 38 when she adopted me. **A shiver runs up my spine as I realize this.** She's now 76, and I just know she won't be here in three months to turn 77. So, she lived 38 years without me and 38 years with me, and I tell myself I can do the same with her. . . . Further, when I turn 76 the year will be 2038!

What an interesting play on numbers! It's also somewhat comforting because of how much of my life I have wished I were dead. Except, I always knew it would kill my Mother, so I couldn't take it seriously. Plus, there was that time I did try when I was sixteen, but for the grace of God I didn't die or get permanently damaged in some way. I had enough drugs and alcohol in me to kill a herd of horses. I went to bed and had an out-of-body experience I can remember like it happened yesterday. I saw myself lying in a casket with my Mother broken-heartedly crying over me. Knowing how much grief this poor woman had already been through in her life, the most recent being my father's death six years earlier, I suddenly couldn't go through with it and fought very hard to snap back into my body. I then sat up with a bang in my bed, drenched in sweat and shaking. When I awoke the next day with a hangover from hell, and remembered everything, I knew I was not in control. Hence, I promised God I would never attempt that again! I only told one friend right away, who was so worried she called a suicide/ drug hotline. When she told them the amounts and types of substances in me, they said to get me to a hospital immediately, since I could still die from the high toxicity levels. Sadly, I was too scared to tell Mom, so I made my friend promise to never tell anyone. I didn't think much or talk about it again for another ten years. It was too embarrassing.

It amazes me to remember how unhappy I was most of my childhood and how much I hated life during my teens. It seems like I'm talking about another person when I remember myself back then. On the other hand, *I have never understood why I have to live in this world, in this lifetime, in this context, or in this human vessel. Is life really just all about Soul lessons? Does it really have to do with learning the right way, taking the right paths, and doing the right things for the right reasons?* Questions kept pouring out of me as I drove into the night. Listening to my old high school music triggered even deeper thoughts. Eagles, Kansas and Steve Miller Band played on as I realized that so many of the intense feelings that I had then, still haunt me today.

Why did I have to be born to a Mother who did not want me? Why did I have a loving adopted family, yet who under the auspices of being a "perfect" Catholic family, were full of discipline, condescending comments, dream clipping, verbal abuse, and personality stifling (along with support and encouragement if it fit in with their strict values)? Why did I have to always be different in school— chubby and biggest in class, only adopted kid, first to have a parent die and only single parent family, first to develop at puberty, first and only kid to get kicked out for unjustified reasons (and banned from childhood friends), only girl in my peer group not to have boyfriends, then to later realize my lesbianism and lose my teen-hood friends over it? Why did I have to be so sensitive, so misunderstood, such a clown, so talkative, so full of energy that others have always wanted to tell me not to be, and continue to do so practically daily? Why do I listen to it? Why do I care?

I tried for years to adapt through different modes: promising myself to be still and quiet, ignoring the comments, becoming the clown—making others laugh to cover up the feelings of rejection, doing drugs to numb the pain plus appear quieter and less active, and making jokes about myself—beating others to the comments so they didn't have to say them. Lately, I've just been more introverted by avoiding social settings altogether, becoming a hermit, and trying instead to just love myself the way I am. I want love mirrored back to me. *So far, that does not seem to be working. Nothing seems to have worked over my lifetime. I am still surrounded by people who want to point out my personality traits in a critical way! It's like I have signs on me. Some people read: "Go ahead and cut me down!" Others see: "Make fun of me!" Still others get the okay to point out how talkative and hyper I am. I've tried to take these signs off. I've tried to stand up for myself and tell people that I don't appreciate these comments. I've tried to stop beating them to the punch lines. I've also tried to not take myself so seriously and just laugh. I've even tried to make sure I don't do that to others in case that's why I get it back. Further, I still try to be quieter at times except then I get teased or asked what's wrong!*

As I drive through the darkness, anger wells up in my gut. If my dogs were not in the car, I would be screaming out the windows to release 38 years of frustration. *I feel so alone and so different from others!* For 20 years I "ran away" from my Mom and two brothers, *thinking I didn't much need them, believing my lovers and friends and co-workers could give me just about everything I needed in life. I felt like my family played too many games and I was not going to be negative like them and in denial like them.* Astonishingly so, I am now finding myself with no one interested in me but my family. **I am realizing that family is always there for you, no matter what, and the connections run deeper than we can know**. And even though I have always had a tremendous amount of anger towards my older brother, I am open to allowing the death of our Mother to shift that for me. Right now, *I just can't believe how long I've been single, how friends have fallen by the wayside, and how coworkers and bosses do not seem to like me much at all.* In fact, creating relationships within this new job setting has been the most difficult for me. Even though they seemed supportive of this trip, *I know they're unhappy with me because of all the comments about my character traits. I just don't get it!*

If I hear one more joke about my personality, I'm going to explode! It's not funny anymore. I've been asked a million times if I was Attention-Deficit-Hyperactivity-Disordered (ADHD) as a kid. Why am I asked this? Why is it looked upon so negatively? Yes, I was hyper. Yes, I was active, yet a very good student! I do have an extremely talkative side, but it has come in handy in my field: leading youth activity programs. I sometimes have a lot of energy, but can stay focused and get impressive projects done: 10 years of college, a Master's thesis, many recreation curriculums, handy-woman home projects, art/crafts, and thousands of writings and poems. I also have a very deep, quiet side that few see. Sometimes, I just don't feel like being around anyone. Sometimes, I am so literally depressed I don't want to live anymore. If people realized how much I hate these comments, how much they make me feel unloved, unaccepted and too different, or how much they make me want to crawl under a rock and die—do you think they would stop saying them? Will it ever stop? Will I ever stop needing it as a Soul lesson?

Just two months prior to this trip, I finally broke down and started taking lots of medications to help me get through this tumultuous time. I just couldn't take life anymore, and it was either die, but I had promised God . . . or try meds. An Oprah show (June 2000) was discussing adults with ADHD and how there are times when medications can help, especially if there are too many stimuli with no support in sight. Oh, God, did I ever identify with that! I listened to a few adults talk about their symptoms and relief, plus the answers to getting healthy again. Before the show was over I was on the phone with my medical provider, trusting God to send me the right help. Synchronicity in action, I received an immediate appointment with a counselor 45 minutes later, and with a psychiatrist in two days, which is usually unheard of. I learned all I could about the way my brain was "wired" and the meds I would be taking. I discovered that amphetamines also help adults to focus better just like children. Moreover, ADHD doesn't necessarily correlate with learning disabilities. In addition, I had never identified myself with all the same symptoms I saw in youth with whom I worked over the years—I was in denial! The doctor prescribed two antidepressants, an amphetamine, an anti-anxiety drug, and a sleeping aid, all which recently started providing me relief and confidence to get through the work challenges and transition time with Mom. Actually, I can't believe how much more even-keeled, focused and non-manic I'm finally beginning to feel.

When I first came to terms with this, I called Mom to talk to her about it, even though I tried to hide the depth of my upset. "I just realized I'm ADHD, Mom," I softly shared with tears streaming down my face like I was admitting I had some horrible disease. "Oh, Kathleen," she chuckled, "I thought you always knew that!" "No, I knew I was hyperactive, but not with an ADHD wired brain," I responded. "It has such a negative connotation. I've worked around it for years, I know!" "Well, I knew you had it when you were a toddler after I read probably one of the first articles on it," she explained, "and I begged our family doctor to try Ritalin which was just coming out then. He told me to manage it by keeping you active, even though I didn't agree. You know, we've always joked about this!"

My heart sunk deeper as I felt even more different and guilty for not being a better, less-wild daughter for my Mother. I knew she was not in a good space to help me through this. Not that she really could help me through much anyway because she always became uncomfortable with me having any emotions. She tended to take them on herself so I never felt validated, rather like I then had to comfort her. This time, however, I felt like I was dying in the pain of more self-discovery. My throat tightened up, as I wanted so desperately to reach out to her for help. Yet, I knew she was so sick. I knew she was dying of lung cancer. In fact, she just happened to be in the hospital during this phone call after having had her lung cavity drained of fluid and narrowly escaping death. We almost lost her and there I was trying to talk to her on an intimate level. Although it was deeper than usual for us, *I still felt so different, lost, and now guilty for mentioning it in her groggy condition. Only, I had longed to talk to someone who had known me since I was born and still loved me.*

~~~

The clock reads 3:20am as I pull into a truck stop in Tucumcari, New Mexico. I fearlessly fill my tank with gas then relieve both the dogs and myself. It doesn't seem like I've been driving over 10 hours at all. I'm so mesmerized by my thoughts mixed with my Divine pull to go home. I breathe in the cool-warm-silent-night air and scrub the bug-scum off the windows. I can't believe I ever had any thoughts of fear of traveling so far alone. Instead, **I feel very peaceful and content with total confidence that the remainder of the trip will continue in this same manner.** As I get back in the car, **I feel a comforting brush across my back and realize how my Angels are dancing around me.** Smiling upward, I thank the Lord for helping me feel this way as I drive towards that Texas panhandle and reminisce to keep time suspended.

I play some upbeat music with which to bounce around as I travel the relatively empty roadways toward my destination. *Strange as it may sound,* **I know Mom is ready to leave this earth and that this is her way of doing it.** It makes perfect sense to me that this woman who had so many heart-breaking experiences, who smoked heavily, overate compulsively, lacked proper check-ups and never exercised nor knew how to really take loving care of herself—should manifest lung cancer. The fact that my family and I now have this "warning time" to heal our relationships is another blessing Mom's giving us. *Many people would think I am crazy to believe something like this. Then again, I'm used to that.* Regardless, she has been so negative about many life issues and depressed deep down for years without choosing to do anything about it, that it had to be easier to checkout in this manner. It's like a grand finale, or a time to say what needs to be said, and to do what has to be done on a Soul level. It is a way to feel less guilt than what a sudden death would have brought, especially for the "black-sheep-prodigal-daughter." I am filled with gratitude for the opportunities she is now affording me.

Mom has had such an interesting life—one that has always fascinated me. She was born November 14, 1923 and was adopted as an only child by a prominent doctor and his wife in the small mid-western town of Danville, Illinois. She was definitely a "daddy's girl" and his "pride and joy" as is evident in the old black and white photos of the time. Sadly enough, it appears she had no maternal bonding. I was struck at how cold her first mother appeared towards her in those photos—holding her out with extended arms like a stinky wet puppy! This mother died when she was just two years old. Her father quickly remarried, then this second mother died ten years later, when Mom was only twelve. (During this period she sometimes played with the now famed Van Dyke brothers whose grandparents lived by her.) After a third marriage to a woman ten years her senior, incredibly, her much adored father died next when she was just sixteen! Remarkably, all parents, including her third mother, died of medical related reasons—polio, TB, stroke, and heart attacks. I also recall her mentioning that her father drank heavily.

To hear her talk of it all from an emotionless stance is amazing. She acts like that's just the way it was and it's no big deal. However, I have always felt her pain. She has an intense, needy way of clinging to all three of us kids, and in particular to me, in a loving/hateful way almost like an emotional vampire. I always felt like she was trying to get some mother-daughter bond out of me that she never got growing up. Now, she would say, "That is just a bunch of hogwash, Kathleen. Just appreciate that you have a mother who loves you dearly!" and would never understand my perspective. I do appreciate her love; only it has always felt like it comes from an unhealthy source of desperation, and no matter what I do it is never quite enough! Even my brothers, whom I see stuck in their own guilt games and negative reinforcing roles with her, would disagree with me on this.

I suddenly notice how the sky has been lightening up around us ever so slowly, snapping me back to the present. Adrenaline rushes through me as I realize how much of a mental fog I am in, and how much I need to wakeup. Dramatically shaking my head, I see a road sign which reads: "Amarillo, next ten exits." I adjust the time with the time zone changes and say aloud, "Ok, it looks like I am just going to miss Friday morning rush hour." As I pour my pre-planned morning coffee out of my thermos, I tell myself to pretend I just awoke and am starting the day. I often feel this tired anyway when leaving early in the morning for a long trip. "Psych the mind and keep on going," I say to my dogs who are also waking with the increase in traffic, then stretching and looking around. "One more hour or so and we'll stop again, ok, babies?" As if they understood what I said, they plop back down after tiring of the cool new smells blowing through the cracked windows.

Jamming to the great sounds of Santana's Supernatural CD, I continue across this beautiful expanse of flat countryside sporadically connecting those sun-topped mini-mountains that seem to magically beckon us on our journey. Feeling relaxed again yet renewed, I think about how Mom would not want to know how long I have been driving (fifteen hours plus as many more as I can stand today). She is supposed to call me at 2pm her time. I plan on telling a little white lie, as usual, to protect her from any extra worry about this drive. She would insist that I stop more often to rest. She always pushes her point until you just have to surrender and say, "Ok, Mother, whatever you say."

She always has had very strong belief systems—something I admire. Yet, I don't appreciate the occasional impositions of her opinions. I am just as strong-willed and stubborn. We sarcastically joke that I learned from the best, however I am proud of the independent nature she instilled in me. She, in fact, was remarkable in her youth. She was a very popular girl, had good grades, voted most likely to succeed and class valedictorian, etc. "Oh, it was such a small school," she would modestly point out. Then after going to nurses training back in the early forties, she worked at hospitals in Chicago until she met my father at age 29. Back then, this age was considered to be an "old maid," yet she didn't care. She operated under the belief that she didn't need anyone to take care of her! After a short romance, she knew he was the perfect man for her and they got married in 1953. She also fell in love with his religion, Catholicism, and soon converted.

~~~

"O-O-O-klahoma! Where the sun comes da da da da da," I find myself bursting in song. I laugh as I recall how many of the cities and states have triggered songs in my mind, regardless of the music playing to keep me alert in my car. " . . . Where it's time for food and time for gas," I continue singing to the tune for my dogs. After 15 minutes of walking around on our break, Charley still won't relieve herself so onward I decide to push. I have trouble stopping for very long anyway knowing Mom is at home anxiously waiting.

How funny it is that she's waiting at home for me. That's the story of my life. I was forever running off somewhere, and there she'd be, just waiting. Bless her heart! My throat gets a lump as I choke back the urge to cry, realizing she won't be waiting much longer. There'll be no more waiting for my phone calls, my cards, my gifts, or my visits. "Please, God let her hold on for me! Dad, be at her side helping her 'til I get there," I pray for the umpteenth time. **A chill up my spine tells me that my prayers are being heard.**

The first time I can remember wandering away from home, I was only four years old. I wanted to explore the neighborhood in a different direction and meet new friends. When I got back home, Mom was very upset and scolded me again. I just felt like there was nothing to worry about, and that I was fine! Of course when I was a teenager, I think I ran around the streets more than I was at home. There were many nights that she didn't even know about because I would sneak out after everyone was asleep or I would say I was staying at a friend's and find all-night parties somewhere. *With regret for what I put her through,* I recall all the times I found her sleeping in the recliner chair in the middle of the night and sometimes she had to go to work the next morning! I can't imagine the stress, wear and tear on her body that I caused. **I have a chance now to make it up to her, and I intend to do just that, then forgive myself and move on!**

I'm starting to feel extremely tired dealing with the miles of I-44W freeway construction. Three lanes go down to two, then go to one lane, back to three again, and then one. We switch into oncoming traffic, over the median, and then back again. Annoyingly, the speed limit goes from 65mph to 45mph to 25mph then up to 55mph! My brain is now swimming. Pressure is increasing on my temples as the air heats up with the noonday sun. Only 85 degrees out, however the humidity is definitely weighing heavy around us. My goal is to last just one more hour where I'll stop to spend the night in Springfield, Missouri. *"I can't believe how slow everyone is going!"* I exclaim, cranky as hell now, *"Oh, come on! Just pass him!"* As I squeeze into the right lane to pass a semi, I see a police car in front of the truck. *"He's messin' with us—gettin' off on a power trip by going 45 when the speed limit is 55!"* I talk as if someone is listening.

Creeping along at 52mph, I very slowly pass this cop. *My eyes widen in disbelief* as I see him pull in behind me and turn on his lights. *"No!"* I whisper in embarrassment, *thinking of how the other drivers must be laughing at me.* As I pull over onto the shoulder of the road, it is evident to me that the traffic is now speeding up. *"You're welcome, guys!"* I sarcastically mutter as I begin to get angry. I knew I had been speeding through the night, but not through these hours of construction and fatigue!

As he approaches my car saying, "Oh, a dog lover," I ask what I had done wrong. He explains that the speed limit is 50mph. So, *I tell him how I have been driving non-stop to get home to take care of my Mother dying of cancer, and that the speed limit was changing so much for the last four hours I swear I thought the last sign read 55.* After checking out my license, registration and plates, he proceeds to say with his southern drawl, "I'm planning on only writing you a warning, ma'am. But, let me give ya a little advice: Never pass a police officer! It's been my experience that only women are gutsy enough to attempt this!" I laugh and explain how traffic does this frequently in Phoenix, before adding, "But yes sir, I understand!" Curiously so, he walks around the front of my car while looking down in the ditch area, and bends to pick something up then comes back to my window. "Now, you'll probably think this is strange, ma'am," he says, "but, I'm very superstitious, and this here rock spoke to me. You keep it close and it will help get you home safely to your Mother!" Surprised by this beautiful gesture as well as amused by the irony (me—thinking this strange?), I take the piece of gravel and thank him. As I pull back onto the freeway, **a chill goes through me as it occurs to me that he may have been an Angel, somehow planted along my path to help me.** "Thank you God," I utter.

Even though he also told me to pullover and get a hot meal at the next stop, I am wide-awake again and determined to make the 50 miles left to the hotel I have on my list. My older brother had told me which places to stay that would take dogs. He has always been a geography buff and travel expert, among other intellectual specialties. I knew Mom would like it that I asked for his input on this drive, besides I had so much to do, I needed the extra help. She has wanted and prayed for us to be closer for as long as I can remember. It has been quite a struggle for me because she could never understand, nor stand up for me on how abusive he has been towards me.

All three of us kids were adopted out of Catholic Charities in Springfield, Illinois. Mom could not have children, therefore, they chose to adopt. In 1958, they brought home Sean, and then in 1961 I came along, followed by Edward in 1964. We lived in Decatur, Illinois until 1968, and then moved to Champaign-Urbana where we remained until I moved to Phoenix in 1988 and Sean to Chicago in 1990. My Mother and my brother, Edward, and his family still reside there.

To hear Mom talk about our relationships, Sean and I were close for two years until Edward came along. Then it broke her heart (and still does) because I turned all my attention to Edward (and still do) and Sean was left out due to differences in interests and senses of humor. The way I see it, Sean and I have always been opposites. Therefore, our personalities, family roles and circumstances would have it that we did not get along well at all. Sean was a quiet-shy-introverted-adult-like-genius-child who was not very interested in social or recreational activities. He preferred staying in his room and reading. I remember our dad always trying to teach him "manly" things. He would drag him along to learn about construction, building things, handyman work, sports, yard work and tool operation. Sean was never much interested and I watched with amazement (and horror at times) at how they would fight over these issues. Albeit a good intention, I believe dad was slowly breaking Sean's Spirit just like his militaristic father had done to him. This did not honor Sean's natural talents and heart's desires. As a result, the lowered self-esteem caused him to turn to over-eating (another compulsion modeled to him by our parents) and social withdrawal. To compound matters, not only did kids taunt him mercilessly at school, he also had this hyper-active-social-enthusiastic-talented-clown of a sister at home always hanging around in the background saying, "Teach me, Dad, I wanna learn! Show me how to do it. Can I, huh? Will you?" And both of us were deeply affected by dad's response. Whether spoken or not, the feeling was that neither of us were quite good enough. It seemed that with Sean it was because of his lack of interest and/or ability, and with me because I was "second choice," and a girl interested in "boys" things.

After our father died of a heart attack in our home on October 23, 1971, our relationships got progressively strained for the worse. This was the time, which I attribute to Sean's becoming downright abusive towards all of us, both mentally and emotionally. Although I understand he felt the need to "act fatherly," he seemed to also possess a power-hungry monster born of inner misery, which he would attach to me in particular. My role of the clown began to turn into the wild-partying-black-sheep-rebel. On the other hand, Edward, who always had similar interests and abilities as me, played the quiet-melt-into-the-background-peacekeeper-ostrich of the family. Not surprisingly, we both sunk into drug abuse as a way to escape the negative tensions.

Edward was the only one in the family to be thin, small-boned yet very tall, with a metabolism of a horse. He was always "the Momma's boy," as are most youngest sons, however, he had an amazing vision the night our father died. Only seven years old, standing in the hallway watching Mom give mouth-to-mouth resuscitation to our unconscious father while waiting for the arrival of the ambulance, he visualized that he'd be the one taking care of Mom during her senior years and nursing her through death. He had a flash and knew then that she would never be with another man again, and would need someone to be there for her to help with her needs. And there he has been! He helped her move out of our "family house" and into her condo in 1989. He always attends the ritualistic Sunday family dinners as well as all holiday celebrations (which mean the world to Mom). Plus, he assists her in countless ways. **I shiver now realizing that I will also be helping her in the end.** My vision just hit me nearly 29 years after his!

∾∾∾

After 20 hours of driving, I arrive at the hotel and check-in. I walk the dogs (Charley finally went potty!), and unpack somewhat. Then, I crash on the seemingly spinning king-size bed cuddled up with my much relieved and equally exhausted babies to watch "The Rosie O'Donnell Show." I can't believe my ears as this eleven-year-old boy, Billy Gilman, belts out one of the most beautiful Angelic melodies I have ever heard. With lyrics reaching deep inside my heart, I am mesmerized by his vocal range and Soul expression. Utterly shocked by this performance, **I get goose bumps hearing the lines,** "We need some help— life's not that simple, down here on earth. A thousand prayers, a million words, but one voice was heard. One voice, one simple word, hearts know what to say. One dream can change the world—keep believing 'til you find your way!" Now, I know I am so beyond exhaustion that this seems like a dream. "Holy, moly! That was freakin' in-cred-i-ble! Oh-my-God," I exclaim slowly with emphasis on each syllable as tears stream down my face. **He is, after all, singing to me and to my special circumstance. He is my precious Angel in this moment, delivering a special message from God to me (no less through the voice of a child which represents pure potentiality): My prayers are being heard! My passions are God-given talents proving I have a purpose to follow. And my desire to nurse Mom and heal family discord is indeed Divinely guided! It feels so right, so awesome, and so peaceful yet moving.** "Thank you God," I whisper as I fall to sleep.

Four hours later, my little Angel, Jamey (he looks like one, too—brown hair with long black hair thinly divided around his mane and shoulder blades where wings would be), wakes me from a deep sleep whining by the door. It's seven o'clock and way past their dinnertime. After a quick sun-setting walk, I settle down again with a peanut butter and honey bagel, cheese and veggie medley with dip. A hot meal would be great, however, I do not want to leave my dogs. They are so freaked out as it is. They act crazy when I just go to the car for a minute—as if I would ever desert them! By 9pm we're back asleep, and incredibly don't awake until 8am! Wow, fifteen total hours of sleep—now that's resting! Then, after all the necessary morning rituals we are ready to checkout and hit the road again! "Ten more hours, Mom. Here we come," I announce to the summer breeze.

We hit St. Louis's crazy freeway system around noon. I am glad it is Saturday or traffic would be so much worse. I miss one exit because of a misleading merge sign (it <u>was</u> the sign, not me). However, I am proud of myself for quickly winding around under the "Arch" and finding my way back to I-70E, my connection to Illinois. Memories again flash through my mind as I recall all the trips our family used to take here. My parents were big Cardinal baseball fans and we came to many games, especially when they played the Chicago Cubs. Throughout my childhood in Illinois, these were the big rival teams. Since Mom and Dad had both lived in Chicago for awhile in their twenties, it would seem more likely for them to be Cub fans.

Having grownup in Indianapolis, my dad then went to the University of Illinois in Urbana/Champaign (as did his father), later followed by Sean and myself. He received a Bachelor's in engineering then worked managing construction sites and businesses. His roofing company helped build the nationally known Assembly Hall in Champaign. I cannot pass by this unique structure without thinking of dad. Just one year before he died, he had finally bought his own business: a sheet metal company. Further, he was in the middle of designing a house for us, to build on land already purchased near our Catholic school/ church. I remember him many a night working on those blueprints and explaining them to me—he was making it a two-story home just for me! Sean now has those prints.

After he died, Mom had to sell his business and the vacant lot. She also had to get a job again and was glad she had a nursing degree upon which to fall. (She ended up working at the County Blood Bank and retired 10 years ago.) In addition, she was grateful that dad had insisted she manage their finances as the housewife, and make life insurance payments even though she thought it was a waste of money. It was almost as if dad knew he would die young, and thus wanted to continue providing for us. Even though he came from a line of men who died young from heart disease, he still smoked a lot, was obese, never exercised and was always working. Unfortunately, it should be no surprise that he died of a massive heart attack at only 43 years of age. Ironically, Mom lost yet another love of her life: the only man she'd ever love. And through this life experience, Mom taught me great lessons on independence and love. Directly she taught that one must be able to ultimately rely only upon oneself, and conversely, that just because a love dies doesn't mean one can't ever love again!

～～～

Finally! After a frustrating extra two hours out-of-the-way due to a wrong turn, I arrive in my hometown only to learn about a big freeway accident in which I would have been stuck, **if Angels had not led me astray**. I am very grateful they were helping me drive that last stretch of I-57N because I was wiped out! "Thank you, God, for getting me and my babies here safely," I say aloud as I pat the dash, "And thank you, car, for purring non-stop like a kitten." **When I felt driven** last February to pull into a Honda dealer and without comparison just buy this brand-new Civic because of my **"vibes,"** my logic had told me many reasons against it. **Now, I understand how I needed it for this trip**, and five months/4500 miles was a perfect break-in period. My 1990-needing-much-work-Prelude would probably not have made the trip. **Again, Divine guidance in action!** Besides, it is the most beautiful shade of bright blue-indigo—colors of the higher chakras—and thus represents a more Spiritual path of Truth that I am now on in my life.

It is 6pm when I pull into Mom's garage. I have to pee like a racehorse after holding it for so long because I didn't want to waste any more time by stopping again. "Hi, Mom! We're home," I yell as I rush through the condo, only to find her sitting on the toilet talking on the phone. "Hey, hello, Honey," she says to me, then into the phone, "Kathleen finally got here," and back to me, "Here, talk to Agnes!" As she holds out the phone, I'm motioning for her to get off the toilet, shaking my head no and doing the little "potty-dance." She continues, "You remember, she's the one I couldn't wait for you to meet—the cleaning lady's sister who brings me all that delicious food!" "Not right now, Mom. I gotta go! Tell her I'll call her back after I get settled in." As I continue to motion for her to please get off that toilet, she flashes me that obviously-embarrassed look and says, "I guess she has to go to the bathroom first, Agnes. We'll call you right back," and mouths "Okay!" to me, as I still wave my arms in frustration at how slow she's moving. I kiss her as she stumbles away trying to pull down her housecoat, plus untangling her oxygen tube and the phone cord, all the while still talking to her friend. I close the bathroom door and start to cry at what just happened.

What the hell am I getting myself into? Just seconds in the door and she's oblivious to my needs, trying to push something on me! I just spent the last 48 hours driving halfway across the country and she acts upset because I need to use the bathroom first. She's just so into her own head she has no concept of where I am coming from! "Please, God, help me. I am so tired, don't let us get off to a bad start or fight at all. Let me feel instantly centered and focused. I am here for Mom!" I breathe deeply several times, and after splashing cold water on my face, I look into my eyes and say, **"Let me always remember why I am here: only to serve her with peace and love!"**

I open the door feeling like a brand new person and say, "Can you believe we're here, Mom? I love you so much! It is great to see you again!" She stands and we hug each other for a long time. She is practically speechless, nodding her head with tears welling in her eyes. "You know I am here for you, Mom. Whatever you need, just ask!" And as she thanks me, full of emotion and love, **I feel the first wave of an Angelic presence helping me deal with this situation and say the perfect things to her!** As I sit down to relax before unpacking the car, I look at her fast-aging body and think about when this all started—when I first found out she was dying of cancer. . . .

~~~~

Oh, Behold Angelic Twilight!

Oh, behold Angelic twilight!
That moment just after sunset when the sky,
Brilliant teal with shades of grayish pink,
Turns an evermore indigo bright blue as one, two, three stars shine out . . .
Oh, and that softly warm summer night breeze—
How it takes the edge off the blazing sun of earlier hour!

Oh, behold Angelic twilight!
That moment when time no longer counts,
With those brilliant colors moving to darkness,
How it penetrates the Soul, releases tribulations,
And gently blows away the days' stressors.
If only for a moment . . . Oh, behold Angelic twilight!

~~~~

3

"Ground Zero"

~back in time~
October 1999—July 2000

I'll never forget that phone call one October night in 1999. We must've been talking for a half-hour before she casually said, "I had a doctor's appointment last week. I was just having a little trouble swallowing because of some swollen glands, so they took a chest x-ray. The doctor said that I have this small spot in my left lung. . . . It's probably nothing, but they want me to go have a biopsy done off the nodule in my neck. Edward is going to take me, however, I'm sure I'll be ok. I don't want you to worry. I just wanted to be sure to tell you now. If I had waited until after the lab test, I know that you would ask, 'Why didn't you tell me sooner?' Just like that time when I fainted in Chicago at your cousin's wedding and didn't tell you about the hospital visit until a week later. But nothing was wrong that time either. I just hadn't eaten much before drinking those couple glasses of wine. I was on that new diet you know, and . . ."

As she continued rambling as if what she had told me was no big deal, I sat stunned. Much as I hate to admit it, sometimes I would just stare at the television while she talked on and on, usually repeating the same old stories to me, or complaining about the same things while doing nothing about them. She was always starving to talk to me, yet always interrupted, or told me "not to feel that way" or wanted to insist on her solution until I would agree. *Thus, I learned not to share much.* And because she really did not do much in her retirement years, and really did not seem to have any close friends, she seldom had "news" to tell me. Therefore, when she threw in this crucial information with all the other chitchat, I almost missed what she had told me.

"Wait a minute, Mom! A spot? In your lung? What do you mean?" I asked. As she explained it in the same minimizing, detached way, my mind started reeling at the seriousness of it all. Then I remembered how one year earlier while visiting my house, she had not seemed well at all. I noticed then that she was aging faster, forgetting so many things, coughing more, getting tired quicker than before, and had a lingering "cold." One night she fell in my backyard and could not get up. That literally *scared* the hell out of both of us. Her heavy weight, bum knee, weak upper body and sore lower back prevented her from being able to stand, even with my assistance. I had to go get a neighbor to come help, *which was embarrassing for both of us, to say the least.* I'll never forget how she politely introduced herself, reaching out her hand for him to shake before we pulled her upright! Afterwards, I let her smoke in my home for the first time, and pampered her differently than before. **I just knew that was the last time she'd be out to Phoenix to visit me, and for the first time ever I did not want her trip to be almost over! I yearned to feel the closeness to her that my Spirit truly knew.**

Upon her return home I insisted she go to a doctor for a complete physical. I called Edward and his wife, Diana and talked several hours about the great need for this. Since they see her all the time, they could not see as big of a change in her. I was concerned about her falling at home, so Edward then became worried. However, she was adamantly against carrying around a medic device or cell phone. It also took her nearly four months to get that physical (I finally stopped nagging her, realizing this was her choice), only to announce that everything was fine—all tests showed normal!

"Wouldn't they have detected it during your physical last February?" I asked. "Well, I didn't have an x-ray and my glands weren't swollen then," she explained. My gut started expanding and my chest tightened. Adrenaline rushed through me as I realized that not only did she not really have a complete physical (what doctor would not give a 75-year-old smoker a chest x-ray?), **she did not want one for this very possibility!** Oh God, I was right. *Something was terribly wrong—I just knew it!* **Yet, I knew this was her life. It was between her and God, and I was not in control here.** In fact, over the years I had gotten much better at just letting her be the way she was, which at times was sad and lonely yet with a good heart and always full of humor!

When she called me a few days later to say they found cancer cells in that biopsy, she seemed so strong and together, it was amazing. "I have an appointment next week with the best doctor in town. He'll explain everything to me then. That's all I know for now," she said as I felt myself growing numb. We then talked about my new job, writing the grant proposal and how I was so excited to be part of a task force creating this opportunity for girls being released from incarceration—something for which I had prayed a long time. As always, when it came to job discussions, Mom was very supportive. "I am so proud of you, Kathleen! You've worked hard a very long time and deserve this. I know you'll do a great job. They don't realize what a treasure they have with you. You are so talented! My God, if I had all the skills you do . . ." she gave me her wonderful little pep talk that *I always seemed to need to hear.*

For three days I went about my routine rather absent-mindedly. It was like being aware that a bomb had been dropped, and although I was at ground zero, it hadn't hit me yet. At work some of my employees were giving me a hard time. One was upset about getting in trouble for something that he had done wrong, but I was the "bad guy" for disciplining him. Another started yelling at me that I didn't communicate clearly, and I didn't spend my time correctly, and I should be doing blah, blah, blah for him. My head was spinning, my eyes felt like they were going to burst out of their sockets. I felt trapped and speechless. *I couldn't believe I was allowing someone to talk this way to me again.* I said to knock it off and take more self-responsibility, and I went to my office. As the tears were bubbling over, the phone rang. It was Leonard, my new soon-to-be "boss" from the Kids Clubs, and *I panicked, not wanting him to know I was crying.*

It was too late, I realized, as he asked what was wrong. I told him my staff were being difficult partly due to them knowing I would be transitioning out of this job in a month or two. This meant that their world was changing and they expressed having "fear of the unknown." As he talked he sounded so empathetic. *Yet, I decided that maybe he would think it weak of me to be upset about something like this.* Then suddenly it occurred to me what was also upsetting me deep inside. "I just found out my Mom was diagnosed with lung cancer!" I announced so quickly that I startled myself. Again, as he became genuinely concerned and explained how his best friend was battling breast cancer, the reality of it all hit me like a ton of bricks. The tears were now streaming down my face, as he allowed me a much needed and important outlet. "Oh, Kathleen! You've got to talk about it. Tell your friends! You need them right now and I'm sure they'd want to know," he said after I told him this was the first time I mentioned it since finding out. *What I didn't tell him was that I felt like I had no close friends to really talk to about it.* Then, when he asked me about my next scheduled visit home, I realized I needed to make a plan, and quickly!

Determined to be there for her next doctor's appointment, I called a travel agent and booked a flight out on Halloween for six days. I then asked two "ex-lovers" and my best buddy, Dick, to stop by to take care of the dogs on a thrice-daily schedule. That way, each one would only have to come once a day. Even though I wasn't real close to the "ex's" and I felt like it was such an imposition on their busy life, my dogs liked them so I knew they would let them in the front door (Jamey's such a ferocious little guard dog with his four inch legs). *Besides, I really didn't have many people I thought I could ask.*

To keep the last-minute cost of the flight down, I flew into Chicago-O'Hare and then rented a car to drive the two-and-a-half hours down to Champaign. After a pattern of "going home" just once every few years over the past decade, it felt strange being back there again so soon. Four months earlier I had been in town for the baptism of my then three-week old nephew, James. Sean and I were both given the honor of being his Godparents, an act Mom had to further complicate with a guilt trip. . . .

I had been so excited about becoming his Godmother, and filled with intense love at seeing my little brother's first natural offspring (Ken was two when Diana and Edward got together). One morning during coffee, Mom started lecturing me about the responsibilities of accepting this role, plus what it really meant to the Catholic Church and in God's eyes. I couldn't believe what I was hearing, and began to feel frustrated. She told me how Edward had to get special permission for me to attend the baptism because the rules "state" that one must be a practicing Catholic. *As my stomach turned, I began to feel "not good enough" again. Rather than show my real emotions, I became defensive and said, "This is between me and them, and they didn't say anything so it must be ok."*

"They probably don't know how to talk to you about it. They don't want to hurt your feelings! Yet if something should happen to them, God forbid, you would get custody and would need to be a good role model to James by attending church. It is an inherent promise that goes along with this honor. Your only saving grace was the fact you were baptized in the Church, however you should be practicing! And you know you'll have to attend Mass in order to officially be part of this baptism—I know how much that means to you!" she added sarcastically, then asserted, "Being a Godmother isn't just all fun and games like you seem to think!" *"I know that!"* I said, visibly irritated by now, *"I'll attend church. No problem!"*

Fuming, I got up and went for a long walk. When I returned, I called Diana to ask if I could come by in a few hours to see the baby. With that confirmed, I heated some leftovers for lunch while Mom was in the shower. As I sat at her kitchen table, *my eyes grew huge* when I noticed "The Catholic Newspaper" folded open to an inside article about the Pope's opinions regarding homosexuality. Now, on the same page was also an article about proper raising of difficult children, one that I could see her wanting to share with Edward to better deal with Ken. I couldn't believe she would have left this page out for me to see, not consciously anyway. Although she has always been desperate for me to return to the Church (I quit as a teen), she's really not that cruel! Moreover, she has always been very nice to my girlfriends, even though we've never discussed it. I tried a few times to bring it up but she always changed the subject. I know it makes her feel uncomfortable *(me too, I guess)*. Hence, I've just learned to accept that we don't verbally acknowledge this aspect of my life.

This article talked about how homosexuality was a sin in God's eyes as stated in the bible, and that the issue of "gay rights," especially marriage, was an abomination to the Catholic Church! The Pope also stated something about how woman was created from man, and that sexuality was meant only for the blessed act of conception within the holy bonds of matrimony in order to procreate in God's image.

The words blurred as I read in disbelief, yet ever-confirming my decision not to be part of this religion. (This decision was actually based on many other reasons and even occurred years before I realized my own sexual preference.) Hearing Mom come out of the bathroom, I quickly grabbed my stuff and disappeared into the "steamed room" before she could see my face. As the hot water intensely battered my head, I cried from a depth of a new corner in my Soul. My whole life came flashing back: *how frustrating it was to stand out as so different during my childhood at that church, to receive no compassion after dad died, and to get kicked out for being a smart-ass asking too many questions in eighth grade. The humiliation and rejection by everyone was very damaging to my self-esteem! Plus, for twenty years Mom tried to get me to go to Mass again, and now I have to go to that very church for the baptism. It's like she's winning because I want so badly to be a Godmother to baby James. Well, I can let her think that.*

While I sat on the floor of the tub hugging my knees close, showerhead still running above, I felt like dying wondering if Edward and Diana had discussed this. My thoughts ran wild as I pictured them talking about *my "lifestyle" and how that might influence their son, or how I might affect him by not "honoring" their religion. Terrible hurt arose from deep within my being as I realized they might not really want me to do this.* Therefore, I could not accept the honor if they had any negative thoughts about it. I would have to discuss it clearly and in-the-open with them to find out. Even though we had talked about my past partners a little, we never went into much detail or debate over it. Now, one thing was clear—they were devout Catholics so I needed to know their views.

After talking with Diana, and later Edward, they both expressed shock at what I had just put myself through. They assured me that they loved me and never once thought negatively about me with James. "Oh Kathleen," they both announced, "We know how good you are with children, and how much you love James. Not once have we had any doubt!" and then added, "Even though we practice Catholicism, we don't necessarily believe everything they preach. Us living together before marriage, for example . . . and we don't agree with them on their homosexuality views. You are a wonderful human being and sister (in-law), and that's all that counts!" When I asked about the qualifying criteria, they admitted Mom had been exaggerating for effect. "We're so sorry you went through this, but it was very simple. We asked and were told 'no problem' if one is non-practicing. We figured they didn't need to know any more than that."

Although **my heart swooned again with appreciation for Edward and his family,** *I still carried so much hurt from the games played with my Mother.* Additionally, **I felt sadness concerning the fact that I would be attending a church where I could not really speak my Truth. This seemed somehow hypocritical of me.** In fact, they would not allow me to be a Godmother had they known I was a "practicing lesbian" and further, did not believe in the doctrine of the Catholic Church! *Ethically in turmoil, I chose to keep family peace.*

∾∾∾

As I arrive at my Mother's condo, Edward and his family are there. It is late afternoon on Halloween, and Ken runs up first, "Hi, Aunt Kathleen!" giving me his typical big bear hug that nearly knocks me over. Even though he's a little guy for a twelve-year-old (his natural father was Japanese), he's chalked full of energy—a lot like me when I was a child. After pulling me inside to see his latest techno-toys and Lego stations, he then follows me around updating me on everything in his life while I manage to hug Mom hello, drop off my suitcases in her guest room, and pick up baby James. Of course I have to give talkative Ken most of my attention. I don't want him to think I am more interested in how much James has grown and what his babble may mean. After acknowledging all the typical commotion that goes on when their whole family is in Mom's small condo, including petting their barking dog turning circles at my feet, I sneak away to the bathroom, then grab myself a beer. Finally I can sit down to admire James while Ken shows me his two different masks. "I can't decide which one to wear, so I'll take both out with me trick-or-treating," he announces for everyone to hear.

He puts on a huge alien head, one with a hand pump that squirts green blood all over the skull and down the face, then walks up closely to each one of us, several times as we're trying to talk to each other. "Ohhh, that's creepy," says Mom, "The people will love that one!" "Hey Aunt Kathleen, will you take me around tonight?" he asks. Before I can answer, Diana says, "Ken, Kathleen just got into town. I'm sure she wants to relax and visit with Grandma." "No, really, it's ok. I'll take him—it'll be fun!" I reply, causing Ken to yell, "Cool!" as he puts on his other mask and runs around. Jumping onto the back of my chair, I say "Careful, Ken, the baby . . ." as he whispers to me how he really intends to go to each house twice with a different mask to get double the candy in half the time! "Oh," I nod, then my inner teacher can't resist pointing out, "Isn't that a little deceitful?" "Yeah, so what!" he smiles and shrugs as I also listen to what Edward is saying in the background about his job situation. I know it is important for me to continue giving Ken as much attention as I can. He has been the only child (grandchild) in our little family for over ten years. Consequently, the two of us have quite a strong bond.

"That's enough, Ken! We're trying to talk here," Mom snaps, reaching her typical saturation point. She wants so desperately to talk with Edward and me, plus obviously loves focusing on her new grandchild so much, that her toleration of Ken is beginning to diminish. Further, the added stress now of her diagnosis creates new eggshells upon which we all must walk. As the now pouting Ken flops down to play with his Nintendo, I feel empathy for his situation. Smart way beyond his years, he is unfortunately very immature due in large part to the first couple years of his life.

Tragically, Ken's real father was a deeply disturbed and abusive man in every way. Baby Ken and his parents were living in California when Diana's best friend moved to Champaign and started working with Edward. One night while the girlfriends were on the phone, Edward was handed the receiver and started talking to Diana. It was love at first sound! They spent the next year talking regularly via telephone, with Edward counseling Diana on what to do about her "situation." Finally, around Ken's second birthday, Diana planned a trip to Illinois so that the three of them could meet. Upon confirming their intense feelings of attraction in person, Diana then made plans for her and Ken to move-in with Edward less than three months later.

Edward and Mom describe Ken as severely stunted at that time, saying he appeared more like a six-month old baby. They said he was unable to talk or walk, and that he would have violent outbursts of banging his head on the floor. Diana, young and naive with low self-esteem at the time, was at a loss for what to do. Thus, Edward took on a very strong parental role: authoritarian and disciplinarian yet loving, playful and building trust. As a result of being removed from his abusive father, plus sensing his mother in a newly supportive relationship, as well as having a new "Grandmother" shower him with love too—Ken flourished! Great strides were made and he was fast becoming more age appropriate when a custody battle took them by surprise one year later. The courts forced them to send then three-year-old Ken, due to lack of "legal proof" of previous abuse, to his father for the remainder of the summer. This man also received custody of his sixteen-month-old baby daughter from another woman, and had both children by himself for one terrifying, life-altering week. The abuse was so violent, so horrific, that the little girl died from head trauma right in front of Ken! When Diana and Edward finally got Ken back, he had totally regressed again. This made their job as parents and our job as a family a million times more difficult. (Ken's father is now spending many years in prison.)

Having always worked with children, and particularly many years with varying degrees of abused children from pre-school through teens, I was acutely aware of Ken's issues from an educational and experiential standpoint. I first met Ken when he was five and just two years after the "incident." It seemed that my family had been around him for so long that they were losing their perspective. Again, they thought he was catching up and doing great, as I'm sure he was, considering. However, I was concerned with how socially far behind and immature he was. Yet, he was also very smart—he knew more about every animal in the zoo than I did. Further, he was so difficult to understand because of his extreme baby talk that I knew they had a long road ahead of them. He was also very affectionate and touchy-feely, and continued to hang all over us until recently. This is something I know that goes hand-in-hand with sexual abuse.

Therefore, it is no surprise how this smart-hyperactive-little-boy captured my heart. And during my next visit when he was seven, we really bonded as we played and ran wild. I have always been the adult who is just a big kid to him, and he expects that of me every time I visit. It is also not surprising that he never made it through a year in any school without problems and getting expelled. His need for attention and his temper tantrums were too much for typical school systems. After years of trying every school in the city as well as home schooling, he finally ended up in a special program for needy children, at a facility where I actually worked a decade earlier as an Outdoor Recreation Supervisor. This school has very small-ratio classrooms, level systems and more creative outlets than traditional schools. Further, it houses the court-mandated children from a variety of backgrounds all mixed together, which also has the possibility of "taking him more astray." This is something Mom, of course, worries about. Thus far, however, he loves it, has great teachers and seems to be doing very well.

~~~

For the next two days, my visit with Mom was very pleasant. We didn't talk much about her cancer. I just let her mandate the discussions. Whatever she wanted to talk about, suddenly took on a whole new meaning. Even if I had heard it before, this time I didn't tell her that, but rather acted interested from a different place. It was about hearing her, not the story. I found myself really listening to her voice fluctuations, her need to ruminate, and her impeccable memory for certain details. She would describe the delicious ingredients of a "best" meal she'd had, the extremely "rare" politeness of a service technician, the "disgraceful" state-of-the-nation affairs, the "irritating" way a friend would treat her, the "most perfect" pine tree out her front window, and the asinine "politics" of the condo association. I observed how she would sit for hours on end, getting up frequently for food or drink yet never once pausing the story. Even when I went to the bathroom, she would often continue talking. She stopped only to watch an Illini game or the Cubs on TV. I studied the way she expressed herself telling these important little stories. She would get so worked up over perceived injustices that I could feel her blood pressure rising from across the room. Then, she would tell a humorous story from a simple point of view, one which most people would not have perceived. This always resulted in a release of stress from the previous story.

It was hard not to notice that she still had a bandage on her neck from the biopsy. That taped-big-white-square-gauze was a constant reminder. I had taken over for Edward, cleaning the incision and putting antibiotic ointment on it. It looked red, slightly puffy and huge: two inches long in a crease on her neck. She said it wasn't painful at all, just made a little pinching sensation sometimes. It was time now to go to the surgeon to have the butterfly tape removed, and I was really ready to discuss her case with him. After waiting nearly an hour in this tiny examination room, a slightly pudgy, rather arrogant man came rushing in. He barely acknowledged me as Mom tried to introduce us. He simply removed the surgical tape and bandage, remarking how well it had healed. I commented on what a good job he had done, and how the scar would be hidden in the fold of her skin. He nodded as Mom surprisingly said, "Well, whoop-tee-do!" He then started to say goodbye and leave when I stopped him and said, "Wait, we have some questions for you." As he stood, one foot in the doorway with his hand on the knob, I asked, "What is her prognosis here? I don't understand." "What's not to understand?" he responded coldly. "Your Mother's in stage four of metastatic lung cancer." Although aghast at his poor "bedside manner," I proceeded to ask, "Well, what about the course of treatment?" With a patronizing tone, he replied, "That's for you to determine with her doctor at the cancer clinic." "I thought you were her doctor," I defended. "No, I am the surgeon," he quickly explained, "I removed several tumors off her lymph glands. She should find some relief in that," and he hurried out the door shuffling papers.

I felt my blood pressure rising. My poor Mom was obviously confused over the entire episode. Her eyes filled with tears as she put on her jacket and I grabbed her purse. I do not think she wanted me to be blasted with the cold reality of her disease quite like that. *I could only think about what an "asshole" he had been towards us, with no regard for our feelings or what challenges we might be personally facing.* On the other hand, Mom could not stop thinking how rude she appeared by her response. She meant to express not caring whether she had a scar on her neck or not. However, she realized it sounded like she did not care about what a good surgical job he had done. I had to listen to her tell one person after another how she probably hurt his feelings and should write to thank him for the great work. *Contrarily, I was totally appalled and tempted to write about his insensitive attitude and egotistical behavior!* This being a good lesson for me in letting-go, I allowed Mom to have her story while, in the meantime, we scheduled and then waited for the "real appointment" two days later at the clinic.

One of those mornings, a good ole friend of hers, Ellen, who recently moved back into town after 20 years, came for a visit. We had a great chat and it was good to see her. I remember them always playing bridge, as part of a four-some throughout the seventies when I was in my teens. Reminiscing over these funny stories was more entertaining than I could have imagined. "I'll never forget how you used to peek around the corner at us, looking all coy, your face just-a-beaming! Boy! That used to crack me up!" she laughingly described. "I always loved your personality. You had such a great way of entertaining us a little each time we came over. Remember that time you came running in saying what a hunk my son Mike was, and I didn't know what 'hunk' meant?" "Really?" I asked with my eyebrows scrunched as I tried to recall what he looked like, "I don't remember that." **It was remarkable for me to listen to this new perspective** of someone from my past. *I tend to remember those years as being depressing with so much shame and embarrassment* that **it was refreshing to hear how some people may have seen the positive. "This is so important for me to realize,"** I thought to myself as I walked her to her car, and thanked her for coming back into my Mom's life at this crucial time. "Oh, I just love your Mother. She's a great gal! Don't you worry now. I'll check in on her every day, but while you're here I'll give you all space." *I had just expressed how worried I was because Mom had been so alone, slowly alienating herself from the world more and more over the years of retirement. I also shared my frustration with her "church" never contacting her.* **I know that's the way Mom liked it,** *yet it really bothered me that this crucial support system in her life, one which she attended for over thirty years and donated God-only-knows how much money to, didn't even have a senior outreach program. And now in light of her illness, I really thought they could increase services.* However, that was just one of the many areas on which Mom and I disagreed.

When the time came for her doctor's visit, I tried to appear calm and cool. I gave Mom a big reassuring hug before we left for the clinic. "I'm so glad you're here, Honey. You can help me remember all my questions," she said, visibly stressed now. Edward and I had made a list of things to discuss, and I patted my pocket to show her I hadn't forgotten as we drove the familiar streets of my old hometown. Mom pointed to a couple new buildings and talked of "changes" along the way. What stood out the most to me were the huge multi-colored deciduous trees lining the roads. They were absolutely breath-taking canopies of auburns, crimsons and gold extending over the roads, something I used to naively take for granted. They certainly were not something you would see in Phoenix!

The clinic had a very friendly atmosphere. While we waited I grabbed at least twenty different American Cancer Society and Lung Association informational brochures and tapes, plus flyers on support groups. We didn't wait long at all when a very thin, red-haired young doctor politely entered the room and introduced himself. Almost immediately, Mom and I were relieved at his gentle and sincere nature. He also had a talent for putting everything in simple terms, and chose his words conscientiously. He explained the good news to be that the cancer had not yet spread to other organs even though it was in her lymph system, which was unusual, and that she had the slow-growing kind of cells. Further, he said that being a "large" woman would be in her favor because of the aggressive chemo and radiation schedule on which he wanted to place her as soon as possible. Mom laughed at that, and looking at me, joked, "I knew there was a benefit to being so fat!" He then stated that he didn't want to give false hope and that she was looking at a short life expectancy at this stage. He added that it was his desire to control the cancer and her pain, and to make her as comfortable as possible. He thought she was a perfect candidate for a new strong chemo of which she would have just two doses, three weeks apart, followed a month later by an intense twelve-day-schedule of radiation. "This type of chemotherapy," he explained, "is supposed to not make people as violently ill, but you can expect to experience lethargy and hair loss." He then gave us information to take home and read, asking us to make a decision soon so we could schedule it. When I asked what the average life expectancy he typically saw at this stage was, our fears were confirmed when he answered, " . . . could be two months, or two years . . ." His explanation of how her 5-centimeter lung tumor had been growing for probably the last eight years or so, and the several ½ to 2cm tumors in her neck that had been removed had also been slowly growing for awhile—was surprising, and tough to hear!

As we drove over to Edward's house after the appointment, I didn't say much as Mom made nervous chitchat about what a wonderful doctor he was. The family was waiting when we walked in. First, I had to look at the reptiles and amphibians in Ken's room where he asked me, "Is my Grandma gonna die?" "Yes, Honey," I had to be honest, "She's very sick." Before I could say another word, he went wailing down the hall and outside. Diana came towards me, quietly mouthing, "What happened?" After telling her, I asked how much they had said thus far. "Not much," she responded, "just that she had lung cancer from smoking, and we'd find out more later," and then, "I'll go talk to him." I felt very awkward, yet not ashamed of the truth. I got Mom a glass of water then showed Edward all the pamphlets. We played with baby James until Ken and Diana returned. Finally, with silence unbeknownst to this family, they all intently stared at me while I bravely gave them the summary.

The look on Edward's face was heartbreaking—first turning red, his Adam's apple grew visibly larger as his eyes became glassy. He reached over and took Mom's hand as she nodded to everything I was saying. **I felt a strengthening of character come over me in order to break all this news to them.** *Yet, I worried about sounding almost cold and too factual. After all, I was the one who flew into town, broke the news to them and then went back to Phoenix the next day leaving them to deal with the aftermath.* I watched the tears now stream down my brother's face as he lovingly gazed at Mom, and I wondered how he would get through this after a lifetime of feeling responsible for her. Mom looked at me most of the time, or at baby James bouncing around in her arms, as she carefully avoided the painful emotions being expressed. "We'll get through this, Mom," Edward choked, clearing his throat before continuing, "Don't you worry about a thing now, hear? I'll help you with every doctor's appointment and the bills and everything, ok?" After Mom nodded with appreciation, she said, "Now, Kathleen! We've got to let them eat their dinner. It's late and I know they're hungry!" She hugged them goodbye, as I stood back and mocked, "Yeah, come on! It's always me that makes them late!" And we laughed knowing Mom had a way of "saying things," when truthfully they did everything late.

∿∿∿

I felt absolutely numb—the worst feeling of shock I had ever felt before— the whole way back to Phoenix. As I walked down the airplane ramp, I realized just how exhausted I was and how little sleep I had had during the entire trip. Mom had coughed and hacked, worse than usual, all night long, every night. I don't know how she slept through it. I saw my best friend Linda, *the only one who had seemed to stand by me and grow with me since we met five years ago,* walking towards me in the distance. She had a big grin across her face like she was up to something. She approached and asked with her silly British accent, "Miss Kathleen, and how was your trip Ma'am?" I nodded while she commenced with telling me about all the funny escapades she had encountered on her recent scuba diving adventure. We often went months without seeing each other, then would get together for a fun night of catch-up, dinner and sometimes a movie. We also had shared several "single" New Years' Eves together, and made plans for yet another. I was so glad she was available to pick me up at the airport; with her busy 60-hour workweek and all her traveling, she was seldom accessible. Nonetheless, I knew I felt the most comfortable with her. I knew she accepted me just the way I was.

As soon as we climbed into her truck, a giant wave of emotion exploded through me as I unexpectedly released a build-up of stress. After being in denial for a few days, then "acting" so strong around Mom and my family for a week, the reality of her disease and what we were about to go through hit me like a lightening bolt from out of nowhere. Putting both hands over my face, I sobbed uncontrollably, saying, "Oh God, oh my God!" several times. Linda sat, waiting to start the jeep. She put her right hand on my upper back, comforting me, and holding a safe space for me while I wept. After what seemed like ten minutes, I lifted my head, blew my nose, and said, "Phew, I need a cigarette!" "Thought you'd never ask!" Linda jokingly replied, lighting one for both of us as she headed out of the parking garage to drive me home.

I have always smoked off and on my whole life, yet never very much. In fact Edward and I both started messing around with cigarettes when we were in grade school, only he has always been a heavy smoker, and I would quit for more years than I smoked. Usually a "break-up" or stressful event would trigger a craving for me, however I only smoked a few each day and would quit after several weeks, months or sometimes a few years. Linda was the same way, a "closet smoker," therefore we would often smoke together. I told myself I needed to quit for good this time, very soon, especially in light of Mom's lung cancer!

I was explaining to Linda how I wanted to go home for five days around Thanksgiving and Christmas, and she found some great deals off the Internet for me. I had to actually return home on those holidays, however I agreed it would be better than the alternatives. Being a computer wiz, to negotiate airline fares was a fun adventure for her. Besides, I was somewhat computer illiterate, and thus grateful for the help. I think I was one of the few at work without a computer. It was the joke of the Institution: "Hey K'earns, ya got e-mail yet?" Regardless, I always knew that working in "social service" fields never paid well and I was used to getting by on a lack of resources. I had been advocating since I started with the Agency to upgrade the facilities to better meet the recreational needs of the youths we served, and to pay the staff better too. It took years, which was common for big budgetary changes within a governmental agency, but I then noticed that all of the goals which I had proposed in the beginning, I had eventually accomplished. If I had gotten any of those other jobs I applied for, I would never have seen the fruition of my labors. I was now waiting for this new team of people with whom I was working to approve the grant proposal so we could turn it in. The longer it took them, the longer my new job hung in the waiting. However, in light of Mom's diagnosis, I thought she would probably die after the first of the year. *So, if my job were to start then, I would be able to devote all my time to it without worrying about her condition back home.*

Mom was so excited to have me coming home for both of the holidays. What a dream come true for a mother! My brothers had never missed these their whole lives, yet I came back for only two Christmases in eleven years. We always talked on the phone for all holidays. Plus, I routinely sent Christmas care-packages for them, full of AZ t-shirts, Phoenix memorabilia, desert creature trinkets, southwestern foods, Native American toys, etc. **However, I just knew that this Thanksgiving and Christmas would be her last and therefore I had to be there.**

~~~

When I arrived in November, Mom had just had her first dose of chemo the day before. She said she felt fine, but by the next day, she was so weak and tired, I was glad I was there for her. **What perfect timing!** She could not have stayed by herself for at least two of the days. She lost her appetite and I had to get very creative trying to get some nutrition down her. She wasn't nauseated per se, yet the thought of food repulsed her. It was strange being there with the condo so ghostly quiet as she slept the days away. This was a very unusual thing for her to do. I took her car to the shop for needed maintenance, and did extra cleaning around the house to whittle away the hours. I was sorting stuff in her garage, when I discovered some old journal entries from her "last mother." Now this lady, who wasn't that much older than Mom, and her husband (Mom's "second dad") had actually disowned Mom after she converted to Catholicism, and didn't speak to her for years. In fact, I don't remember really meeting or seeing them until after my dad died. Then, I guess, they decided forgiveness was the Christian thing to do, and they all got closer again until the "mom's" death from pancreatic cancer in 1984. The "dad" ended up living until 1998, and Mom was the only one who took care of his estate. She also visited him regularly for over a decade after putting him in a good nursing home an hour away. **She's very blessed in heaven for this selfless work!**

One evening during sunset, I went into her bedroom and curled up behind her. The house was getting darker and colder with the mid-western winter encroaching. We must have lain there several hours, me asking her all about this "mother" with all her problems and the surgeries I had read about. It somehow comforted the little girl inside of me to listen to my Mother like this. She talked a lot about her own childhood as well as this third mother. It felt reminiscent of a bedtime story, feeling her warmth next to me and cuddling together in a way we hadn't done in years. As I fought back urges to fall asleep, I listened trying to understand what this mother must have gone through in her lifetime to have had all those medical problems and been so judgmental towards other people. When I asked Mom if she knew what her dreams had been, I was told she really wanted to be an artist and that some of her oil paintings were in the closet. I jumped from the bed and pulled out these interesting still life paintings, as we talked about them for some time.

The only light on in the house now was from her closet, and I laughed as I discovered some of her 1970 clothes. "Oh my God," I exclaimed, "I remember this from when I was in seventh grade!" As I modeled a loud polka dot turtleneck, and multi-colored crocheted vest, I continued, "Oh hey, Mom, this will really attract those older gentlemen when we go for a walk after you feel better!" Always easy to entertain, she started laughing to where the tears came to her eyes as I swished my hips in a seersucker skirt declaring, "Yeah, baby—I am a hot momma!" I then asked her when the last time was that she "purged" her clothing, and if she wanted me to help her get rid of any of those archaic clothes (many of which were yellowed with tobacco stains). She started laughing even more hysterically, so that she couldn't even answer me. "All-right-y, then! That explains it perfectly. You need not say another word," I kept egging her on as we shared this typical, comical mother/daughter moment.

We were planning to have Thanksgiving dinner around noon, more like a brunch, because my flight left at 2:30pm. The day before, I had begun preparing and Mom was still too weak and spacey to help much. This really disturbed her, and it hurt me to see her this way. Additionally, I was tired from a lack of sleep. Her coughing was continuing to scare me; *it sounded like she might die in the middle of the night.* However, the chemo made her not want cigarettes at all so she quit smoking without really trying. This was the first time in my life I hadn't seen her smoke, plus my clothes didn't get stinky being around her. Even when I smoked, it was mainly outdoors. I was very conscious of not wanting to smell like it and thus had developed great habits as such. I had actually quit (again) a few days after the Halloween trip. I decided to trick myself whenever I craved one by saying, "I am a non-smoker! Always have been, always will be!" I then would force myself to think of other things. I also hung on my refrigerator a list of health improvements by the day, week, month and eventually year, which I had gotten from the cancer pamphlets. It helped to further motivate me daily by reading the cumulative effects of abstinence. *This trip was very trying on my nerves, and my craving was intense!* I realized just how much I numbed emotions around Mom by smoking, but if she could refrain, so could I.

I tried to get instructions from her on the way she prepared the turkey and how to make her special stuffing recipe. We started getting frustrated with each other because she was too tired to come into the kitchen and too groggy to give me complete directions. So, I had to combine my way of doing things over the past decade with what she could manage to instruct. Then, when she would ask me what I was doing, it was always somehow wrong! I had arisen at 4am to start cooking everything, and by 8am Sean had arrived. I usually froze around him. *His emotional walls clashed with mine and I never knew what he was going to criticize next.* He said, "What, no coffee?" to which I responded, "You'll have to make some." Mom was feeling too ill for the first time and didn't have his pot ready. I already drank mine hours before. When he didn't make any and I saw Mom attempt to, I grudgingly took over and told her to go rest.

While they sat in the living room and talked like nothing was different— even though she was still in her nightgown, I was busy preparing for the meal and packing for the flight home. Sean was also deeply connected to Mom, yet did not want to talk about her illness. They always talked more like equals, friends almost; instead of, as Mother and child like with Edward and I. *Further, Sean had pretty much been a loner. It was my understanding he had never been in a relationship, and I worried about the impact her death would also have on his life.* **I actually prayed for all of us to heal and grow into the beautiful Beings we were meant to be on this earth. I knew that Mom's passing would somehow give wings to all of our hearts.** For the time being, however, it seemed that *we remained somehow stuck and stifled.*

Even though I was attached to old resentments toward him, kept alive by hearing his occasional critical comments towards me, I never fought with nor criticized him (to his face) as an adult. On the other hand, he seemed stuck on verbal negativity towards me. It was almost like he tried to trigger my hurt and anger, *so I learned to hide emotions.* This was an absurd game, which I prayed to God to transcend. I just hadn't discovered how yet. What was astonishing was that Mom never heard his comments! She only saw my resistance towards him and lectured me to grow up, let go of the past, and love him. She thought he had outgrown his old ways. And on several occasions I had to remind her of the time he started cutting down my Master's thesis. I was thirty then and had worked harder on that project than any other in my life thus far. It was my precious baby for which I had tremendous pride. Even Edward stuck up for me by saying, "Oh Sean, don't you even . . ." *I had to leave the room and go outside for a long walk, chokingly not able to say anything because of my promise to myself to never fight again. Nonetheless, I couldn't believe the feeling like he was reading my diary all over again, and how absolutely invaded and degraded I felt deep down.*

Mom always tried to manipulate me to be closer to him, which caused my gut to constrict worse. She never understood his invasion of my privacy and my sensitivity to his criticisms. Thus, she never respected my need to establish boundaries with him as an adult. For example, when I'd call on holidays, she'd say, "Do you want to talk to Sean now?" and as I'd answer, "No," she'd then hold out the receiver and yell, "Sean! Your sister wants to talk to you!" Other times she would tell me to hug him goodbye, and even though the energy exchange felt very uncomfortable to me, I'd do it anyway.

By 10am Edward's family came blasting in the condo. Diana brought her special carrot cake and was offering to help me while Ken ran around wild as usual showing us his latest gadgets and wanting me to play with him. "Not this time, Honey. I have too much to do here," I explained as he pouted and rolled outside on his in-line skates.

As Mom and my brothers were making over baby James, Diana and I arranged the meal. We then sat around the table, and Ken started grabbing the gravy, spilling a line of it across the tablecloth then dumping three servings worth onto his plate. I snapped, "Ken, could you wait until after prayers, please!" I had spent so long making that gravy, plus there wasn't very much to begin with. "I was probably just like this when I was young," I told myself. Then he jumped up and started lighting candles as Edward ordered him to not play with matches. I smirked inside remembering how much Edward used to be a little "pyro." "Can we please say prayers now?" Mom asked with irritation in her voice. However, when Ken started slyly grabbing other food, sneaking it onto his plate so that no one else saw, I couldn't play my typical role of "big-kid" with him this time. "Ken!" I surprised myself by yelling, then after taking a breath, I said softer yet firmer, "Please, I don't have any patience—I'm just grumpy since I haven't slept in a week." "Whad'ya mean you haven't slept?" Mom inquired as Sean sarcastically added, "So what was your excuse the rest of your life?" Another deep breath or two later, Mom was still saying, " . . . but I thought you slept fine," as I shook my head "never-mind," and we started our prayers.

Mom cried as she thanked God for having her wonderful children all together again, of course after saying the typical Catholic "BlessusOhLord-an'these-thygifts . . ." This was one of the many "rote" prayers which I wondered if they really knew what they were saying. I then suggested that we all take turns saying something we were thankful for, and I felt a bunch of eyes stare at me like I was an alien. The uncomfortable feeling this request generated amazed me. They obviously weren't used to my kind of genuine spontaneity. First, **I thanked God for the gift of family for Soul growth issues, for bringing all our hearts together, and for sending Mom extra Angels at this time.** Edward then broke the tension, as usual, by saying, "And thank you for Kathleen being here and making us this delicious meal—now let's eat!"

"Where are the black olives?" Sean asked, "They're usually on the relish tray!" My blood pressure started rising as I thought about saying, "If you would have offered to help out earlier . . ." Instead, Mom said, "Oh, Diana, could you open a can and bring it in here, please?" Then I felt myself absolutely fume when I heard him say next, "What happened to the rolls? We always have rolls at Thanksgiving dinner!" "Well, Honey, I'm sorry but Kathleen forgot to buy them this time," Mom replied as my heart sunk. *That same old feeling of not being good enough, or not doing something quite right returned like an inner bomb. As an adult I'd gotten really good at keeping my negative thoughts to myself, however, I couldn't believe how much power I gave to this man. It was like a subtle thing.*

He didn't ever say anything positive to me, and often nobody else noticed. Even Diana couldn't see it until I pointed it out each time to her. After ignoring (but not really) one last cutting remark about how "we had to change our whole Thanksgiving Day schedule just to accommodate Kathleen"—it was finally time to leave.

This time when I returned home and Linda was waiting at the gate, I was pretty drunk. I had spent a three-hour layover in Detroit, and the airport was practically empty. There were two other women in the bar near my gate with an equally long wait. They happened to be flirting with the bartender, and I got in on his generous holiday spirit. He was whipping up sweet potent concoctions in the blender for us, and we were downing them. It was a fun, let-loose time; one I desperately needed after my experience at home. Then on the flight to Phoenix, I also drank a free little bottle of wine with the Thanksgiving dinner they served. The plane was so empty that I stretched my legs across three seats and had a blast. Linda was so surprised at my incessant giggling and obvious different mood than when she'd picked me up the last time. "Oh, who wants to talk about that," I sarcastically answered when she asked how things were at home, "Let's just party instead, girlfriend!" Then, rolling down the window, I yelled out into the night sky as the freeway traffic whirred by, "Yeee-high! Hello Phoenix! It's so good to see you again!"

~~~

Up until the Christmas trip, I stayed busy trying to learn all I could about my new job assignment: studying about the girls at their institution, going to meetings in the Clubs, meeting staff I'd be working with, and preparing my employees for my absence. The grant had been initially approved and it looked like the money would come in after the first of the year, just like I predicted. I was getting very excited about sitting on a rare opportunity like this. We were the first in the country to receive monies to help transition girls out of Corrections, and then set them up with mentors plus a program in the community.

At one of the Club staff meetings, the art coordinator, Rudy, an eccentric passionate black woman with fiery red hair, started to catch my enthusiasm as we discussed the project. I needed staff to help and she felt a calling to be involved. Our boss said, "Great!" and everything seemed to be falling into place. I was feeling grateful to God, like my time was finally here after a very long wait. As

I watched her artistically doodle during the meeting, **I felt myself being inspired to get in touch with my inner-artist, something I had long neglected. I sat intently for the remainder of the hour, drawing an Angel of Compassion next to the following poem, which simply flowed out:**

In Preparation of Death

The chill in the air . . .   No, the flash of heat . . .
Encompasses my sad spirit and binds my brain—
From functioning . . .

Deep thoughts a scatter . . .   No, intense feelings abound . . .
Infiltrate my broken heart and trigger the tears—
Of near grief . . .

Maternal energy connections . . .   No, karmic Soul agreements . . .
Snap my sunken solar plexus and prepare to bid a physical farewell—
To my Mother . . .

As I packed for yet a third trip in two months, my dogs were visibly upset. The last time, Charley had had an accident. My dog-sitters were doing the best they could but if one arrives early, and the next late, it can make the dogs wait entirely too long. Poor things! They were getting terribly lonely and depressed, plus I couldn't seem to find anyone willing to spend the night. Even the kennel at their vets (whom they love) was booked for the holidays. So, I begged some coworkers, "ex's" and other friends to stop by, spreading it out as thin as possible. *It was a nightmare for me because I felt like no one really cared the way I wished someone would. It didn't make sense to me when I had dog-sat for many friends in the past, and now that I needed people, where were they?*

I was mad, very angry at times in fact, because I was alone during this time in my life. Most of my adult life I had been in monogamous relationships, anywhere from one to four years, with very little "single" time in between. I didn't really look for this, it just happened that way. After each break-up, I'd meet someone else and "fall in love." *At this point, if I had been with someone I wouldn't have had to worry about dog-sitters! Plus, I could've used the intimate support to get through my Mother's death.* However, it looked like **God intended for me to go through all of this on my own.**

Christmas time in Illinois was full of snow and cheer. Surprisingly, Mom didn't have a bad reaction to the second dose of chemo and thus was feeling good this time. I suspect it also had to do with her having all her kids together again for her favorite holiday. She wanted it to be special, as did we. I was really enjoying myself, feeling like an excited child again as I ran around with Diana buying presents, loving on the ever-growing James (6 months now), and hearing the music of the season everywhere. I was also decorating Mom's house for her as if it would be the last . . . **because it would be.**

One evening about 9pm I went out, against Mom's advice, for a walk around the winding sidewalks between the condos. I was dressed in Mom's big coat, gloves and hat, with a scarf around my face and her boots on my feet. It was starting to snow really thick fluffy flakes and the wind was getting stronger. I could barely see a few feet in front of me. I couldn't remember the last time I dressed like this. **Memories of Mom bundling me when I was young came flashing back to me as my heart opened wide, and feelings of love kept swirling to the rhythm of the blowing snow.** Around the huge pine trees and under the glowing yellow lights **I danced like a little girl, feeling lost in wonderland. The inner warmth and peacefulness I felt in this scene was comforting to my aching Soul, and I felt many Angels laughing with me as I flopped onto the pure white virgin snow to make snow-Angels.** Nobody else was out and about to watch my silliness, yet I wouldn't have cared if they had been. Sinking down onto a large, deep snowdrift, **I felt cradled in warmth and magically hypnotized, almost like I could fall asleep and die right there. And I remembered feeling and thinking that often as a child.**

When I opened the front door then quickly closed it behind me, Mom asked, "Honey, where've you been? I was getting worried about you. Ohhh, it's really getting cold out there!" she added as she felt the crisp winter night air that snuck in with me chill her body. I stood by the doorway, slightly leaning towards her, with a barely visible goofy half-smile on my face under the drooping wet scarf, waiting for her to really look at me. "You know you shouldn't be out so late," she continued to scold me some more until she at last understood what I was doing. She started laughing, "Well, don't you look cute! Just like when you were a little girl!" I began to shake all the snow off me like a dog—I was totally covered in white. She then stood to give me a hug saying, "You're so sweet, Kathleen! I just love you so much!"

The next morning I had a very difficult task ahead of me. Mom had been wearing a cap now because her hair was coming out in clumps, and falling fast! I pretended that it did not bother me, and I offered to cut what was left. She had not been able to wash it for a while because she didn't want that much hair going down the drain. As I lifted and cut her hair as close to the scalp as possible, Mom admitted to me that this was probably the worst thing that could happen to her. She had always loved her hair. Whenever her weight depressed her, she always thought, "At least I have great hair!" Her whole life, she had always been complimented on how thick and wavy it was, and easy to cut, style or perm however she liked. She expressed being afraid to see herself bald. Being empathetic, I told her I'd feel the same way. I also told her how beautiful she was. **She honestly did have a vulnerable beauty glowing about her.** Afterwards, however, when she looked in the mirror, I heard her exclaim, "Oh Kathleen! It is not beautiful! To think I actually started believing you! Oh my God! This is scary!" Then, that became a joke she told everyone, about how she couldn't trust my perspective anymore.

When Christmas Eve rolled around, she asked me if I was going to Mass with the family. It was just like she had asked me for over twenty years, only this time I answered yes. Taken aback, she paused, and tearfully said, "Oh that's great, Honey, just wonderful!" I knew it was like **giving her a dying wish**, and even though I did not want to go back into that church again, I figured I'd have to for her funeral eventually, so why not with her alive as well? This was also a tough decision because I had felt pressured into it.

It had happened the Sunday before Thanksgiving when I was home. Edward and his family had gone to church with Mom. That was the service they decided to tell her favorite priest after Mass she had cancer. Teary eyed, she then got into the car and said to them, "I wish Kathleen had been here." I was standing in the kitchen when they got home, and first Ken ran through weeping, "Aunt Kathleen, Grandma's crying because of you!" Then Diana walked by me and said, "Kathleen, at Christmas you have got to go to Mass for your Mother!" Next, Mom walked in crying and said, "I wish you could have been there, it would have meant so much to me! Edward told Father Edmondson about my condition and he was so wonderful. He'll be saying a special Mass and prayers for me!" She was truly touched. *I, conversely, was utterly incensed by this major guilt trip thrown at me.* Pride aside, there I was at Christmas Mass. This trip seemed to go the fastest, with minimal family discomfort, which was a relief after the frustrations from Thanksgiving. We exchanged gifts Christmas Eve, and it was a wonderful time for Mom. Before I knew it, I was flying back home.

Christmas evening I arrived at my house with Linda as my escort again. This time, however, I was in a deeply quiet mood. At first I was hoping she'd leave because I thought I didn't feel like having any company. My dog-sitters had left me some presents, and she encouraged me to open them along with her gifts! The first, a bottle of "tequila rose" which tastes like strawberry cream, sounded awfully good. We started drinking it as I played this absolutely awesome CD: "Wallela" by Rita Coolidge and her sister and niece singing wonderful Cherokee honoring tunes. It caught my ear in the airport and I just had to buy it. **The Soulful native harmonies really reached in and caressed my heart while the lyrics somehow enriched my Spirit with a renewed sense of strength. Remarkably, Linda had the exact same reaction, as we both got goose bumps and let the songs decorate the background to this now festive occasion. Adorning our bodies with Christmas bows and decorations, suddenly I was really glad she stayed. I felt my mood rising and we giggled as we shared family stories and got caught up on things. And I told her how I would be at peace if Mom died now by knowing I had done all I'd done.**

≈≈≈

A New Year's Affirmation Ditty: To Me With Love

I love my house and all my space; I love my puppies in my face.
I love my friends and those to come; I love my family and my Mom.
I love my job, I do it well; I love my life as time does tell.
I love myself, my passionate fire; I love my God and my heart's desire!

It hit me, one hour before New Year's Eve at midnight. I was listening to two friends discuss how they talk to their Mom about menopause. *And I realized . . . I would not be able to, nor any other topic in the future.* It hit me, looking at some paperwork, that my beneficiary is my Mom. *And I realized . . . I don't know whom to put down now.* It hit me, watching TV the other night. Every show was about relationships with mothers, and I reflected on the deep struggle and pain my Mom must be going through now. *And I realized . . . there's no one to hold her—nor am I capable, strong enough, or responsible.* But God does it hurt . . . really . . . deep. And it has just hit me, like a shock wave: **my Mother has done the best she could and meant well,** *even though she really never accepted me, knew me, or loved me.* **And I realized . . . I did the same thing! So now I need to mother myself, and heal my inner children. And then, I realized . . . it's too late for her to do that!**

I want 2000 to be so different! I want to find people who will support and nurture me. I want to think positive, and act only for my Highest Good. I want to stop thinking that I'd rather be dead. **"Can you see the truth in it?"** echoes in my mind. Finally, it just occurred to me that the visualization of killing myself is okay. **It's really about trying to kill the part of me that does not work for me anymore.** Although, this also seems to be part of who I am and all I know right now. I don't quite know how to kill it off, embrace it, or let it go. The intense pain I get sometimes, feels like something's being ripped out of my gut, like I had surgery and have a big wound healing. *I know it takes time to heal, but a whole lifetime? How much more ripping out will I feel until it's out, gone, not held onto, released, or shifted? And what is "IT" anyway? A big horrible monster?* **It—that which does not serve me, It—those childish games I play, It—hurtful memories of my past, It—my belief systems.** *Oh my God, all of IT? Please God, help me, I don't know what to believe. I feel shaky and unsure. I'm struggling and can't quite see. The walls are tearing, slowly. Ahhh—It hurts!*

Yet, from this depth, I still see myself as an experienced-mature-Spiritual-grounded-woman sharing my True self with those in need. I see myself filling a void in this country. I'll be called upon to share my thoughts, experiences, beliefs and research with groups of people desiring change in the policies, procedures and Spiritual programs for all children. I envision myself writing wonderful children's stories, in addition to poetry, inspirational books and research texts, and being respected as a publisher of such. As well I affirm that I'll be greatly compensated for these transactions. I see myself with the passion and drive needed to succeed. This is my grandiose dream, my ultimate visualization!

~~~

By the end of March, I was getting ready for yet another trip to see Mom for five days, even though the timing was tough. I managed to squeeze it in right before my classes for the girls started. I'd been talking with Mom several times a week now, sometimes every night, and usually for a couple hours. This took a lot of time, as did my new job, leaving little time left for me. *I was really surprised Mom lasted this long*; **watching baby James grow had given her extra will to live.** The radiation she underwent in January was extremely difficult on her. She had to drive with friends help, to the clinic twenty minutes away, three times a day for twelve working days in a row. They zapped the cancerous lymph nodes in her neck and chest cavity along her sternum, plus the large tumor in her left lung. Although the tumors showed a great reduction in size at the end of all this treatment, she was left feeling very depressed, drained and depleted. The radiation also killed her good cells, which left her throat and esophagus raw. Thus, she had great difficulty and pain swallowing, especially with acid reflux. She also had not eaten much for the last couple months, so her obesity definitely helped. After strong steroids and liquid pain medication with an antacid, she slowly got better. We all questioned: which was ultimately worse—to die naturally from the cancer, or to die from treatment effects?

This time when I left Phoenix, I felt blessed because I had my cousin's son, who recently moved to town, dog-sit for me. This was an answer to that prayer! What a relief for me to know he was staying at the house and being so loving to my babies. Thank you, God! It was the first time I visited Mom without having to worry. I could give her more undivided attention. Remarkably, she surprised me this trip because she had scheduled Fr. Edmondson to meet with us. *A little apprehensive*, I went along with her **admirable gesture. She was attempting to help me heal** through my old childhood resentment of having been expelled from grade school.

I never really cried around my Mother ever since my father died and she had told me to be strong, not to cry. Only I stopped, and she started. However, when I was there last Christmas, she saw me choke up as I talked about how painful it was to get kicked out, and how much it hurt that the teachers were so cold and uncompassionate after dad's death. I shared with her how I remembered getting sent to the hallway in sixth grade because of excessive giggling, and then this nun was yelling at me about how bad I was while I was trying not to cry. Suddenly, my fourth grade teacher—the grade I was in when dad died—walked down the hall, called the nun over and I heard her say, " . . . she's just a little girl!" It was the only moment of empathy I ever felt at that school for nearly eight years. When Mom saw my emotion attached to this story, she said, "Honey, that was a long time ago. You need to move on." And now she's decided that was the root of me leaving the church, and was hoping this wonderful-creative-loving-new priest could help me.

When he came in and sat down at the kitchen table, I instantly liked this man, too. Mom was right about him. He was so laid back and from the heart, with refreshingly liberal views. He made it clear, again, that he would play no part in trying to "convert" anyone, to which Mom nodded in agreement, however we both felt her dual intent. **I was just remaining open to one of the bravest, emotionally honoring gestures my Mother had ever attempted: to help me heal my old wounds.** After I told him about my work with disadvantaged youth, he then asked what happened to me at Catholic school. I explained how I tended to ask too many questions, and clowned around too much. Then, as I got older and more resentful of the lack of compassion around me, I became a bit more sarcastic.

The third day of eighth grade, the "new" teacher asked us to write our accomplishments over the summer, and I said, "Why don't you do it too?" She then replied, "Ok Miss K'earns—to the principal's office! I was warned about you and I'm not putting up with you. You are out of here!" Flabbergasted, I went to the office, only to have the very obese Sr. Roselyn Little (you can imagine the jokes) jerk me in, yelling in front of one of my friend's mothers. "I warned you to never speak out of turn again or we'd kick you out of here so fast your head would spin! Now I'm calling your Mother!" Next, I sat in absolute humiliation and horror as she called the blood bank, telling whoever answered the phone, "Yes, I have Kathleen K'earns in my office here, and she just smarted off for the last time! So we're kicking her out of this school, and I need to talk to her Mother right now!"

As I told him the rest of the story, Mom started crying. She expressed regret for not helping me then, nor sticking up more for me. She then stated how she believed that the experience turned me against the Catholic Church. I responded by honoring her intentions while pointing out the many other reasons I was not comfortable with this "religion," nor any religion for that matter. I explained how I see myself **integrating the main principles from many doctrines,** and believe that I have a stronger relationship with God than I saw in many people who practiced Catholicism. Further, I continued that I was actually grateful for every experience I ever had, no matter how rough. **They all provided me with the very passion and intensity of desire I use to help youth through**

their own difficulties; I am able to offer genuine compassion as a gift. I need to tune in to that pain, my pain—our pain, in order to identify with these incarcerated "street kids" and have them know it's legit. My sensitivity can be a blessing!

Fr. Edmondson then said, "Well, Kathleen, I'd just like to say, that I can tell from your story that you were treated very unfairly, and on behalf of all those priests and nuns from your past, and on behalf of the entire Catholic Church, I would like to apologize to you for this. I know you have turned it into a blessing, but I also hope you can accept this apology into your heart and heal any ill-feeling you may have." Then he turned to Mom and continued, "I want you to know you have absolutely nothing to worry about!" (I wondered just what she had said to him as I held her hand.) "Your daughter is a beautiful person, who is following her heart and doing God's work here on this earth. The gift she gives all those children she touches is recognized in heaven, so trust this and know that her Spirit is truly blessed!"

That trip touched my heart so deeply, and I am very grateful to have had that opportunity. It felt like Mom really made up for so many times of not wanting to help me through something, or rather, not knowing how. **For her to have made this gesture,** albeit with some ulterior motives, **was her Spirit speaking to mine with pure love. She always thought just her love would be enough for me, and in some ways, it was.**

This time when Linda picked me up, we were both so exhausted that we laid down on my couch after loving on my dogs, and fell asleep in each other's arms. It felt so comforting and secure, plus I was impressed with the level of intimacy we could show each other. Although she held me once while I cried after the Thanksgiving trip, this time felt like pure nurturing. **What a good friend to have opened her heart this way!**

~~~

Mother's Day came quickly and **I knew it would be her last**, even though she was actually feeling pretty good. She even went out to a wedding party with her friends from the blood bank. Her hair was finally long enough, an inch or so, that she felt confident to stop wearing hats. Unfortunately she ended up with food poisoning, which set her back. However, I spent an entire week making a special card for her. I figured my first card ever to her was probably out of construction paper, why not the last. I also knew it would mean so much more to both her and me to create a beautiful work of art. It consisted of three pages folded into twelve sides, with magazine pictures glued down collage style. It represented some of her favorite things, Spiritual blessings, words that describe her, memories of my childhood, and advice she gave me. Included as well was an Angel prayer I wrote for her (which I will read at her funeral):

TO THE ANGELS AMONG US

Thank you for guiding our lives together,
Thank you for binding our hearts forever.

Protect my family; stay with us always,
Remind us of LOVE on cold and dark days.

Keep us on God's path; help us see the light,
Wipe away the tears and hold us through the night.

Oh, Angels among us, listen to this prayer—
Please comfort my Mother; always keep her near,
Especially at this time, be there by her side,
Through her sun-setting days, to love, care and guide!

As the summer months were rolling by, the stress from my family situation compounded with the frustrations at my new job, began to take its toll on me. It appeared that my Agency and the Clubs were unable to develop and align their visions, or follow through with appropriate methods to implement this project. I did like my two main coworkers, Angela and Rudy, who came from the Clubs to help me with this grant. We seemed like a good team! Additionally, I still believed in the project, yet had difficulty making it happen especially in light of what was occurring around me. I had so many hindering thoughts swirling around in my head I decided to write them down. *"I can't believe all the walls I've hit, the personalities with whom I've clashed, and the resistance I've encountered trying to get this new project going. I am so angry at all the disrespect I see, and the lack of support I receive. I resent all the delays and interruptions, the micro-managing, the criticizing of my work, the procrastination, power plays, canceling of meetings or showing up late, saying one thing but doing another, changing the plans, and lack of follow-through plus direction.*

"I don't know how to establish boundaries without creating more problems. When I stick up for myself I'm being told that I take things too personally, I am too sensitive, I'm playing a victim, or I just need to toughen up and work things out! This organization feels so alien to me, so strange. Yet it is so huge, so institutional, so affecting of young kids' lives, so controlled by seemingly insecure-bitter people, and worked by so many needy-inappropriate-acting people. Oh dear God, are they really mirrors of me? I must attract this or it wouldn't be here. I somehow ask for it to learn some stupid lesson, but what? It must be a pattern ingrained in my psyche, a karmic lesson perhaps or a deep feeling that I deserve this, but why!?"

Dear Lord, please hear my prayer. Let me move through this stage with love and grace. Let me move forward to that place in the Universe that shows me my true inner beauty, reflects back my passion for love and laughter, and mirrors secure-appropriate-hard-working people to better serve our youth, all in forums of mutual respect. Oh, and God, please send me extra Angels right now to hold me during this dying process with my Mother. *She seems like my only support,* and I love her so much.

As soon as I spoke this prayer towards the dark heavens over my home, **I felt a cool breeze stir up goose bumps over my skin,** although it was still around 100 degrees at night in July. **I knew this to be an Angelic validation, a reminder that Spirit is ever-present and listening.** Thus, I fell to the ground on my knees, feeling humbled, yet so lost. . . .

~~~~

STILL

I'm still standing here,
Still trying to find myself,
Still striving to unbind myself,
Still standing behind myself.

I wanna die still,
I wanna cry still,
I don't know why still,
I'm still alive.

Still,
It remains still,
In God's hands still.

~~~~

4

"The Process"

~present day~
April 2001

*H*ere it is, the fourth month of my freedom, and the fourth month of the year truly starting this new millennium. This represents to me my favorite number: four. I was born on December fourth. Numerically as a twelve, December contains three fours, plus one four for the day equals four fours. This **speaks of balance** to me, just like a table rests best on four legs. Four also represents the main directions: north, south, east, and west; or elements of nature: earth, air, fire, and water. Most importantly, **the fourth chakra contains the heart. It governs our ability to receive and give the greatest gift—"love," as well as connects our body to our Spirit.** Thus, I feel drawn to the number four. Even the number 38, which I referred to earlier with its synchronistic play in my life, can creatively be looked at as a four. The symbol "3" appears to be "half" of the symbol 8, which then translates to four. Most numerology definitions say 38 (3+8) =11, which represents a **Spiritual domain and creativity quest. How apropos to my life right now!** Further, 11 (1+1) =2, which also signifies balance (and cooperation), and is half of and the square root of my favorite number. I'm growing very partial to elevens now, too!

Obviously, I love playing around with numbers. Another metaphysical author, "Way of the Peaceful Warrior" Dan Millman also wrote "The Life You Were Born to Live." This book uses a numerological system based on one's date of birth to determine life purpose, and it defines the number 4 as stability through process. **(Is it mere coincidence that I titled this chapter 4 as "The Process" <u>four</u> months before reading his text and writing this chapter? In fact, while** meditating one morning last January, before I started writing this book, the titles to nine chapters were given to me. I heard Spirit speak them into my mind, and I quickly wrote them down. Simultaneously, the sequencing-of-time format was also made clear to me and felt Divinely inspired.) Therefore, playing with my birth numbers of 12/4/1961, they add up to 24 (1+2+4+1+9+6+1=24). Both the 2 and the 4 are "significant forces" along my life path, as is 6, the sum of these (2+4=6). All three birth numbers interplay in one's life. The latter actually represents "true destiny." According to this text, one tends to work in a chronological style with the issues and potentials of each digit, from left to right and from negative to positive aspects of each of these numbers. Interestingly enough, this indicates that I first need to establish good personal boundaries and rise above codependency and resentment into a more balanced sense of diplomacy (the #2). Next, I must learn to patiently follow a step-by-step process towards my heart's desires in order to manifest my destiny. I'll move from indecisiveness to organization, while building a strong foundation and trusting Spirit to guide the process (#4). Finally, by reconciling issues of perfectionism and demonstrating <u>total</u> self-acceptance, I can then embrace my high ideals and create my "Spiritual Utopia" in life through practical down-to-earth means (#6). These great descriptions of my birth numbers definitely resonate with me.

Being a visionary and dreamer, I feel called upon to motivate others to reach their potentials. I feel inspired to weave images of hope, love, and peace on this planet yet desire to do it in logical, realistic ways. It makes sense to me that I need to reconcile the many issues of my past, which I've been doing through the death of my Mother, so that I can learn to form healthy boundaries and have better relationships with others. It is also relevant for me to develop patience and trust in this arduous process, as I one-day-at-a-time work towards my Soul's purpose. Most importantly, I must learn to love myself unconditionally, and treat myself like the true treasure and special gift from God that I am. This means <u>total</u> self-acceptance, whether I sometimes talk excessively, or passionately express myself, or accidentally push people away. This means <u>totally</u> embracing who I am, whether that means being a lesbian, a Spiritual adventurer, a child-like adult, and/or an emotionally sensitive woman.

I can't believe how much **I am growing**! Each month seems like a year. The amount of things **I am learning**, without being in school, is phenomenal.

The speed, at which **I am processing** without as much rumination as in the past, is incredible. The intensity at which **I am honoring myself,** and attempting to assert myself in healthy ways, is amazing to me. Finally, **I am feeling more peace.** *Of course I know that is easy to say sitting at home a lot and not dealing with near as many people as in the past.* Nonetheless, I truly am turning things over to God. I really am learning to discern between my *critical, fearful self* and **the voice of my Soul.** There are still moments I feel stumped, yet even during those times **faith exists because I know I am improving. As I actively try to balance my chakras and meditate on my intuition, I feel the ability to believe in myself growing, and the reliance on others' approval and advice diminishing.** Additionally, as I continue to let the words of my struggles and my darkest thoughts flow through my fingertips and onto these pages, **I feel my Spirit ever-strengthening and my will to live rising out of the ashes of my past.**

≈≈≈

"Ok, time for the critic to step in again. I don't know who she thinks she is, but this 'writing a book' process and thinking it is what God wants her to do is going a little too far! Just because she bares her Soul and is a good writer does not mean anyone is going to want to read about her life. Look around, she has hardly had any people in her life in the last few years who cared to hear about any of the issues and situations she is now writing about, much less go through them with her, so what makes her think anyone will want to read about it? People have enough emotional dramas going on in their own lives that they don't need to take on any of hers. Besides, there are plenty of books already floating around out there as it is. Many people dream of being a published author; everyone has a story to tell. It's not that I mind her writing a story, however, exposing her whole life so intimately like this is only going to backfire. Just like any other time she tried to open up to people—they ran! She should try publishing less risky subject matter first and then see. But just watch, they'll use the information against her . . . always have, always will. Exposing weaknesses only encourages others to strike out, which she has seen over and over. She's pouring her heart out here and I'm so afraid that it's all in vain. Then she'll really have nothing left. Nothing . . ."

When I think back to last spring and summer, going on one year now, I am in awe at the vast difference in my life. It was undoubtedly the most emotionally and Spiritually challenging time of my life, leading up to, of course, the death of my Mother. Indeed, that ordeal seemed like a breeze to go through compared to my job situation. Her death, after all, was a natural part of life, out of my control, and something I needed to experience. The *absurd* job tribulations were not, yet somehow seemed to be. *I just felt like I could not communicate well with anyone! It seemed that everyone in my world played games with me, or misunderstood me, or caused trouble behind my back when I was not expecting it.*

I'll never forget the day my "boss" Nicolas called me in to his office after just two months of my working there. He asked, "Do you remember at the training last week, talking with Ms. Bentley at the break?" and "Do you recall saying to her that her brother had 'big Negro lips, and bugged-out eyes?'" I *gasped in horror* and stuttered "No!" as he continued to read from the "write-up" paper on his desk, "And did you tell her you believed 'light-skinned Black people are prettier than dark?'" As Nicolas looked up at me and deeply through me, stoically studying me with no sign of reaction one way or the other, I felt my heart flop out on the floor and bounce around. The tears welled up as I fought the urge to cry, and redness spread throughout my face as *I felt the anger of being misunderstood quickly rise.* I did remember comparing her to her brother who worked at the boy's institution (someone with whom I got along fine) and saying she had finer features with lighter skin and was much prettier. I also recalled how she stood there nicely talking to me about my job, then I told her how I'd love to have her assigned to work this new Project with me, as she was aptly qualified. I thought we hit it off great. In fact, she never once indicated discomfort with any of my comments (we could have cleared it up right then). Now, I was on brain overload and could hardly understand what was happening or how something like this could have arisen.

I found myself going into my typical defensive mode, explaining, *"This is just a major misunderstanding. I am not prejudiced like that. In fact, I've always identified very strongly with the plight of Blacks in this country."* (As a child I read tons of "underground railroad" books, feeling strangely drawn to them as if I had been a runaway slave in a past life. But I never told anyone that when I was young.) I went on to say, *"While working on my Master's degree, my major was studying multicultural recreation patterns, particularly Blacks,*

Hispanics and Native Americans all of which I am very passionate about when discussing disparities and inequities in this country. I even frequently watch specials on TV that leave me crying at the plight of disadvantaged minority youth in impoverished areas. Plus, two of my closest buddies who work at the boy's institution and who have been my dog-sitters, are Black and understand where I come from. I cannot believe that I, of all people, got called in here like this and written up in this manner!"

Nicolas then told me to talk to Ms. Bentley to clear it up and apologize for the misunderstanding. After this I felt totally exasperated. All night long I could not sleep, ruminating over and over what had happened. There they were again, all those ego voices in my head battling for my attention. I could hardly tune in to Spirit. Plus, humiliation burned through my veins as I saw how this "write-up" climbed up four levels of the chain of command with my "colleagues." *Could it be true that all these people would think I was capable of being that blatant? Could everyone really think I was that stupid to have said those things even if I was that prejudiced?* I knew I was inappropriate for comparing her to her brother, and I realized that even inferring she was "pretty" could have been construed as sexual harassment (which would not have knocked the air out of me like "racism" did). Hence, I made a mental note not to make comments like that ever again.

This event discouraged me tremendously, and from the depths of despair **I felt a little voice seriously question if I was where I was supposed to be in life.** Additionally, I wondered: if Nicolas honestly thought I was capable of making such comments, then why would he support me in running a program in his institution for mostly minority youth? Plus, I couldn't understand why he did not have the lower levels deal with this complaint. **I knew, from somewhere in my Soul, that I deserved better than this** and thus drug myself into his office the next morning ready to quit if he responded in any unsupportive way.

"Do you honestly believe that I am capable of making those statements?" I forcefully asked. As he slowly looked up at me, carefully pausing as always, he replied, "It doesn't matter what I think." "It does to me!" I responded with a lifetime of emotion, "I need to know if you really think I would say things like that?" After a brief pause and studying my face, he slowly answered "No," to which I replied, "Good, because I could not work for someone who would think that of me!" I then exited his office, **feeling proud of standing up for myself for once in my life**, not to mention being elated at not having to quit my job. *After* *all, I lived paycheck to paycheck and didn't know what I'd have done if I had to walk away then.*

My two coworkers, Angela and Rudy, kept telling me: "You are too trusting and sensitive, and divulge too much information to other staff. This puts things on too personal of a level, and sets you up for getting hurt. Don't be so friendly or worried about creating good relationships with everyone. You just need to do your job, and stay very professional." Hearing this feedback further annoyed me. Even though I was trying to be more detached, I found my natural personality in conflict with "left-brained professionalism." And I believed that I did need to develop good relationships with everyone because the success of my program depended on staff helping in many ways. This had always worked in the past for me. In fact, it was one of my strong points. However, this time with this job, it seemed *I was slowly and miserably failing.*

Another frustrating, reoccurring theme at work during this time period was the difficulty getting girls to participate in our new classes. This was not because they weren't interested but rather due to conflicts with the many other programs at the institution, as well as staff who wouldn't allow them to attend consistently. With the girls who were about to be released, it was crucial for us to continue working with them despite their behavior or schedule conflicts. This was necessary in order to develop trusting relationships that could be transferred to the community. Plus, some girls had phenomenal talents for which we were working on developing appropriate resources for them. Understandably however, most employees were not too trusting of any "new programs" (which came and went regularly) and frankly seemed apathetic. Therefore, we had quite a challenge ahead of us.

One housing unit manager, Tom and I had a particularly hard time compromising our agendas. He would agree to allow a couple of girls to participate. Then when they were in the middle of an art project, for example, he would just pull them out for a myriad of reasons that seemed like power plays to me. One time he came charging into my office yelling at me in front of others. He said he didn't appreciate me questioning his authority in front of his staff then calling him at home during his free time, and pitting the youth against him. I sat stunned for a moment then tried to be the peacemaker by validating feelings, apologizing, and giving a little teamwork speech. He left and I thought we were fine. Yet this happened several times with various youth in his unit over the next few months. He even "wrote me up" and "jumped command" by sending a "carbon copy" downtown to the Directors of our Agency. He was questioning my motives for youth membership! This time we were forced to do a conflict resolution, and I was looking down to keep from crying as he apologized for over-reacting. After he left, Nicolas had the gall to inform me that he thought I was the one being insincere because I had my arms crossed and no eye contact. Once again, *I was shocked. Tom had twisted things around and tried to make me look bad to everyone! I just wanted my program to be successful and for the girls to receive more help in transitioning—and now I was the bad guy!* Nicolas even told me to go apologize to him for my body language! *"Why me?" I kept asking God, feeling such the victim,* **yet slowly becoming aware that I must also be creating this.**

Just when I thought things couldn't get worse, Louise, my boss from downtown, walked into my office and started chewing me out. She asserted, "When I call you to come meet me downtown, I expect you to drop everything and get your ass to my office! The last couple of times, your excuse of being too busy with programming just doesn't cut it. The Director needed information on this Club-Project, and you're not keeping me well enough informed about the various activities going on. Just remember, young lady, the Director and I pay your salary!" She sat down and continued, "Furthermore, if you are supposed to be at a special staff meeting, you need to be there and I better not get any more reports about you not attending." Scenes like this had happened so many times before, that I decided I could not tolerate it anymore. *Amongst all the defensive, angry, and hurt voices in my head,* **I felt my Spirit softly coaching me, "Do not allow anyone to talk inappropriately to you. Gently stand up for yourself at all times, with love."** Again, I felt prepared to quit if she didn't like it.

Then, shaking on the inside, I heard the competing voices say: *"Be careful. This is your boss. You don't want to piss her off. You'll get in worse trouble. Just apologize, validate and try to keep the peace."* **"No!" an inner Spirit interjected, "You can state your case, and assert your boundaries without playing the game back."** I then numbly found myself standing up from my desk and **heard a new voice from within explaining,** "All copies of the calendars, memos, flyers, and monthly reports which I send you regularly, should suffice with any information regarding Club activities that you or the Director might need. I am very busy, and as assigned, my priorities now are running this Club. Thus, I require all downtown meetings to be pre-arranged, unless there's an emergency. I also must insist that if we do meet, you will be on time and notify me in advance if you cannot attend."

Unbelievably, she sat there calmly taking in my whole response. I heard myself continuing while my inner confidence grew. "And as for that staff meeting that I missed, *are you also aware that I had just worked twelve long days straight, without benefit of staff assistance like I was supposed to have received?* This made our ratios of staff to youth way off, too. Plus, when I saw that I was signed up for that meeting, I let everyone know it was my day off, and I would not be able to attend." Girls were now starting to come through the doorway for class, as I concluded, *"What a shame. It seems that you only hear negative reports, and not all the positive things we are doing.* If you really want to know more, just ask the girls." I pointed behind her to the gathering crowd of high-energy teens as I walked out of my office and started greeting them. She followed me out and after talking to many very-excited-anxious-to-share-their-whole-lives-not-just-their-projects girls, she approached me and said, "Keep up the good work," as she left. Amazingly, she never spoke inappropriately to me again!

I also had to stand up, only very differently, to my other boss, Leonard from the Kids Clubs Administrative Office. He had been pressuring me to get the Project going faster than we were able to due to lack of assistance and cooperation. He just didn't understand our Agency's bureaucratic ways well enough, and thought that by giving me a "loud" pep talk, I would get motivated. *Instead, it sent me into self-doubt and more procrastination. I was afraid I could not please anyone. They were all on different pages and had vastly different personal agendas. The walls were incredible, all of the demands intense, and the hierarchies incomprehensible. All this with no support was making my ADHD personality falter like never before. I couldn't joke my way out of this one. After three weeks of sinking into worse depression,* I called up Leonard and told him, "I need a different style of supervision from you, one more of coaching in a supportive way, or I will not be able to work this Project with you." Once more, I found myself having to be ready to let the job go for a matter of principle. After telling me in a nice way, "I cannot and will not change my way of supervising just for you—now, take care of your problems with authority and self-esteem and just do your job," he actually ended up never reaming me out again. So, incredibly, it worked once more!

I realized after these last two encounters that maybe the "bosses" needed to see the fighter in me to show me more respect. I was too nice and accommodating for months in the beginning, and was trying to please everyone. I also understood my ADHD personality better because of this and was seeing these conflicts as blessings in disguise. In my past, whether in school or at work, there was always someone giving me the support I needed to get the tasks done, so I flourished. *But, without clear guidelines and positive reinforcement in this situation, I was sinking fast.* **I also knew that things didn't have to be this difficult. I should not have to take abuse to then reach the point of having to fight.** I just kept praying for God to put in my life, only those people who will support me and treat me with respect (and I will do the same in return). It was obvious that I had to **be patient**.

Nobody really knew how strange this new job was for me. I felt as though I was going through a private hell. All pathways had so many obstacles, like doors being shut everywhere I looked. It's hard to believe how just one year ago when I would drive to work, *I could barely make my exit off the freeway without breaking down and crying. "Oh God, help me! I can't do this! I can't go in there again!" My car would slow down as thoughts of "turn around and go home," and "God, I'd rather be dead!" ran through my mind. Then with gut-wrenching agony,* I'd force myself to dry my face and keep driving forward. "Oh, please let us all get along. Let today be a good day! Oh dear God, get me through this!" And each day it seemed, something else would happen, and my depression would get deeper yet. Since there were personality conflicts going on all around me, I was becoming painfully aware of how **I needed to learn to communicate more effectively.**

A good example was this Native American co-worker, Frank, whom I allowed to repeatedly "walk all over me." *He tended to be too quick to run and scream discrimination—to the point, in my opinion, of reverse discrimination.* And he was quickly rising up the administrative ladder of the department, as we were in desperate need of minorities at higher levels to be more representative of the disproportional minority youth and families we served. *Frank was known for always pointing out other peoples' weaknesses and lack of following proper protocol, as he walked in late to almost every meeting! Staff had a way of dummying up around him, falling silent as he droned on, driving his opinions home and making his threats to inform the Director or other administrative top-dog if things didn't change.*

At one meeting, I volunteered to be part of a gender-specific training team for employees. This was a new program, which we were starting to help provide better sensitivity to females' needs and issues. Frank snapped, "That is for Master's level therapists only! Danielle and I are the ones doing it." *I felt my throat close up as I sat in disbelief to his response, and then to the lack of redirection from any "bosses" around that table.* When I later talked to them about his *demeaning* comments (especially since most employees didn't have a Bachelor's much less a Master's degree), they merely stated that they couldn't do anything about it because someone downtown supervised him and it would be inappropriate! *I told them that even though I did have the degrees and knew I was more than qualified for the assignment, I did not speak up because I was not the type to throw my Master's around. I also did not want to put "academic" wedges between people.* After staring blankly at me, I realized that they obviously were not going to stick up for me *like I had hoped.* **Deep inside, I also realized that I needed to stick up for me.**

I tried to let that incident go. There were too many other priorities on which to focus. *From then on, I made sure I was nice and respectful to Frank so as not to attract more of the same. I always made sure to introduce him to everyone I showed around the institution.* One time alone I asked him if I might have the honor of helping to rebuild the Native American sweat lodge on the premises; it would have meant a great deal to me. Before I could explain more, he gasped, "Of course not! That is for us Natives only!" *Again I said nothing and just walked away thinking how sad it was that people could be that way. If things were turned around, he would have been down at the "Affirmative Action" office filing a discrimination suit against me. Imagine—if I wanted to teach a white only cultural pride activity and didn't allow minorities to be involved!*

Then, on my last day of employment with the Agency, during a large staff meeting, **I could no longer stay quiet.** When the subject arose of youth wearing religious wristbands, Nicolas pointed out that girls were hiding gang graffiti on the inside, and to confiscate them. I chuckled and shook my head at the ambiguity of that: What Would Jesus Do? Once more, and clearly misinterpreting my reaction, Frank barked, "You don't know anything! You haven't gone through all the gang training." **Without even thinking, I somehow stared him in the eye as I found my voice loud and clear replying with passion, "You do not talk to me that way!" Echoing in my head was my Mother's voice saying, "Nobody talks to my daughter like that!" It seemed as though Mom's energy was helping me assert myself.** Afterwards, I had many staff members congratulate me. It felt great!

In my personal life over the past year, the relationships were not much better. There were just far fewer of them requiring my attention. Many

95

acquaintances over the years had faded, many "ex's" suddenly were out of the picture, and many friends *appeared to not like me nor understand me anymore.* Linda, my regular airport "picker-upper," *seemed like my only friend since 1995 to weather the storms of life with me. Sadly it now seems I have lost her since I quit my job and embarked on my new adventures.*

Only Dick, my Black buddy from the "Boy's Institution" has consistently acted like he cares, and still keeps in touch regularly. This man has graciously house-sat for me many times. He has spent endless hours over the years listening to me ruminate about every detail of my job frustrations, and some about my private life as well. A few times he dropped what he was doing and came to be at my side when the world was getting me down. He has shown up at my front door with a six-pack of beer and a reason or two to celebrate when I needed it most, yet didn't realize it. I am so grateful for his friendship and often thank him and God. *Every time I was feeling down, wanting to die, feeling like no one in the world really cared, I would have to add: "Oh, all but Dick that is." I never thought a man would end up being there for me more than a woman,* however, I'm awfully glad that I've been open to it.

Dick and I are so different it is amazing we are even friends. He is not metaphysical at all, although he seems interested and allows me to share without judgment, as I try to do in return. He is also a big-time player of women and with all due respect, this man knows how to get his "Mack-Daddy" on! He has a very quiet, low-key personality and appears so serious and professional at work. I, on the other hand, have been known to be a little wild and crazy, and believe "if ya gots to do it, ya might as well be havin' fun!" Also contrary to Dick, I'm not into casual sex, and similar to many women, I desire and deserve a loving committed monogamous relationship. (In fact, I've been waiting for over three years, and believe I have even more to offer now as a result.) So, while I'm sharing my latest Spiritual revelation or describing something that happened to me, Dick's cheering to his latest sexual conquest or talking about the great programs he's starting at work. He's always so optimistic and upbeat for me!

Besides Dick, there is one woman, Brenda, who has stepped forward lately and seemed very interested in being friends. However, **I'm taking it slow since my gut feels slightly uncomfortable around her.** It has to do with the fact that she thinks we're soul mates, but I don't. And s*ince I've been so hungry for companionship, I want to be careful. I also do not want to push a potential friend away and then feel more alone.* She is interested in a lot of the same Spiritual concepts and creative endeavors as I, plus has volunteered to dog-sit for me, which is a Godsend! I've found myself sharing a lot about my life and my path with her lately, and we've gotten along pretty well. On the other hand, she offers to do more for me **than I feel is appropriate**, and she's expressed her attraction to me several times, even though **I've told her my viewpoint. Because of this, I feel hesitant, which I interpret as a sign from Spirit steering me in the direction of my Highest Good. I sense this friendship is a lesson for taking baby steps at establishing new boundaries and communicating better, and I pray daily for assistance.**

Otherwise, since I quit my job, I have been pretty much on my own, which has **fortunately caused me to connect stronger with Spirit**. *Yet I still struggle with feelings of loneliness and hence pray for God to send me my Spiritual family. Of course, I also ask for a "life partner" after being single so long.* Although, more important to me, is a few good friends with the mutual intention of having supportive, loving and fun relationships. I know I'm a good person and deserve these people, *however, especially after Mom's death it was hard to accept that there was no one around with whom I could really identify.* **I just have to trust that they'll come. And I have to believe that I'm supposed to be alone to get this book done with fewer distractions.** I also pray to release whatever I may have caused to subconsciously push people away. Everything I read, study or hear lately is how important it is to have people supporting you. *I can't help but have my heart sink when I realize I haven't and don't. "Why me Lord? I'm not that bad," I cry.*

Since Mom died, I have made several attempts to reach out to past acquaintances as well as try to make new friends. *Sadly, none (except Brenda and Dick) have worked.* Even when I was back home, I made no connection with people from my past. Most calls were not returned, and of ones that were **I could intuit they were not interested, merely being polite. (The question, "Was I really interested?" now echoes in my head.)** Two gals I used to hang out with for several years and whom are also from my same hometown, called back and we scheduled a couple of happy hours. However, they kept canceling so I said, "never-mind." One of those women, when we were trying to find time to get together, asked me what my work schedule was going to be like the following week. When I reminded her that I had quit my job and that my writing schedule was flexible, she replied, "Well, ya gotta work again sometime!" *I then* *sat in awe at all the implications of that statement, feeling unable to respond to my new situation.*

During the last month at my job, I became acquainted with three women who were more Spiritually aware than other staff and were being friendlier to me. Although they said they wanted to do lunches and get together after I quit, every initial contact I made produced no results, therefore, I let it go. One of these women, however, set me up with a friend of hers with whom she thought I would click. Well, I thought so too at first, and we talked several times and met once. I could see had great healing abilities and herbal knowledge, and surprisingly I heard myself ask, "Will you help me with my Charley?" Unfortunately, it seems she also disappeared from my life. *I think she was searching for a "partner," not a friend.*

I also contacted two massage therapists whom I met a few years back. We went through a women's Spiritual program together for over six months. We even saw each other several times over the years, primarily when I called to schedule an appointment with them. Unfortunately, I soon realized that again I was the only one initiating and finally gave up, yet not after a struggle. *I was just feeling so lonely after quitting my job* and I thought they'd be interested in my new adventures, as we always said we'd support each other's endeavors in life. We had scheduled a little potluck type get-together at my home, and I had declared the theme to be manifesting our hearts' desires. Unbeknownst to them I had purchased and prepared some materials for us to artistically create alchemy or "God" boxes, with magazine cuttings, colored markers, stickers, etc. for decorum.

The first date one woman cancelled, and the second date the other one did. Both times I then scheduled a massage with the opposite one in order to have personal contact. *"I can always use the bodywork,"* I told myself, but **my True intent** was that I really *needed the company*. It seemed I was trying to buy friendship because my heart longed to connect with another. Hence, we scheduled a third date, yet while out to lunch with one of them, I realized she was pointing out my weaknesses. She told me what I should be doing or feeling, and showed irritability with the things I was sharing with her. Later at home, I finally "woke up" and left them messages canceling out, and I never heard from them again. **"You know they won't call because they're not true friends of yours," my Higher Self had lovingly warned, "but know that soon you will meet wonderful, loving people to support you on your path!"**

One of those ladies had also given another woman, Teri, my phone number because she thought we'd hit it off. Well, she was right, for several hours anyway. Teri was friendly on the phone and we talked for hours like we had already known each other. We decided to meet the next evening with a few of her friends for dinner. As she walked towards me for the first time, **I could tell** from her quickly averted eye contact and body language that she was disappointed with what she saw. I tried to ignore that **first gut feeling** she gave me, instead I joked around and enjoyed myself for the next couple hours at the table. I was proud of myself for not going into self-doubt and feeling like leaving when she spent most of the time talking to the other women. All the while, a little voice kept saying, **"You deserve better than this . . ."** *"But maybe she's just shy in person,"* my pride argued back, *"I'll be patient and see if we connect like on the phone."*

After dinner, Teri and I had made plans to be spontaneous and go "out on the town." Much to my chagrin, she told me that a bunch of personal issues had just come up for her and she needed to end our date. **"Graciously go home right now,"** **went through my brain** but instead I heard myself say, "Well, maybe as quickly as this mood came over you, it will shift again after talking a little and then we can still go out . . ." Next thing I know we're sitting at a dirty table outside a food store, with her smoking and talking about her ex-lover and all the problems associated with letting go of that situation. After an hour I realized I needed to end this disturbing outcome to a potentially great evening. So I left, actually still hoping that we could be friends and hiking buddies like she had agreed to. After all, I wouldn't want someone to just give up on me if I had some issues arise.

The next evening she called and again we talked for a long time, yet it seemed to be a little more "forced" than before. When she hung up, I was taken back as she said, "I gotta get up early and go to work. Of course you can just sleep in 'cause all you have to do is write!" Well, *I couldn't believe how much I let that statement bug me. All night long I ruminated about how tired I was of comments like that. In my head I kept hearing the rude statements or personal questions from people at my last job. I felt choked again remembering how I told people I was just exploring options or was following some job leads. I felt frustrated for not being able to simply speak my Truth. I was afraid of others' negative energy judgments affecting my new life and my book.* I realized how much my work ethic was bothering me. I kept hearing my ego say, *"You're not valid if you don't work for somebody, or not established if you haven't published."*

The next morning I decided to speak up for myself, and I prayed for guidance to do this lovingly. After all, I wanted friendship yet **knew I was to practice staying in my power, asking for what I need, and setting my boundaries.** After telling Teri how her last comment made me feel, she replied, "I am just so envious! I wish I could quit my job and just write books!" *I told her I needed her support, and not to make this stage in my life sound so easy. I reminded her that I was writing about the recent death of my Mother!* As we talked, I got this **eerie feeling** that I was *over-explaining out of a need to feel understood.* She finally stated, "Look, I've decided you're not for my Higher Good. I have enough reiki clients that are too deep and heavy, I don't need a friend to do that," and then hung up. Well, *I cried at hearing it put quite that way, and was frustrated with the whole situation. "Why me God? I would've been fine just continuing on my own,"* I later asked out loud in the empty steam room at my gym, then affirmed, "I want to meet friends that will last, not just tease me then dump me!" After swimming forty laps to remove the sting of her words, I went home and called a counselor-Angel to get clarity. She told me to never let someone say something like that to me. It's like saying they're better than me, on a higher plane, when in reality we're all on the same level. And after she reminded me **of how beautiful and special I was, and that my friends who could see my Truth were on their way—just to be patient,** I wiped away my tears and got back to writing!

A month later when I walked into a bookstore and saw Teri standing there, I felt awkward but took advantage of the "meeting" to tell her a couple things. It didn't take long for her to retell of her disappointment with how quickly our friendship had gotten deep and heavy. She also said if we would have met after I was done writing this book then perhaps I'd be in a better place for her. *My anger started rising; I felt that if she couldn't be a friend then, there was no way I'd be interested when I was "better!" I also wanted to call her bluff, because deep down I knew she was disappointed that there was no "physical attraction."* Instead I said, " *I told you right up front that my Mom had just died four months earlier, and what a rough time I had just been through. If you really think I would be just all light and breezy through the process of writing about this, then you're not being realistic or allowing me to be human! Furthermore, I wasn't the first one who took this friendship to a 'deep-heavy' place. If you recall, I was in the mood to laugh, dance and party that night and it was you who had issues come up to process."* She stood there for a moment as though she were letting that sink in. Then, I was *absolutely flabbergasted* as she inquired, "Well, would you like me to read and edit your book for you?" *Oh, I wanted to say, "If you don't want to be my friend because the subject matter seems too much, why in the hell would I want you to read it and critique it?"* Instead I found myself saying, **"No, but thanks anyway!"** The whole conversation was really gentle yet firm. I was proud of my inner strength as I left. In the past I wouldn't have been able to speak up, **so this was a little practice.** "Thank you, God, for the lessons in my life," I exclaimed skipping down the street, glad to be following the voice of my Soul.

Figuring out where and how I stand with people has been and still is quite a process. Yet I know **I am stepping into my own** a little more every day. Somehow through all these frustrating trials with people, I am **finding an inner strength** boring out of me. Just because I made mammoth changes in my life recently doesn't mean every problem will magically go away. I know it takes time to rewrite a lifetime of patterning and scripts. And I am determined to do it! I know that a big part of this process involves both **gratefulness and forgiveness** exercises.

Oprah is known for advocating the importance of gratitude in one's life for attracting more inner peace and happiness. Even if you're having problems, she stresses the importance of expressing thanks anyway for you know the lesson will come soon. She also recommends keeping a gratitude journal, as this was something that helped turn her life around. **I now wakeup every morning and instantly thank God for everything in my life, and I continue thanking all throughout the day, as it is habit forming! This really helps me feel much happier as a result!**

I also have worked very hard on releasing all resentment, anger and hurt I've been carrying around towards other people. I made a list and then did a forgiveness meditation with each person I described in this book, as well as anyone else I could remember. Doreen Virtue recommends this in her seminars and books, and I actually followed these guidelines adapted from her work. First, I visualize the person in front of me (in my mind's eye) after a relaxing prayer time. Next, I picture their inner light, starting out small then slowly growing bigger and brighter until it encompasses their entire body. This light glows so large around them that I cannot really see their body anymore and they appear translucent and Spirit-like to me. Then I lovingly walk into their light with them and sincerely say the following words: "I am willing to let go of all resentment towards you. I hold no un-forgiveness back. My Soul recognizes your Soul, and I love you. I release you and we are both free now!"

Also under Doreen's direction, I have been learning to call upon my Angels for assistance. In particular, I call Archangel Michael to help clear away any negative energy and Archangel Raphael to help speed up the healing process for me. At first, I called in these Angels during meditations then I also found myself taking notes on answers I knew they were giving me. Finally, I felt my relationship grow to where I quite frequently have dialogue with them, and especially with Michael. **I have such a sense of protection and unconditional love when I tune into his energy.** Nonetheless, they all have been extremely instrumental with my healing process. And I am realizing through this process that **the way I see others, so I shall see myself**. Therefore, now when I start to get frustrated with someone, I instantly stop and pray. Since I do not want to attract more negative or unsupportive people, I must **make sure I am positive and being totally supportive myself**. It truly is getting easier, and I trust **with continued gratefulness and quick forgiveness, of myself as well, that I will finish working out the cobwebs of my Soul and radiate pure clean light instead. Deep down I know I have to follow my heart's desires, bring out all my creative talents, pour my passions into my work,** and then I will meet new Spiritually minded people on a similar path with whom I can phenomenally relate. Somehow, **I feel my Mother's Spirit urging me on, trying to speak through me, and encouraging me to follow this new path**. Humbly, I accept the mission. After all it is because of her that I can take a long sabbatical to even do this!

I have never been more grateful in my life. **Mom is actually serving me better in Spirit than she ever could in person. It feels like a lifetime of healing energy coming through all at once. We now have the close relationship that both of us always craved but never could achieve. She knows me and accepts me now just the way I am. She greatly admires all those traits she used to try to stifle; she accepts all those parts of me that used to shock or humiliate her.** I love her so much for giving me the means, both monetarily and Spiritually, to move to where I need to be in my life. **I believe her Soul will heal along with mine as I embark on this new journey. I feel she wants to use me as a vessel to spread messages about the importance of mother-daughter relationships, and how to stop controlling and start loving from the heart! This is why she is now proud that I am such an articulate, honest writer and so at ease on**

stage. Finally she understands how those very traits that used to embarrass her are ones that will help her get these messages across!

I am so grateful for allowing myself to be released from my prison, and taking the time needed to lovingly heal myself while appreciating my home, my belongings and my dogs. I am astonished at how well Charley is doing. She has surpassed any vet's expectations, even my own. I can tell she has more energy again, and is very happy. Could it be that **she truly is a mirror of me**? It seems that **her miraculous kidney improvement is simply the result of me taking better loving care of myself!**

One year ago I was so depressed, I literally wanted to drop off the face of the earth. My journaling at the time reflects a very different woman than who I feel I am today. I even wanted to write a book called "Crying Heart / Dying Spirit." It was supposed to be about *my life with undiagnosed and untreated ADHD. It would have included all the negative things I ever heard about myself and how my own self-talk then reflected most of the same condemnations. It would've also exemplified how I was stuck in a pattern of attracting people who wanted to repeat the negative comments in my face, more than the positive traits of which I also heard and was aware.* At that time, I started giving myself hope to "hang on" by *planning how to exit earth after Mom passed away. Even though I had promised God, I felt that life just didn't make sense and I couldn't take it anymore. God would understand. I figured so few people really cared, no one would notice if I just disappeared. I thought I'd quit my job, sell my house and belongings, and pack my dogs in my car. Then I'd tell my brothers and anyone who asked that I was going on a several year Spiritual sabbatical to a land far, far away and would not be in touch for some time. This would not have been that surprising, therefore I knew I could have pulled it off and no one would've noticed for years. I did not want to leave a mess so I fantasized about driving off somewhere into a big body of water where no one could find me.* **Only, there was always this little voice telling me to never throw my writings away. Spirit guided me to write my books first, and then go through with "the plan" if I must.** I figured I might as well publish at least my poetry and journals to leave behind. And I now wonder if this was **the True voice of my Soul**? Could this have been **my Higher-Self giving me a clue as to what would make me happy**?

Ironically, **my Mother's death has graced me with a new will to live**. The more hurt I encounter and the more walls I see put up now only fuels my desires. I don't feel beaten-up and knocked around anymore. I often feel a little confused over what I really do feel, but that's because I've been so far out of tune with my real inner voice that I have trouble hearing my intuition. Yet, I'm quickly learning. **Mom's death has definitely given wings to my heart. I am now learning to rejoice in my uniqueness, revel in my creativity, and radiate my sensitivity within a whole new perspective. I somehow feel driven to remember my Soul agreement with God,** and not waste any more time. I no longer want to live for Mom. **I desire to live for me and for my True purpose on this earth as God's child**. I first got in touch with this feeling when Mom so graciously shared the last six weeks of her life with me. Then, as I felt her Soul so serenely leave her body, and as she finally allowed me to cry unconditionally in her arms, **my Spirit was reborn and my heart filled with a love that I'd never known in this lifetime. . . .**

~~~~

OF MIND NOT MERCY

Be it of mind not mercy-me,
When an illusive dichotomy,
Like separateness doth prevail,
Falls victim; emotions entail!

Oh those days of younger years,
Bears a strength through absent tears,
Stifling passions as they soar,
Whence a father's passing o'er!

Oh young girl, bruised heart in hand,
Feeling lost, yet to understand,
Dispassionate eyes is all to find,
While choking throat and legs that bind!

Oh grown woman, alone again,
How patterns repeat, despite refrain,
Past holding of Mom in final days—
So affects the Spirit, myriad ways!

Why is, that to look around,
Closed hearts it seems, all are found?
Yet giving gentle, loving touch,
Surely doth not cost that much?

Be it of bliss, be of joy,
Trusting the Angels to employ;
Follow heart thus it shall lead,
Oh gardens of love, my Soul to feed!

~~~~

DARK DAY OF THE SOUL

5

"6 Weeks with Mom"

~back in time~
August—September 2000

*M*y Mother never cried, when I was young. At least I never thought she did. In fact, I never saw my parents fighting. My dad was often stern, and sometimes "barked out" commands, but only a couple of times did I see them having slightly heated discussions. Then, it seemed like Mom would be holding back tears, and dad would appear irritated yet in control. I was always told to leave after stumbling onto those moments.

I was nine years old in October of 1971 when I awoke at 2am to a loud thump and a lot of scurrying around. Paralyzed with fear, I couldn't move out of my bed for a while as I gathered my wits about me. Slowly, heart pounding loudly, I crept to my doorway. I saw then12-year-old Sean down the hall in our parent's bedroom on the phone, and Edward who was 7, standing helplessly watching something happening, both of them obviously upset. Taking four more agonizing steps, I felt like I was in a nightmare as I cautiously peered around the corner while sensing it strange how my brothers never looked at me. There on the floor, sprawled on his back, was my father with blood running off his forehead, and my Mother was hovering over him, frantically trying to give him CPR.

Quickly I scurried back to my bed and dove between the covers, pulling them over my head! "No, no, no, no, oh God, no," I dryly pleaded in whispers, while in shock at what I had just seen. I tried to wakeup and to tell myself it was just a bad dream. I tried to find my voice to call out for Mom to come comfort me like she had done in the past when I had scary dreams, yet nothing came out. I waited, trying to go back to sleep so I could awake once again, but still the hurried movements persisted and the panicked voices continued. I found myself numbly getting up again and watching Mom still work on dad. I felt frozen in time, standing statuesque with my little brother. Only now the next-door neighbor had arrived, and before I knew it a siren was blasting through the silent dark night, coming this time to our house. As chills ran up my spine, I hurried back to bed, while hearing Mom say something about going to the hospital. Then, there were a lot more strange noises, men's voices, and doors banging—things I'd never heard before. I got up and peeked out my window in time to see the ambulance doors close. Then it drove off with blaring sirens, which frightened me right back into the safety net of my bed.

I don't know how much time passed as I stayed in bed silently crying while fading in and out of slumber, sadness and shock. I vaguely remember the neighbor lady trying to get me up. At one point, I finally got curious enough to creep back out to see what was occurring, only to find Mom, my brothers and our family priest sitting on the couch speaking in low-key, somber and deep tones. As soon as my Mom saw me looking around the corner, her face contorted with love and pain. She held out her hands to beckon me to join them as she nodded her head: the nod of death! Instead I found myself again turning on my heels and heading back to the security of my bed. Only this time I was crying hard. I was so shaken by that look on Mom's face. Tears now streaming, I quietly sobbed, "God, I didn't really want dad to die. I didn't mean to be bad or to make him mad!"

Mom sat on my bed and said, "Now, Kathleen, your father had a heart attack and died. There was nothing we could do. He must've hit his head on the bookshelf as he fell, which is why he was bleeding. Stop crying now, Honey, come on. We'll get through this. You must be strong—for him, for all of us. Tears won't help any, just come join us in the living room. Father Mason came all the way over here in the middle of the night to be with us and you need to be a part of this. Ok? Now dry those tears and let's go!"

The next couple days were a blur. Mom was on the phone, monotone, telling everyone how dad had died and providing all the funeral information. Hundreds of people kept coming to the house, bringing so much food, and looking at us like something horrible had happened. I kept hearing adults exclaim over and over, "He was so young!" and "The poor children!" and "How will she take care of everything by herself?" then they'd look at us again with that disgusting pity. I don't remember anyone being gentle and loving, putting an arm around me, or trying to explain anything. I just recall being told what we had to do next, or to eat this or that, or to be polite to all the nice people, or to clean those messes, or go serve so and so something.

I do remember being told we were going to see dad in his casket because that's what people do to pay respect when a loved one dies, and how strange that concept seemed to me! In fact, during the whole drive over I studied how everyone acted like nothing out of the ordinary was happening, even my brothers. Yet in my head I was thinking, "We are about to see dad dead!" When we got to the funeral home, I remember how everybody just filed in like they had always done this kind of thing. My stomach turned with anxiety. I did not want to see dad dead! I was "scared to death" to walk in there. I couldn't just pretend and be herded along like everyone else. Feeling incredibly alone, somehow I managed to take up the rear then proceeded to sit on the steps outside the door in fear. Next thing I knew my grandmother (dad's mom) came flying outside yelling back, "Here she is! Out here!" She then commanded, "Get up this minute! Who do you think you are? Out here just trying to get attention like always! You march in there and pay your respects to your father like everyone else!" as she pulled on my arm. I was shaking my head "no" in terror, my eyes wide with a panic that she could not see, when at last my Mom appeared saying, "It's ok, Mary, I've got her. Let me talk to her." My grandma went back in muttering what a disrespectful, disobedient, spoiled little brat I was as Mom quickly, yet sweetly told me I needed to be inside. It helped when she explained how I wouldn't have to see him if I stayed towards the back.

Furthermore, I recall thinking how strange it was watching so many people cry at the visitation, the funeral, and the burial, while we numbly went through the whole crazy process. And I remember how the chaos ended as quickly as it had started. We were all left alone, to deal with our grief as a family. Others seldom discussed it, and never showed their tears again.

My mother never used to cry. But after dad died, she cried regularly, and I found myself trying to comfort her. She was often in the living room crying on the couch for hours, while my brothers sat helplessly watching TV in the family room. She would tell me, "I just miss your father pulling up in the driveway, coming home from work everyday. I keep watching for his headlights and they don't come!" She cried about needing to get a job to take care of us. She also cried about taking care of his business and property matters, which I did not understand. I would just put my arm around her, and say, "It'll be ok, Mom. We'll get through this together. We'll help you. Don't cry, Mom. We can all be strong, just like you said." And slowly over the years I watched this amazing woman rise out of her grief, go to work, and get through everything she had feared.

I never cried again, around my Mother that is. Something inside of me turned off that night my father died. Even when I was younger, it never felt right to cry anyway because Mom would either tell me to stop, or take on my pain and get teary eyed herself. This made me want to stop to help her pain. What a cycle of co-dependence! She always took on our emotions. She often subconsciously invaded our boundaries in the name of love. Thus, *we learned to hide real feelings and deep troubles so she wouldn't feel responsible or be shocked. For some reason we felt safest expressing negativity, anger and sarcasm, which we did entirely too much of!* All of us suffered from horrible depression *yet it seemed like no one wanted to admit it or deal with it, except me.* (In fact, I've been the only one getting "professional help" for it off and on my whole life. *Sometimes I wonder just how much good that did!*) Lately, however, I have to believe that the help I've been getting for my suicidal ideology and ADHD is helping.

Now as I sit in Mom's condo, watching her stare out the window and talk about how nice everyone in hospice is and how busy her schedule has been lately because of all the visitors, I snap out of my mental digression and **am aware of how much I just want to hug her and cry**. However this of all times, I believe that I need to be strong. I am here for her, to help her get through this last stage of her life, and I know it would upset her to see me cry. *So as always I just sit, achingly holding back the pain in my gut.*

We are drinking coffee, this second morning after my drive out here to be with her. We are both still in awe that I'm even here and I am trying to adjust to the time warp. "I was thinking you could take me to the bank today, and then we could stop at IGA and pick up some sandwich food and things to serve for when company comes." She explains, telling me of all the sale items, as I give myself a pep talk from the heart. **"You can do this, Kath, just relax and breathe. God will help give you courage. Tune in to the Angels—feel them, they're all around."** *"But she looks so much older, every day,"* my head interrupts. *"She's so weak and out of breath, she can hardly move around. Look at her hands shaking as she tries to write the grocery list. And she keeps falling asleep in the middle of conversations. Then she gets irritated when she awakes and I'm not still here in this chair. She doesn't realize how much she's nodding off. Then when she plays mind games with me, can I keep from getting mad? I just don't want to feel any* *more guilt than I have to after she dies. Oh, I'm scared. Can I really take care of her? Please, help me God," my fearful voice prays.* **Just then I feel a soft breeze blow past my head, and for a moment I forget my worries. Somehow I shift as a renewed strength and jovial confidence arise.**

"Oh, hey Mom, I'm sorry to inform you, but I cannot step foot into another car and drive until my trip back home. I'm on at least a six-week hiatus, or however long I stay. You'll just have to find yourself another driver!" I hear myself joke to further change the mood. She looks at me a minute, trying to figure out if I'm teasing or not, then laughs and says, "Oh, Kathleen! We're not going that far!" So I push the issue and respond, "Oh no, I'm serious. My body will not allow me to sit behind the wheel again. I have a mind block now from that thirty-hour drive. You'll have to drug me, and place me in the driver's seat. But then I couldn't drive 'cause of the drugs anyway!"

I went on teasing her about this for several days. Even while in the car, I insisted I couldn't drive as if I didn't realize I was doing it. Whenever she asked me to run an errand for her I had the same response, just to loosen things up a little. It eventually got old, and I switched to other jokes, all of which seemed to cheer her up. As I drove her to various appointments and errands, I was *painfully* aware of the wheel chair in my trunk, along with the spare oxygen tank (just in case). When I would see her having an extra rough day moving around, I would insist on helping her to use the wheelchair even though it embarrassed her. She didn't want me to take her out around the condo to see the lake or the pretty flower gardens because she didn't want neighbors to see her like that. I did surprise her one-day and take her to this huge floral garden a couple miles away, which she always liked to see. It was difficult to push her over the gently rolling hills and wood chip walkways, yet I pretended otherwise. I also took her twice around a huge natural prairie. Thankfully, a sidewalk had recently been placed around the perimeter to make it accessible. She so thoroughly enjoyed these few outings, she told everyone about them.

I also made her laugh a few other times that she loved telling people about over and over again. As if I were a kid, she had me show them. "Kathleen," she would say, "Do your paper bag dance!" or "Show how you put on your armored-guard!" The bag dance happened one evening when I was out on her patio raking the leaves and putting them in the special recycling bags that the city required. These were long, tall and narrow paper sacks. As I worked, I kept looking through the sliding glass door at her sitting in her recliner watching TV.

This was a position in which she spent most of her waking hours, and had for years. As the sadness rolled over me, I got the idea of how to cheer up both of us. I put an empty bag down over my body with my arms above my head, and shimmied until it reached my knees. Not being able to see, but trusting, I knocked on the door through the sack, then assuming she could see me, I started dancing around the patio. I did big circles bending at the waist, kicked around leaves with my feet, and then wiggled my paper butt at her. Finally, I pulled it off only to find her laughing with tears in her eyes. She started clapping just like when I was a child. Then as I choked back tears, I put some leaves on top of my head, made a goofy face against the glass door, and took a big curtsy-bow.

For the armored-guard, she had asked me to cut her toenails because she could no longer reach down that far. Now, her nails had been progressively getting thicker and harder over the years and she had clippers that looked almost like wire cutters. I had cut them when I was visiting in July and knew how dangerous of a job it was. One clipping went flying off her toe at such a high speed I heard it zing past my ear. Another ricocheted off the glass before landing by the fireplace across the room. She never believed me, but I swore it! I also told people that one got lodged in my cheek, however I was kidding about that. Since this was another joke between us, I decided to "gear-up" for the event this time. I put on a white dust mask, sun glasses, hat and gloves, and buttoned my shirt up to the neck so no skin was exposed. I then came out holding the clippers, saying, "Ok, I'm ready." Well, she laughed so hard I thought I'd have to get her the adult diapers! I'm not too sure if other people found it that amusing though.

Additionally, I loved bringing her food to eat, and making it so she'd smile. For example, I'd slice some homegrown tomatoes and place them on top of cottage cheese forming a big smiley face, with pepper for freckles. I also shaped a serving of rice into a big heart, plus made fancy fruit bowls for her, always eliciting the response: "Oh Kathleen! This looks too pretty to eat! Thank you so much, Honey!" I enjoyed cooking for her and a couple times a week I would make some of my specialty dishes, as well as concoct a few of our family favorites: lemon chicken, spinach-garlic pizza, potato salad, meat loaf, and banana cake. No matter what I brought her, she always said it tasted better because I had prepared it for her, with love.

She had been eating well since taking Prednisone for the last six months, yet was starting to dislike the puffiness and fluid retention so her dose got reduced. The hospice nurse, Evelyn, was coming once a week when I first arrived, but I asked to move it to twice. Mom had a way of saying, "I'm doing real good, eating great, sleeping fine—no problems." *Then I felt like the bad guy in the background, correcting her.* "Mom, what about that pain-spell you had last night?" or "Well, she's falling asleep all the time and not realizing it!" or "I've noticed just in the two weeks I've been here that she's gotten much more short of breath and has to rest just walking from room to room." I eventually felt like I was depressing Mom, keeping her from enjoying her natural denial disguised as optimism. Therefore, I started to talk to the hospice staff more on the way out of the house, instead of in front of her. After all, that was why I was there, to be the objective caregiver, as best I could.

At first, Nurse Evelyn didn't think Mom was "eminent death" and thought her doctor was getting me out here too early. "He's been wrong before you know," she pointed out. *At times my stomach constricted thinking I was maybe wasting my leave-time and personal energy.* However **when I asked God in my heart each time, the tingle up my spine indicated a clear answer to me. I needed to be there!** I told Nurse Evelyn about Mom playing some mind games with me the night before and she arranged to have the social worker begin meeting with us weekly. Mom also had an assistant come to give her a shower, twice weekly before I arrived, down to once a week now because I wanted to help although it strained my back. Mom said she loved my showers the best. They made me nervous because she was so weak, pale, out of breath, and obese without all the proper bathroom equipment to safely bathe her.

Last Christmas when I had been visiting, I went to the local home improvement store and bought a shower seat, bars to install on the bathtub walls, a removable hand-held shower head, all the proper hardware, and even anti-slip stickers for the tub floor. At that time, she was not ready to accept being in that much "need" and started yelling at me when she saw it all. *I did not let her see my intense disappointment with her negative reaction to my helpful gesture.* "Oh, Kathleen! I do not need that stuff! I am fine! I like my shower the way it is! You will not drill holes in the liner walls! It will lower the resale value of this home! I like to stand up to take showers and will not sit down! I like the metal showerhead I have. Those plastic things break too fast! I don't need stickers on the floor. You just take all that stuff back right now! My God!" So I did, or actually had Edward do it for me. The timing wasn't right for her then.

Now hospice actually provided most of the equipment she needed, thus it saved me the money. Mom was realizing lately that she couldn't stand long enough to really wash herself, or even to let someone else do it. She was starting to feel afraid to be alone, and to slip and fall. I could see it on her face. It broke my heart, yet I would rather have been there to help than to have had strangers always doing it for her. She, of course, preferred that I do them all. I had the routine down good: put towel over the toilet seat for afterwards, turn on lukewarm water at tub spout, help her out of her nightgown (clean one ready hanging) and onto the new tub seat, turn on shower head, help wash her hair, then hand her a soapy wash cloth to wash her front. Meanwhile, I would scrub her back with a brush I bought that she just loves. "Mmmm, ohhhh, Honey, that feels so good! Ohhh, gosh," she would say slumping forward to concentrate on the feeling while I lovingly swept the brush all over her back, neck, shoulders, arms and buttocks. Then, I would turn the water back down to wash her feet for her, carefully working the shower curtain so I didn't get too wet!

Showers became some of our most intimate times together. Helping her dry off as she struggled to breathe tugged royally at my heartstrings. I would watch her sweet face contort in pain while verbally saying, "I'm fine," yet moaning and groaning through the whole process like it was the most difficult thing she had to do. She became like my big baby. I would rub the towel over her helpless frame while she weakly tried to tell me, "I can do it, Honey, you don't have to. Just give me a moment to catch my breath." Then she'd add, "Oh, you're so sweet. Thank you Kathleen. I'm so glad to have you here," as her head limply swung side-to-side, eyes still closed. I always kissed her forehead over and over saying, "It's ok, Mom, that's why I'm here. I don't mind. I love you very much!"

It would literally take her all morning and sometimes all afternoon to get the strength needed to face the shower scene, as I sat trying to be patient while motivating her to do it. This was a delicate balance to maintain. Sometimes she would say, "Ok, Kathleen, don't push me!" in an irritated tone, yet I'd been waiting eight hours! Often, I would let it go until the next day, but then I had to insist. When the assistant came to give her a shower, however, she couldn't procrastinate. Thus, I found myself appreciating the help in more ways than one. Mom liked this lady, but told me she was too fast, didn't let Mom help at all, and did not use the back brush like I did. Of course, I knew that I also showered her with love.

I actually took her to only one doctor's appointment. He said she was doing great overall, and saw improvement since I'd been taking care of her. When we asked him about her occasional pain attacks in her ribs and up her neck, he examined her. The place on her rib cage where she had had the tube draining her lung, left a huge nodule of scar tissue, and her glands seemed to be swelling again. He told us, "Well, it looks like the cancer is growing there again. Cells often leak out around the drain tube and start spreading through the lymph system. There is nothing to do at this point except manage how you feel. Take all the pain and anxiety medications you want, with trade off's on how alert you want to be. It's up to you. We'll see you in six weeks!" And for some reason Mom told everybody how she was doing so well now, that he didn't need to see her in the usual "every three weeks" pattern as he had in the last six months! Conversely, I heard: "This is the end. There's nothing more we can do!"

Mom did start to get confused about all the different medications she was taking. Each nurse's visit seemed to result in more of this and less of that. The times were staggered, some with food and some without. I helped her keep track, which was another reason I was so glad I was there. She would sit and ponder it for an hour, "Are you sure she said just half a pill twice a day now? I don't remember her saying that!" "Yes, Mom, I'm sure," I would try very patiently to repeat over and over without getting mad. It amazed me how different we were. I could pop a fist full of pills and not blink an eye, while Mom was afraid of being a micro-milligram off. It was in part her nurses training and personality that made her an "exact dosage" person. *Contrarily, my low self-esteem and tendency towards abuse made me a "the more it hurts, the more I take" kind of gal.*

I found myself (just like when I was a kid) sneaking out to her garage and smoking cigarettes within a week after arrival to deal with the stress of being there and holding back my feelings around her. I really didn't want to start smoking again, and for some strange reason, I didn't want to tell her. I don't know why. I'd always told her before and she didn't care. She, like the rest of my family, never believed it was a big deal for me because I quit so often. Yet, I knew that the older I got the more difficult it became each time to quit. *Nonetheless, it was simply too much for me to care about at that point.*

I also felt so tired after I first arrived that I wanted Mom to continue with her monthly cleaning lady, Becky. She always talked about how much she enjoyed her visits and how much of a hard worker this lady was. For example, she'd move furniture to vacuum and take things off the refrigerator to wipe it down. I wanted Mom to continue with her important little socialization patterns that she had before I came home. Plus, I knew with my dogs staying there, the place was going to get dirty faster. Therefore, I liked the thought of a monthly helper in this area too. Yet, Becky had told Mom that since I was home she shouldn't need her services. She said she'd still stop by to visit like her sister Agnes who brings us all the great home-cooked goodies. For some reason, we both thought that maybe Becky didn't feel needed anymore, so I encouraged Mom to call her and tell her I could really use the extra hand once a month.

Meanwhile, I was walking the dogs probably six times a day, all around the beautiful grounds, enjoying the great weather and exercise. Even though it was a little humid, it felt wonderful compared to the 100+ heat in Phoenix. And the dogs seemed to be getting used to the walks, with all the new smells, although Charley had a couple of accidents inside the house. I just assumed the timing and stress of the whole trip and different environment were just too much for her.

Over two weeks now into my stay and I'm making sandwiches in the kitchen when I hear Mom say, "Kathleen, something's wrong with Charley. She keeps sitting down hard on the floor and turning circles!" I come out to see her run towards the door and start to poop. I grab her leash and quickly take her outside, where just a few steps from the house she poops some more only to then lay down, completely, on her side. I panic and say, "Charley! What's wrong Honey?" As I shake her I realize she's passed out, totally. Terror runs through my veins as I try to analyze the situation and get her up. She feels too heavy. I cannot lift her and thus keep trying to wake her. I look around and see no one, then realize how Mom lives amongst mostly senior citizens *and I feel very helpless*. I look up to the sky one quick time and say, "Oh please, God!" as **I pull upon some hidden strength from deep within me**. I scoop my hands under her neck and hips and mightily lift her up, bouncing her to get my grip on her "dead" weight. I'm wondering if she ate something poisonous. "Don't let her die, God, oh please! Hang in there, baby!"

I then lay her down next to my car and run into the house. "Mom, I got to take Charley to the emergency clinic! She's passed out, maybe dying . . . How do I get there again?" Next thing I know, Mom is in the car with me directing us to my old University grounds, where one of the best animal clinics in the world exists! We should know. Our family dog was their first patient when they opened their doors back in 1973. That was indeed a horrible incident to remember.

I had actually found this puppy we named Ernie, a sheep-dog-spaniel mix, who was only a year old when he got hit by a car. It was my fault because I let him out at lunchtime and forgot to let him back inside. Plus, it was cold that

December, just one day after my twelfth birthday, with snow on the ground. As I was walking home from school, I spotted him across the busy street waiting for us. The minute he saw me he started to run towards me at the crosswalk, as the cars appeared to be stopped. I yelled out, "No Ernie, stay!" But it was too late. Traffic had just started up on a green light and a Volkswagen hit him broadside right in front of me. I lost all my senses and ran wildly across the street, weaving between honking cars and nearly getting hit by every lane of traffic myself. I pulled him over to the side of the road and ran to the neighbor's house for help. They brought out a blanket to roll him in, and meanwhile a carload of kids from the grade school stopped and the driver offered to take him to this new clinic. Edward had come onto the scene by then and went along. I got scared and said I had to get back to school for basketball practice. Actually, I cried the whole time. I just couldn't face the fact I might have killed him. When I left, he seemed already dead!

One of the hardest things I ever had to face was coming home later that evening to see what happened, and to face my family. We loved him so much and it would have been terrible to lose him just two years after dad had died. Even though Ernie would turn out to be fine, things were worse than I feared because my family was so mad at me. I had to listen to Sean say, "Kathleen tried to kill our dog," and "Poor thing was so cold he dug holes in the yard trying to keep warm." Mom would sarcastically point out how my friends and practice were more important to me, and Edward just said, "How could you?" They all basically ignored me for a long time. And the story got told over and over because of the extent of his injuries and what a miracle survivor he was. He had a broken back, ribs, rear legs, and collapsed lungs with internal bleeding. If it weren't for the new 24-hour service at the clinic, he would have died. I, on the other hand, had always wished it were me that got hit instead of Ernie. I distinctly remember from that moment on wishing I were dead, deep down. I had to watch his back sway from side to side for years, and listen to his occasional whimper because of pain. I felt so much shame upon condemnation while never receiving any compassion from anyone on the horror I went through and felt.

"This clinic should have a plaque on the wall dedicated to Ernie," I think as I run in to tell the clerk about Charley. Then a team comes out to my car with a gurney on which to put the now awaking Charley, and my heart sinks as I watch them wheel her away. "My baby, look at her! Oh my God!" I start to cry, forgetting who was with me. But not for long as Mom responds, "Well, Kathleen!"

(As if I had an abnormal reaction!) "She's gonna be ok!" I stop, the tears dead in their tracks, and look at Mom. I want to say a lot yet instead calmly ask, "How do you know?" "Oh, I'm sure she just ate something and will be fine," she answers, totally detached. Next, I park the car and help her walk into the waiting room. I feel so conflicted: thankful to have her support, *angry she doesn't know how to support me!* **"Just be grateful for what she can give you," a little Angel whispers to me as I feel a slight tickle upon my neck.**

I was grateful that she sat patiently in the waiting room, without her oxygen, for four hours while I was in the back with the doctors! *However, I felt hurt that the few times I came out to check on her she always started to talk to me about something else, never once asking how Charley was. "Lack of oxygen?" I thought to myself, "Too many meds? Early Alzheimer's? I shook my head in amazement*, and prayed for patience to get through this. Charley was groggy, but showed nothing abnormal, until they did that ultrasound. Then, the doctor was talking to me privately like Charley might die any minute due to kidney failure. What stumped them all though, was that the unconsciousness had nothing to do with her kidneys. Astonishingly enough, she had no toxins in her blood stream to cause that. Her urine was not concentrated as it should be, however, and that was the only symptom she had. They suggested that she passed out due to holding her bowels too long. Then they told me in her condition, there wasn't much left to do except wait for her to lose her appetite and thirst. And it would probably be sooner than later, as statistics show, before she would die.

After we went back to the condo, I could not help but be depressed no matter how hard I tried to hide it around Mom. I took extra naps, holding Charley and crying. I prayed for God not to take one of my last little support systems in life right now. I sobbed for days thinking that she may not make the drive back home. I was dealing with the thoughts of *how lonely that drive would feel, what Jamey would feel, and how my house would be without her in it. I thought I'd have to have a friend remove all her toys, as I couldn't bear to see them upon coming home. I was in constant fear she would pass out again during every walk, and therefore kept her closer to home. I kept hearing the vet say that in order to prevent further damage, encourage her to pee often and keep her out of stress as much as possible. "Did I bring this on because of the trip?" I kept asking, "Did I make her hold it too long?" This new slump I was in, on top of everything, was killing me (good thing I was on meds). And to top it off, Mom actually got mad at me for it.*

For the next couple weeks, it seemed like everyday when someone would stop by, they'd ask about Charley, naturally. And I could tell Mom was tired of me getting the attention. This was very difficult for me to go through in this setting since I needed support too. I spoke to the wonderful social worker who explained that when cancer patients are at this stage, it is hard for them to focus on anything else except their illness. I was able to have more compassion after our talk, but what bothered me most were Mom's cutting comments towards Charley. Her insensitivity in light of Charley's illness really perturbed me. She would tell people how she just didn't care much for dogs, and how Charley was not very loving or friendly. (I think Charley just sensed that she wasn't a dog-lover.) I asked her to stop saying those things in front of me, however, she just didn't understand and it wasn't worth fighting about. I learned to ignore her comments, although they saddened me. I know it would have been best to have not brought the dogs, yet I had no alternative. It was my dogs with me, or none of us at all, and she knew that.

One evening after two of Mom's friends, Mindy and Carla, brought us dinner, I went to lie down after eating and left them talking at the table. An hour later, I heard Mom demandingly and sarcastically saying to me through the door, "Kath-le-en? Our guests are doing the dishes and cleaning up our dinner!" I lay there and sadly thought, "Now what is the best response to that statement?" I heard them say, "It's ok—we got it!" Yet, again Mom hollered, "Kathleen!" I chose to ignore her and relax until I felt like coming out. My body's craving for a moment of peace and space prevailed.

As those ladies were leaving, Mindy could see my pain over Charley. She said, "If there's anything you need, Sweetheart, you call. I'm so sorry you're going through this. We'll be praying for you," to which Mom then emotionally added, "Yeah, I just hate seeing her this depressed and sad. She shouldn't let it get her down for so long! I wish I could make her pain go away!" I understood that she was really trying, but *I was boiling inside* and looking for a diplomatic response to say in front of our company. "Mom, my feelings are ok, no matter what they are. I appreciate you wishing my sadness gone," (God, if she only knew how much I hid from her!) "However, it's just as healthy for me to feel as my happiness!" There, I'd said it! Whew, that felt good. Even though Mom and her friends seemed a little awkward, I was proud of my response and thanked my Angels again for their support.

The next morning Mom's cleaning lady, Becky, came over. This was the first time I had met her, and I *assumed* she was anxious to get an update like everyone else that came to visit. I told her how Mom was having some anxiety attacks and pain spells, and how the cancer was back, growing in her rib scar tissue and neck lymph nodes. She said she was sure Mom would tell her these things, if she wanted her to know. **I started picking up weird vibes** yet *dismissed them.* I also told her how grateful we both were that she was there. Mom really missed seeing her. Plus, I could use the help, especially in light of what was going on with Charley. She mumbled some comment about dogs not belonging in the house. As I talked I noticed her eye contact leave me, and she started cleaning, almost like she didn't care to hear. Thus, I concluded by telling her that she didn't have to pull out the furniture this time to vacuum, or change Mom's sheets, because I had just done those things a couple of days ago. She suddenly stopped doing dishes, put her hands on her hips, and replied with an irritated tone, "Well, why am I here then?"

I felt my throat tighten as I chokingly answered, "Because we need you. I'm so exhausted . . ." "Well, I want you to know that I don't clean for people anymore! Just your Mother because she is such a special lady," she cut in, "and what you need is to get out of here more often, give yourself and your Mother a break! She's used to living alone you know. Now let me get to work!" *Confused at the interaction and implications, I shook my head as I went to the bedroom to lie down until she was gone. It was obvious she thought she should not be there, cleaning, when Mom had a perfectly healthy daughter sitting around who could do it all. It was clear she felt like I was imposing on her quality time with Mom, as well as invading Mom's space. It was evident that she did not like me, or my dogs and had strong opinions on the subject. What I didn't tell her was that I had to change Mom's sheets several times already because of "little accidents." What I didn't say was that I have to do much more cleaning because of Mom's messes now, both vacuuming and mopping. What I didn't tell her was that I did not realize just how old she was. Mom sure presented her as "young and vibrant" always cleaning up a storm, as well as such a nice caring lady. I was starting to wonder.*

I was not so lucky when an hour later, Mom called me out to come meet her husband. I sat and politely chatted with this couple for the next half-hour, all the while realizing that Becky had rearranged things back to the way they had been before I arrived. I had set up Mom's gifts, trinkets and cards differently on all the tables one day, and arranged them in altar fashions, which Mom appreciated. And *it was as if she thought that I took over Mom's house, so she was doing Mom a favor by putting things back!* I could also tell she had moved the furniture around and done whatever she wanted. *"Unbelievable!" I thought to myself, "We definitely don't need her assistance here anymore!"* And her sister Agnes, who stopped by several times a week bringing great home-cooked food gifts, seemed like such a wonderful lady. *I began wondering if she's resentful of me too, because we talked about how good her cooking was and I joked about eating it all myself. If Becky knew this she'd really think it was true and add that to her obvious impression of me as a jerk. I couldn't believe these feelings were arising in me. All the other guests were very nice and honoring of what I was doing for Mom. Here Becky was looking at me like I moved back in for no reason. Yet, I shouldn't even care what she thinks! Ah, I did not need this!*

I anxiously awaited for Diana's visit later that afternoon to "switch gears." She regularly brought over baby James, several times a week, which Mom looked forward to with joy. **We believed James had given her more will to live. He was such a hyper-genius little guy, rarely letting anyone cuddle him while awake. Yet, whenever in Grandma's arms, he held still and stared into her eyes. It was almost eerie to watch, like they were bonding Spiritually with Mom letting him know that she will soon be his Guardian Angel.** I was also glad to see them and have Diana to talk to. She always listened to all my frustrations with my family, plus validated my feelings about Mom. Sometimes after Mom said or did something that infuriated me, I would run to my bedroom and call Diana to vent because I was dedicated to keeping peace.

"You won't believe what Mom said this time," I said to her the previous day. "She was talking about the political candidates and asked what I thought. When I said, 'I don't know and don't really care,' she said, 'Well, you should care. This is your country, your responsibility, blah, blah, blah.' So after tuning out this same old lecture again, I heard her say, 'Can you imagine if every young person was like you and didn't care about the political state of this nation?' Then she grumbled something about hell in a hand-basket. I blew up inside, but calmly said, 'Can you imagine if every young person cared more about abused, neglected children in this country like I do, than they cared about materialism and getting ahead in corporate America?' Well, you know her. She just changed the subject like nothing happened and started talking about the pretty birds outside. God, she makes me so mad sometimes!" As the tears rolled down my face, Diana responded, "You know she loves you though, Kathleen, and is proud of you. She always talks about that to us. Just remember, when she goes off on her tangents, it's not really about you. She merely wishes you two had more in common to talk about sometimes, that's all. I don't know how you're doing this, Kathleen. You used to go crazy every few hours, now you're in there for weeks taking care of her dying. I really admire you. That's got to be hard. Anytime you need anything, just call. Let me know how I can help." "You do, Diana, by listening to me and visiting us," I replied with renewed vigor, "Thanks, I feel better. Oops, gotta go, she's calling me again. . . ."

Nearly every day, Mom had this habit of talking about Edward's family, sometimes for hours. I noticed this pattern getting worse over the years. As she had less happening in her life, she lived more vicariously through their lives. It was like listening to a soap opera. She was addicted to ruminating over and over again, the same old issues about them, only with new ones added now because of baby James. Probably like most Grandmothers, she thought James didn't get enough proper nutrition or sleep, and that he was too coddled. I had to listen to these details time and again. So, I found myself playing around with different responses to see if she'd stop. "Ok, you're concerned because he doesn't get enough . . ." or "I'm sure Diana's doing the best she can," or "Well, that's their business. They'll figure things out the way they need to." But to no avail, it didn't really matter what I said. Mom was obsessed with her opinions.

She also would go on about Ken: what the best course of treatment was and how he needed counseling, better discipline, and consistency. She was really worried about him, and truly loved him. She always mentioned how they had this special bond, as well how much she loved having him come visit. In the last year, during a time when twelve-year-olds typically start to pull away, she also became much harder on him. She began nagging him about everything. "Ken, did you write those thank-you letters? You really should. It's so important. You need to learn . . ." and "You spent more money on what? How much are you saving? Kids these days . . ." and "You have another creature? Oh, it belongs in the wild. Your house is crowded enough." She seldom saw his tears of frustration and screwed-up expression as he walked away exclaiming, "Ok, Grandma!"

This subject was hard for me not to get pulled into because of my background and expertise. It hit very close to home. I agreed with Mom on the counseling, and struggled with Edward and Diana seeming in denial about Ken's past sexual abuse. They hold an "it's in the past now—we're over that" attitude.

This is understandable. They have been through hell because of everything. Diana is also naturally very sensitive, struggling with her own guilt issues over it. I hope to God they are right, and I do not want to focus on the negative. Nonetheless, I have seen patterns repeat themselves exponentially. Thus, I would be playing my cards differently if I had Ken and baby James. I talked with Edward right after James was born, about statistics and the warning signs in which to heed. I suggested getting it out in the open and talking to Ken candidly about any feelings he might have come up from his past. He's seeing Edward, whom he loves dearly, with his now biological child, showering him with love in a way he did not receive during his first couple years. Ken may not realize his feelings of animosity and anger that may surface in hidden or outward ways. It may seem like normal sibling rivalry, yet with hormones about to hit, I warned him to watch for the symptoms. Edward didn't feel comfortable talking with Ken about it unless something came up, and I have to respect that. I will not say anything again. I have to let them run their own lives, for their Soul growth issues are not in my control. I said my piece and that is enough.

Mom worried about it from a different perspective. She had a hard time dealing with issues of sexual abuse, and frankly would not talk about the subject hardly at all. I always wondered if she might have been, but it wasn't any of my business. Once when I mentioned it in regards to Ken, she replied, "Oh, he was not, just physically." I realized they might have kept that detail from her, yet felt I needed to be honest. "Yes, he was Mom. I won't go into it but he was," I gently repeated. Then in her typical uncomfortable demeanor, she responded with, "Oh, everybody thinks they're sexually abused these days!" and changed the subject. I really don't think I was, although I seem to have some of the symptoms. *Regardless, I sure as hell could never have talked to her about it, had I been!*

Of course she spent hours daily talking about (her "Momma's boy") Edward. He regularly called her from work to discuss all the stressors going on there as well as at home. After getting off the phone, she would always tell me how worried she was about him, particularly his heart condition, and how he didn't need that much stress. Nothing was good enough for her. So, although she truly loved Diana and treated her like a daughter (she'd been my replacement since I moved away), she got upset because she wished Diana would help Edward out more. "He works such long exhausting days, putting up with . . ." she routinely commented, and "He makes that long drive to and from work," and "He comes home to that messy house, full of noisy animals, Ken needing discipline, and

James wanting attention," and "He has to buy or make dinner late at night when they all need to get to bed sooner," and "I'm so worried about his weak heart . . . his diet . . . his smoking . . ."

I listened to all this and kept repeating, "They'll get through this ok," or "Don't you remember how messy he was growing up? It's how he feels comfortable," or "I hear ya," or "It's in God's hands," or "Edward is choosing this lifestyle, you know? It's his Soul path here and his family's. He obviously isn't ready to change, Mom, or he would." A few times, I felt a little shame knowing how much it would hurt them to hear this after all they've done for Mom. Therefore, I became bolder by stating, "It's really none of our business, Mom. I do not want to discuss their lives like this anymore," and would change the subject. That still didn't seem to faze her because she was too addicted to discussing it. I began getting up and doing work around the house whenever she would start again.

Three weeks into my visit, I noticed that Diana had gotten visibly irritated with Edward spending time with Mom as her cancer progresses. I could see each of their points, and understood the validity of their feelings. They had difficulty seeing the whole dynamic. Diana would have jealousy arise because Edward talked about everything with Mom, leaving little to share with her about his day. She would wait at home all day for him, only to have him stay late at Mom's helping her. One of the reasons I felt compelled to come out there was because of the strain I saw on their relationship. Mom and Edward both had an incredibly co-dependent relationship as their days were filled with constant worry about the other all in the name of love. It troubled me though I understood. As well it helped me painfully see Diana's position of craving her husband's attention more all the time to the point of her self-esteem falling over the years. Since I arrived, Edward cut his visits down to two or three a week instead of daily, and the phone calls to end of workday (4-5pm) only, unless something came up. He was so relieved to have me there to give him these breaks.

Mom, on the other hand, showed signs of missing him, even though she was glad I was there. One day I came back into her condo at twilight after walking the dogs and found Edward on the couch gazing into Mom's crying eyes while holding her hands. Instantly I wondered what was wrong and why he was there. I heard Mom say as she shook her head, "I don't know. I just was missing you for some reason. Then to hear your voice come in through the kitchen surprised me and made me cry somehow. Nothing's wrong. I'm fine. It's just so good to hear your voice and see you. These are tears of joy." Edward sweetly replied, "Oh, Mom, I can stop by more if you need me to. Ok?"

The depth of their bond really hit me at that moment. *I even had some anger come up at times because I felt like she was playing emotional bonding games with Edward, keeping him from feeling totally free in his life as an adult.* Nonetheless, I knew he chose it, and also needed it. He'd say, "Well, someone's got to do it! You and Sean moved away. Somebody has to look after her! That's just life!" And over the years of us talking about this, I thought he didn't know how to draw the line with her. Now, I was starting to see my own boundary issues and unhealthy type of relationship with Mom.

I quickly realized living there how she also organized her days around both my brothers' visits and phone calls (Sean's was daily around noon). I was sure she did with mine as well, although mine were more spontaneous and sporadic. However, we could not run an errand if she thought it would cut into her calls from them. Often giving herself an extra hour before they usually called, she sat, waiting by the phone, telling anyone who would listen all about their lives and how proud of them she was. She arranged all her appointments and visits from other people, including hospice, around those lunch and dinner calls. *It amazed me and angered me how we truly were her whole life.* I always wished that she had more pursuits of her own interests. I would have loved for her to be a better role model at **standing up for herself, following her heart's desires, and putting herself first! I knew my lesson here was about acceptance. I needed her to accept me the way I am just as much as I needed to do the same!**

Today during Diana's visit, I sense that she doesn't really want to be here. I may be reading her wrong, yet it seems like her resentment towards Mom is conflicting with her love for her, and she appears frustrated. I can almost take it personally, because I've noticed lately this habit she's developing of correcting so many things I say. As I'm talking to James, reading him books or playing with his toys, I invariably refer to something with the wrong name or species, to which she replies, usually in baby talk, "No, that's Furbee, not Gismo, Aunt Kathleen!" or "Tell your Aunt that's a marsupial not a mammal!" or "Cocadile, not awigator" or "Gecko, not lizard!" "AAAhhhhhh!" my head silently screams back, louder the more she corrects me, but I just shake it off. *I can see that she is lonely and spending way too many hours with "kids stuff." The funny thing is that I don't notice her doing it with other people.*

As Diana is getting ready to leave, Mom starts to get up to hug her goodbye. We can tell Mom is extra tired during this visit, having just dozed off for the first time ever while her grandbaby is here. "It's ok, don't get up. I'll hug you in your chair," Diana says as she leans down and puts her arms around Mom. Yet, Mom still rocks herself into a standing position to follow Diana and James to the door. My dogs are also jumping around, as they always do when activity is going on at the door, and Charley is licking at James' face as he giggles and turns away. They often play this game. He will lean in to kiss Charley then she knocks him over with kisses. As Mom is pulling out her oxygen cord, she tries to step over it just as Charley runs underfoot while chasing James to the door. Mom loses her balance and falls to the ground with a thud and a moan! Her right knee buckles under and takes the brunt of her weight. "Oh dear! Oh gosh," Mom painfully starts mumbling. "Are you ok?" we both ask. "Let us help you up!" "Wait a minute, my knee," she groans and shifts around a little. "You two both have bad backs! You can't lift me!" "Yes we can, Mom, now come on," I coax, as fear actually pierces through my veins. "One, two, three, up!" I coach, as our adrenaline helps to pull her off the floor. Then we assist her as she limps back to the recliner.

After Diana leaves, Mom starts to silently cry. I put ice on her knee, and encourage her to take ibuprofen as well as her anxiety medication. She is refusing all pain meds lately because they make her too groggy to talk to us kids. She wants to wait until the pain is unbearable, which actually is a good policy so she won't build up a tolerance. I hold her hand and say, "I'm so sorry Charley tripped you! Are you sure you're ok? Does your hip hurt at all?" I probe. "I'm fine, Honey. I think my feelings are more hurt than my body," she insightfully answers. "I understand, Mom. That's embarrassing and scary to fall like that and not be able to get up, huh?" She nods as tears continue to run down her face. I kiss her forehead and tell her again how much I love her until she falls asleep. Then, I go to my bedroom and collapse on the bed crying. I realize how much my back aches, between carrying Charley the other day, giving Mom showers and now lifting her. It feels so strained that I actually pop one of Mom's pills. Then fear soars through me alongside the thought: *if I were alone when she fell, what would I do? I couldn't just pick her up. "Dear God, don't let her fall again, please?" I beg.* **Then once again I feel the comforting wings of an Angel wrap around me as I drift off to sleep.**

~~~

Mom was very excited that Sean was coming for Labor Day weekend! She had me run around shopping for all the goodies she wanted on hand. Whenever I was there and Sean would drive down from Chicago, Edward's family always came over. Together it was a crazy yet fun madhouse, especially since James was born! Along with my dogs, this little condo was going to be crowded. I had my normal trepidation arise at the thought of Sean's visit. A part of me knew I loved him as a brother, yet I always felt uncomfortable inside. Not knowing how Mom may play guilt games now that she was dying of cancer, my stomach was really turning. I had been staying in the spare bedroom, but because he was too heavy to sleep on the old sofa, I moved to the living room. Since I had built a beautiful altar and didn't like the thought of him being amongst my things, I packed it up too. Sadly, Sean was in denial about Mom's condition. He didn't really understand why I was taking care of her, even though several times on the phone I had explained my gut feelings on her condition as well as her "attacks." She would tell him, just like everyone else, how good she was doing. Having always been so independent, she didn't want anyone to think she needed help. And he wanted to believe it. He just couldn't face losing her yet. Diana also seemed to be in denial at first. Edward and I were the only ones seeing her go down fast.

The morning after Sean arrived, I was taking a shower and piddling around in the guest room. Then, for the first time in my life, I heard him talking about gay people. He sounded very open to the lifestyle, which was a relief to me as I always assumed he would criticize that too. I was surprised at how he kept discussing it in various manners with Mom. First he talked about TV shows he liked with gay characters then about his class reunion and how many classmates turned out to be gay. I wondered if he was partly doing this for my benefit. *(Thanks, but I was not going near that conversation!)* Mom was just "uh-huhing," not too interested herself, yet not being critical either. I took a deep breath and came out asking, "Are you guys ready for our drive to the park?" Sean finished by saying something about how all the women in our extended family have always been down-to-earth, not real dressy feminine types. Like tomboys for life, they all seemed to enjoy hanging out more with men. Astonishingly, Mom replied, "Well, Kathleen prefers the company of women!" after which I said, "All-right-y then, let's get going!"

I noticed how Sean just got into the car right away as I helped Mom slowly walk down the two steps and across the garage floor, holding her elbow for support. Then I assisted her with sitting in the passenger side, swinging her large legs over in front of her, and putting her seatbelt on for her. I also noticed that after we arrived at the park, he stood looking out at everything. Meanwhile, I popped the trunk, lifted out the wheel chair, put it together, helped Mom out of the car and into the chair. I also wondered why he never once offered to help push her as we walked the two-mile path around the diverse landscape. I'm sure that it was hard for him to see her like this, as for all of us, and he obviously felt unsure of what to do. Towards the end of the hike, Mom started to get a headache so we went home instead of for a drive in the country like we had planned.

Sean went right into the kitchen to fix something to eat as I helped Mom out of the car. Saying she was okay on her own, I then carried some stuff into the kitchen as Mom walked unassisted. When she lifted her legs to make the two steps up, one leg didn't quit clear and she started to teeter. I looked up to see her about to fall as I yelled to Sean who was closer, "Help Mom!" He jumped and started towards her just as she steadied herself on the door jam, and said, "I'm alright." *Anger raced through me* as I watched him seem unable to help her finish the last step. "Lord, help me get through this without animosity. I'm here for Mom, no matter who else is visiting, even my brother," I silently prayed. I also thanked God for Edward being so loving and nurturing to Mom then made a compassionate note that Sean is unfortunately just not "that way."

Once sitting in her recliner, Mom's pain attack became increasingly worse. As Sean sat staring forward into space, I got Mom her pills and made her an ice pack. Surprisingly, she took half of a pain pill, then agreed to take the other half twenty minutes later, which indicated just how severe her pain was. It was shooting up her neck and down her arm, so I applied the ice in between. **I also placed my hands on her shoulders and prayed for God to help me heal her with Divine loving energy. A tingling down my arms was validation of such.** With the soft jazz sounds on in the background, she eventually fell asleep. An hour later she awoke and incredibly felt fine again.

A day later now, Edward and his clan arrive for the holiday full of bags of toys and extra food to share. We all fall into our normal routine, which starts in the living room getting caught up and having refreshments. Soon we'll take turns bouncing around, except Mom who stays in her chair the whole time. Ken's off first to go skate around the neighborhood, and I tell him I'll join him after I finish my beer. Then Edward leaves to go start the grill, and I know we won't see him sitting still inside again until after dinner. As usual I want to follow, for I always feel at home next to him, yet find myself watching the dynamics in the living room instead this time. I think about how Sean and Diana have a pretty good relationship. It seems that when Sean and Mom aren't discussing current events or family history, he's making Diana laugh until she cries. He's great at talking in various accents and doing funny imitations of famous people. It's a refreshing side I never used to see of him, and one of the reasons Diana has had trouble seeing his rudeness towards me or picturing past abuse by him. I feel sad wondering how many people he has really ever let in to see his goodness, his heart, and his humor.

He's asking Mom again when she can come visit his new condo in Chicago. She saw it once right after he moved in, yet he really wants her to see it again. "Hey, I was a little worried about making that drive by myself, but since Kathleen's here, she can take me up there next weekend. Right, Honey?" she asks me. "Well, I guess," I sputter as my gut turns, "But, the dogs, and Charley's not supposed to have extra stress, and . . ." "Oh, Charley will be fine! That's not a stressful drive," she cuts me off. Sean adds, "Yeah, dogs are allowed at my condo. Some neighbors have them so it won't be a problem." I mumble, "Ok, whatever you want Mother. I am here to serve you!" Then I go join Edward for our typical powwow: just a-smoking-up-a-storm in the garage. It's our refuge, our way to gather our senses together as the people, noises, arguments as well as laughter waft in and out of the stressful family environment.

"God, Sean is bugging me again! He's pushing for Mom to come visit and you know she can't make that drive," I vent to him as he hands me a smoke. "Will you please talk to him?" Ken keeps rolling up on his in-line skates trying to talk to me about things happening in his life, in between saying, "Hey Aunt Kathleen, watch this trick . . . See how I do this one!" Meanwhile Edward and I keep trying to privately discuss what is going on with Mom. "Oh, now you know I can't get involved! That's between you all," he replies from his usual peacemaker stance. "But you know Mom's too weak," I argue, "and what if she has another pain attack, or little accident, or . . ." "Hey Edward! Will you watch your son a minute while I clean up his mess in here," Diana yells, poking her head out into the garage. Attached to her legs, James is now wailing at the top of his lungs. "He wants his daddy! I tried to tell him you were busy giving yourself lung cancer too, but he doesn't seem to understand," Diana sarcastically digs. After a quick roll of the eyes at me, Edward says lovingly, "Come here little man. What is it? Huh? You miss your daddy?" He scoops him up to play with him while Ken rolls back up. "Whad'ya think, Aunt Kath? Think you could do that? Did you see how fast I was goin'? This kid at school . . ." I nod as my mind wanders thinking about *Mom and my fear at making the trip. My gut aches for assistance and understanding; I find so little.* "Hey, I thought you quit smoking," Ken ponders aloud as I reply, "I did!"

The dogs are now barking louder than usual inside and Sean pokes his head out to say, "Kathleen, will you shut your dogs up? Mom's trying to sleep and they're driving us crazy! Hey Edward! When's that barbeque gonna be ready? Mom needs the table set up and the salad made!" The door slams as Edward answers, "Give me ten minutes!" I'm thinking to myself, *"You asshole, do it yourself!"* while Ken continues talking to me. Edward breaks in to say, "Ken, watch your brother while I flip this meat. Ken! He's heading for the street!" As James' toddling picks up full speed, it appears that the slant of the driveway is going to make him fall forward. Ken replies, "You mean flip the blackened-crispy-charred-used-to-be-meat!" as he rolls off and scoops up his little brother with one arm, speeding around the cul-de-sac with him sideways like that. "Ken! Be careful! You'll hurt him! Put him down!" Edward yells as James shrieks with sheer delight. Ken pulls back up and says, "See he likes it!" then skates off once more in a big circle before setting James down. The momentum is a little too fast and the timing a little off. James scrapes his knee and bumps his head a little on the concrete, screaming now in pain. As Edward picks him up to quiet him down, he demands, "Ken, get those skates off, wash up and set the table for Grandma!" "After one more time around," Ken states as he heads back out. Edward yells, "Now!" and the sweaty faced Ken finally rolls into the garage and says smartly, "Yes, father!"

The tensions are building as we settle down to dinner. Mom is quieter than usual, appearing stressed and tired of all the normal commotion our family musters. Baby James is fussing and nothing Diana does seems to calm his whining as he kicks and writhes in his high chair. It's obvious that Mom is thinking he didn't get his nap ("He never gets enough sleep, poor thing!"). Edward is getting last minute condiments, utensils and drinks for the rest of us already seated. Mom, while looking down at her plate and trying to be patient, finally says above our bantering back and forth, "Can we just say prayers please?" Sean, also visibly frustrated by all the noise, sarcastically comments, "Apparently not," while looking squint-eyed at all of us.

After a little prayer and passing of food, *I find my silly clown mood coming out stronger to cover up for the uncomfortable body language of Mom and Sean.* I start singing "beans and cornbread," and "let's go out to the lobby, to get ourselves a treat" and then "give me my baby back baby back baby back, ribs" all the while with Ken joining me. "No, Aunt Kathleen," he laughingly says, almost with coke coming out of his nose. I point and laugh for him to be careful not to spew it out across the table. "We should sing: 'give me that burnt chicken, burnt chicken . . .'" "Oh, thanks a lot," Edward teases back, "Next time Ken, remind me and I won't make you any!" "That'd be fine with me," Ken retorts, "Grandma would let me eat something out of the fridge." "All-right-y then," Diana jokingly says and picks up Ken's plate to remove it. Mom yells out, "Oh, no I wouldn't! You either eat what's made for you or you don't eat at all, Buster!" Ken grabs his plate back from Diana as he awkwardly says, "Just kiddin' guys," and throws me a pleading-for-understanding look. After winking at Ken, I say, "Do you know that when we were growing up, our dad did not allow us to sing or joke at the table?" After scrunching up his face in disbelief, Ken replies, "Really? That's stupid. Why?" However, before I could answer, Sean, who had been brewing for some time, finally explodes, "Because that's the way it should be! Families have traditions for discipline and self-control, something we could use more of around here! It's a matter of respect, so start showing some right now!"

Ken almost drops his fork in shock. There is an incredible awkwardness at the table. Even baby James stops eating for a moment. I haven't heard him yell quite like this since we were growing up, which he did regularly then. It amazes me how after twenty-some years, that feels like yesterday again. It is obvious to me that Diana and Ken have never seen Sean like this even after hanging around him off and on for twelve years now. The way they are studying everyone's reaction is very interesting. Mom and Edward just act like nothing happened. I give Ken an understanding wink and nod; one that says it is time to be quiet for a while. Ken starts to do a little uncomfortable laugh out loud as he looks at his mom, then thwarts it on second thought. He looks down at his food and eats in silence like the rest of us for the next five minutes, until Sean pushes his dishes out of his way, and storms out of the kitchen. We all look at each other and shrug as we hear the spare bedroom door slam shut.

133

I can't believe how Sean still commands his way, and we give it to him. Is this really what they want? Does this make us seem like a happy cozy family now? Being afraid to say anything out of fear, tiptoeing around, being misunderstood and not allowed to really express oneself—the story of my life! I try to explain all this to Diana as we do the dishes. She says that now she really understands more of what I'd been telling her about our relationships, especially growing up. I'm describing to her about the patterns and roles we all play in our family, and how Sean would often explode like that. Mom then would always try to get Edward to go in to talk to Sean to make things better. Suddenly, Diana holds up her hand for me to be quiet as we lean in to listen to Mom saying just exactly that to Edward in the living room. "Oh my God, Kathleen, you sure called that one. That's incredible!" We listen to Edward reply, as I mockingly shake my head no, "Oh, Mom, I wouldn't know what to say. He'll be ok—don't worry. He just needs time." Then we jump back and giggle like two schoolgirls as Edward walks by us to go have a cigarette in the garage. "And what are you two up to in here?" he asks, quickly adding, "No good, I'm sure!"

Next, I whisper to Diana, "Now watch. Mom will try to comfort Sean on her own," as we tiptoe back to the edge of the dining room. Sure enough, we see Mom slowly walk to the door. After knocking with no reply, she inquires anyway, "Sean? Honey, won't you come back out and join us? They're gonna be leaving soon, and we'd sure like to have you out here with us." I finish the story by saying, "He won't come out. He'll pout all night, then Mom will be extra sweet to him in the morning and they'll act like nothing happened. It never gets talked about. I've always thought that was a bunch of bullshit!" Not sure if we hear a grumble or not, Mom discouragingly walks away and sits back down in her recliner with a heavy sigh; in a manner I've sadly heard my whole life.

One of the biggest frustrations I had growing up with Sean was how he would always go through my stuff, personal things, in my bedroom when I wasn't home. This absolutely drove me crazy. It angered me more than anything else I knew. I could not stand feeling like someone had been looking through my things, especially from a place of faultfinding. It felt so invasive; it was an emotional rape of sorts. I remember one time when I came home he had not only busted into my diary again, but had read a very personal account of my first kiss with my boyfriend. What I did with that young man was nobody's business, except mine. What happened between us, and what I wrote was actually very sweet. Further, it was a very normal twelve-year-old perspective and experience. Sean however, turned it into a major embarrassing and humiliating incident. As he was mockingly calling me a slut in the background, Mom was trying to lecture me on being inappropriate with boys! This was stuff I would only share with best girlfriends, not my Mother and definitely not my older brother! *And to think she didn't trust me felt hurtful. She wasn't even mad at him for reading my diary. She was more interested in scolding me for something they shouldn't even know about, something I did not even do wrong!*

From then on, *I was so angry inside I actually thought I hated him.* He would always kick my friends out and treat us abusively (Edward's too, although he forgets). Over the years *my rage built as my drug usage to escape reality increased.* One night when I was barely eighteen, I had a reoccurring dream again: I was axing him to death, chopping at him over and over until he finally died. *I awoke in a drug-stupor sweat, and honestly believed I had just done it. It was horribly frightening to think that I might do that in a blackout or something,* therefore I went to get professional help. She told me I had to ignore him until I moved away from home (six months later), which took all the strength I had to do so. For example, I remember him coming into the family room, plopping down in front of the TV and changing the channel I had been watching, just to try to trigger me. I took a deep breath and went to my room. Eventually it did get easier and I stopped screaming and asserting my will over his. I never had that nightmare again. *I also vowed to never be personal with him again.*

~~~

Mom is really slowing down now, her breathing is more labored, and she pauses a lot when attempting to get from one room to another. She often sits at the sink for an hour just trying to brush her teeth. Sometimes, she seems to fall asleep on the toilet. I have to check in regularly and help her get up most of the time. She's losing track of time, but she's still very alert and smart-assed as always, trying to be humorous in light of so much difficulty. This morning she was so excited because a long-time friend of hers, Clara, was coming again to give her communion. She loves it when this lady visits, because unlike the couple of priests who have stopped by, Clara spends an hour talking to Mom. She also shares an inspirational story with her, like a mini-sermon. Today, Clara gave Mom a 30-day meditation book, and Mom turns to me and says, "Oh, I just love this book! Wasn't that so nice of her? She is such a wonderful person! Would you

135

like to read a passage out of this book with me everyday?" I agree as I thumb through it, thinking about all the affirmation books I've used over the years. Something Mom never got into before, yet I'm glad it has meaning to her now.

For the next few weeks, we weren't as consistent at reading it daily as we had hoped. Some days she would forget, others I would. One night I was feeling exhausted, *irritated* with Mom, and needing space. After I went to bed early, I heard a knock at the bedroom door. "Yeah?" I called out. "Kathleen, would you like me to read you the thought for the day?" she asked me so sweetly. *Unable to pull myself out of my slump like usual, I replied, "No, Mom. Remember, Ken already read it at the dinner table tonight? But thanks anyway."* "Oh, he did?" I heard her mumble, then, "Well, ok Honey, you get a good night sleep then." "Ok, Mom, you too." "I will, and it's so good to have you here. Thank you for all that you've done. I love you!" **I tried to be patient** as *my head yelled, "Please just leave me alone,"* yet **my voice said, "I love you, too."**

The next morning I kept feeling a little guilty about having turned her away the night before. I was trying to be very careful. I didn't want to do anything I might regret if she were to die soon, but sometimes the pressure of being perfect around her plus not taking proper care of myself was getting to me. Nonetheless, I was extra nice to her all day. And when she had another pain attack later that night, I was very glad I had been. This time, it took several hours for me to convince her to take more meds and then for the drugs to take effect. Thus, she was wiped-out, as was I. She kept changing positions, from lying to sitting, turning this way and that. When the pain finally subsided, I sat holding her on the bed. She looked at me with so much love and thanked me from a deeper place than I'd ever seen before. "You are such a sweet daughter, just the best! A mother couldn't ask for better," she sincerely said. I jokingly replied, "Oh yeah, well I'll remind you of that the next time I do something that you don't like!" She then retorted, "Well, the next time you get upset with me, I'll remind you of what a great patient I am!" We both laughed at that; yep, Mom was back!

The next day, two old blood bank buddies of hers came over. They had been stopping by fairly regularly, and had been in touch a lot since Mom had been diagnosed. One of them, Carla, a nurse who went with Mom on many doctors visits, upon hearing of Mom's attack, told me to call her if that ever happened again. I was beginning to think I might need help or advice when these attacks hit. Mom would listen to Carla better than me about taking more medication, too. The other lady, Alyssa, was closer to my age and we hit it off immediately. She was always such a relief for me when she would visit. We could giggle and be on the same wavelength about many things. Her own mother was currently in remission from breast cancer, and she had been fighting that battle for several years. Both Alyssa and her Mother had been very good to Mom in the last year. Alyssa also told me to call anytime I needed help. They both meant it.

A few nights later, while Mom was in the bathroom, I snuck in her room to write **special messages** on the top of a bunch of crossword book pages. Mom loved to sit and relax doing crossword puzzles, and **I knew she'd appreciate some Spiritual notes** from me. I was hoping she'd read only the one on top of each puzzle so that the messages would last awhile. However, later that night, after I tucked her in and said goodnight, it was evident she had flipped through the book and read all of them. "Kath-leen," I heard her chokingly try to say, "May I come in?" "Sure!" I answered, smiling with a warm heart as I watched her being so deeply touched by my notes. She slowly walked over to my bed and sat down, shaking her head in amazement while trying not to cry in gratitude. "Thank you so much, Honey," the tears came anyway, "This was very sweet of you, just more than you'll know . . ." She tried to express herself as her fingers stroked the cover of the book. "You weren't supposed to read all of them at once, silly," I teased her. She chuckled and replied, still crying, "Well, I couldn't help it. They were so nice, I just had to!" "I understand, Mom, but it really wasn't me! **An Angel overtook my body and wrote those things! Even though they're from my heart, they're really from God!"** She laughed again and jokingly said, "Uh, huh, I know—you and that Angel again!" (This was something I often claimed when she was thanking me.) As Mom sat looking around the room, it hit me that the entire month I'd been there she had never seen the special altar I created. For some reason, I still did not feel like explaining much. I merely listened to her. "That's really neat, the way you have that set up there! I like your Angels, and that's the prayer card I gave you, huh?" she pointed out. Then her attention turned to a southwestern designed fuzzy blanket of hers and said, "Isn't this blanket beautiful! These colors—teals and lavenders—I just love them, don't you?" I smiled at her and nodded yes, as they are also some of my favorite colors. Then we hugged goodnight.

By morning, she was talking about going to Chicago again, thus I suggested we take a drive around town to see how she did short-term. I knew she'd never last, and was furious that Sean was blindly still asking her. She barely made it out for one errand per week with me, and then was so exhausted she slept for hours afterwards. Plus, these weren't "walking around" type of errands either. For instance, we'd go to the bank drive-through, or I'd run in a store while she waited in the car. I took her out driving all over the country roads for an hour. *I wanted her to decide for herself that she couldn't go, that it would be too much. I knew if I put my foot down and said that, I'd be the bad guy, and I wasn't going to allow that to happen. I knew if I called the trip off, she'd think it was about sibling rivalry, and accuse me of not wanting to go visit Sean (which was only a small part).* I honestly cared about her condition, and was seriously concerned about handling her by myself, and with my dogs, on a two and a half-hour drive to Chicago. I knew the stress on her system would be tremendous. I tried to tell Sean, however he thought I was being *overly protective or lazy or something. I was so adamant about wanting to convince her, that I drove a little wilder than I should have. I sped around those country roads, purposely hitting little potholes and dirt bumps to shake the car up a bit. I drove slightly faster than the speed limit then lied to Mom when she inquired about it. I told her she just wasn't used to driving and that her perception was off. Finally, I stopped the charade, trying not to feel guilty, while seeing her pain start to travel up her neck again.* She tried very hard to be strong. She wanted so badly to make that trip and be healthy now for us kids . . . she just never wanted it bad enough for herself before.

We ended the excursion by visiting Edward's house. I pulled up and jumped out to play with baby James running barefoot around the front yard. We started playing peek-a-boo in his cardboard playhouse while chasing around a ball, and then I drove him in his toy truck. Mom just opened the passenger door and hung out her legs, watching and smiling at us, saying, "I'm ok, I just need to rest here a minute." Although the sun was streaming down hotter than usual on this September afternoon, she didn't want to budge from the seat. Meanwhile Diana talked with her for a while, then Ken's school bus dropped him off and he slowly showed her his artwork and homework. It was obvious she had no concept of how long she sat there. Two hours later, I drove us to Arby's (it's what she asked for) where we got chicken sandwiches and fries. Then, we ate in the car at a big park, where I happened to spend many years of my childhood and teen years "hanging out." I reminisced about the years on the swim-team there, admitting to all the partying I used to do over on the picnic tables when I should have been in school, and then commenting on the addition of the water slide and other park amenities. Although she was nodding, I could tell she was not really interested. She kept asking me what time it was, or when she had her last pill, or when Alyssa would be coming over later. I sullenly pulled out of the lot and we drove home in silence, as I asked God to forgive me for being so hard on her.

The following day she still talked about going to Chicago, even after that drive plus Diana's warning against it. Therefore, I went to discuss it with the nurse and social worker at hospice. This time I was almost hysterically crying as I told them the whole story. Even they had thought that she'd be fine for the trip, based on what they had observed and what she had told them. When I described how tired she was, her little incontinence problem, and her difficulty getting from one room to the other without turning pale and losing breath, Nurse Evelyn agreed to come the next day to evaluate and tell Mom her decision.

For the first time, the nurse had Mom walk across the condo, while checking her vitals. She saw her stop frequently and get long-winded. I noticed her surprise at how much Mom's oxygen level decreased with just that little movement. When they sat back down, Evelyn told Mom she did not think she was fit enough to make the trip at this time. She also told us to turn up the oxygen machine for whenever Mom was moving about. I couldn't believe how Mom almost seemed relieved! She just sweetly nodded and said, "Ok." I was dumbfounded at how easy it turned out, and grateful to have those wonderful hospice staff available to help!

I had grown really fond of the hospice ladies, as well as Alyssa, one of whom was stopping by every day. Carla was also starting to visit regularly now, and although Mom just loved her, I felt a little guarded around her due to her slightly tough exterior. It seemed I could really be myself, with emotions and all, around the other ladies. One day Mom was crying in front of Nurse Evelyn, saying, "I'm just really worried about leaving my children behind. I don't want them to be upset and have problems with my dying." We were so proud of her for sharing her feelings like that. I said, "Mom, I told you that we'll be ok. Sure, we'll miss you in person, and we'll go through grief—it's part of life—but you'll be our Guardian helping us out." She nodded, the whole time her fingernails were tracing circles on her right knee like she always did when deep in thought. "I know you'll be ok. I'm more worried about your brothers . . ." she choked up again. I understood exactly what she meant and *at the same time felt a little hurt.* Evelyn acknowledged Mom's feelings and assured her that hospice would help take care of us. "We have grief counseling and an after-death program. Don't worry. We'll be here for your children just like we've been here for you. That's what hospice is all about: before, during and after—all through family involvement." I saw Mom's whole demeanor soften and relax as she heard these comforting words. I found myself feeling touched to hear this as well. I hadn't realized how much I had opened myself up to receiving help from hospice. I hadn't realized how much I needed help too after struggling alone with so many issues for so long, and now putting all my focus on helping my Mother.

Later that night, Mom had another bad pain attack. We were up half the night with her moaning and going from room to room. I found out that was something she had done many nights without telling me; she didn't want to disturb my sleep! Her body would ache lying down, so she'd move to her recliner in the living room, and then back again. The sad part about this was that she had to drag that oxygen tube around, trying not to trip over it, as well she wanted her glass of water and all her meds with her, just in case. This entailed at least two trips when the poor lady could barely walk five steps by herself as it was. Recently, however, I had heard her groaning and walking more clumsily when she moved about in the night. Thus, it had been awakening me.

I was starting to get a little worried now. Would she need to go to the hospital? Would she pass into a stage I couldn't deal with? Did I really know how to take care of her or should I hire a professional who may better help her? While the panic soared through my gut and I prayed to God for assistance, I wiped her forehead with cool washcloths as she moaned appreciatively. **Then I felt calmness come over me. An Angel invaded my body again and I knew just what to do. I found myself setting up a picture of Jesus plus an Angel statue from my altar, and lighting a candle that Alyssa had given her, all on the table next to her. Then I held my hands over her areas of pain and prayed for healing energy to flow from God through me to help comfort her. An hour later (at 3am) when I finally saw her sleeping peacefully, I blew out the candle and tiptoed to bed.**

The next morning when Carla arrived, I was still in bed and could hear Mom talking about the beautiful little altar I had created, and how good I'd been to her. I came out and smiled hello, then announced that it was time to finally cut her curly locks! She had procrastinated long enough. "Carla," I jokingly said, "since you're here, you hold her down while I cut that mop. And if she's real good, she'll get a sucker when I'm done!" Mom laughed and explained to Carla that they had to say that to me when I was little. "Kathleen was such a little flibbertigibbet!" "Still is it seems, huh?" Carla responded, then, "I'll keep her busy with answering a crossword puzzle." I was pretty nervous. I hadn't cut hair in a long time although I used to do it for fun for friends as well as Edward and Mom all the time when I was in my teens and twenties. I was pretty good for being self-trained. Now, with Carla watching and all this curly hair, I was a little shaky. It took me about an hour, and I was very pleased, although Mom was getting pretty pale without her oxygen hooked up. We got her sitting back in the chair quickly and she dozed off as I rubbed lotion all over her body.

A little while later, when Nurse Evelyn came by, she checked her oxygen level to discover it was only 89! That was dangerously low, and we immediately turned up the tank. Fear soared through me as I realized that I had her off oxygen for a whole hour; something I wouldn't have done had I'd known. Evelyn heard more fluid in her lungs too, which would cause a lower oxygen level as well as more frequent pain attacks. At least her appetite was still good. She'd been at this place before. She just slept it off, so she should snap out of it again. She definitely earned that sucker earlier!

When I spoke with Edward, he asked if Mom was going downhill fast. I said that I'd been too close to the situation for over five weeks and had lost my perspective. When she was awake, sitting down, she seemed fine and could fool just about anyone into thinking she was healthy (if you ignored the tube in her nose). Edward had decided a week ago to visit almost daily again since Mom was starting to have more pain attacks. We were both glad Sean was coming in a couple days. It was hard to believe it had been almost three weeks since his Labor Day visit already. We talked about how excited Mom was that he was coming, and how he would probably come more often if he realized how bad she really was. And yet, maybe she'd improve. We surely couldn't know.

The following day I kept trying to talk Mom into getting a hospital bed. Evelyn had actually started this conversation by saying how much easier it would be to help her manage her pain attacks. At first Mom was adamantly against it. She had worked too many years in a hospital and swore she'd never be in one of those beds, especially in her house! When I suggested how it would give us a spare bed for when Sean came, she finally agreed. She was sleeping so much that we were merely catching her in between naps. She kept asking me, and whoever was visiting at the time, why she couldn't stay awake very long. We would explain how pain itself is tiring, plus the build up of toxins, lack of oxygen, and medications all make one drowsy. Now that she hadn't had much pain in a couple days, her system should be just about completely rested. She hoped we were right because she wanted to be alert for Sean's visit. However, her "awake and alert" time was still minimal. Even when Alyssa and I took her to the bathroom, she kept falling asleep while we held her. "Mom, did you go yet?" I kept asking. "Mmmm, hmmm," she mumbled but we knew she hadn't. "Come on, Hun, go potty or we'll take you back to the recliner," Alyssa coaxed. **I looked at Alyssa with an intense amount of gratitude.** There she was holding up my Mother with me! I was so glad she had been able to come over. I mouthed to her, "Please, don't leave me!" with an expression of need I've never felt on my face before and tears welling up in my eyes. A couple of hours later, Mom seemed fine for the night, hence Alyssa went home to be with her family (husband and three kids), promising to return when she got off work.

The next day, a Friday, hospice delivered both a bed and a portable toilet. It was just becoming so difficult to get Mom to and from the bathroom, that I told them to bring a toilet too. When she awoke and saw it, she demanded, "What the hell is that thing doing in here?" I tried to explain, "Now Mom, it's just in case you are too tired. You don't have to use it if you don't want. I'll hide it away, don't worry." She snapped, "Well, send it back!" Then she glanced around and exclaimed, "Oh Kathleen, it looks like a hospital in here! There's no room for that bed! I don't want all my visitors to see that, or me in it!" "I know, Mom," was all I could really say. Soon Sean came walking in the door and did a double, no, quadruple take seeing the furniture moved about and the hospital stuff added. It must've been quite a shock; poor guy awkwardly kissed Mom hello then went to her bedroom to put his luggage down.

We eventually got settled in. Sean seemed to be getting used to Mom trying to stay awake and talking in spurts with him. As well he was adapting to Carla and Alyssa hanging around ready to help walk Mom to the bathroom or do whatever was needed. I think they could see her slipping and knew how desperately I needed the assistance. At one point, Mom thought there was something wrong with her oxygen tube. "It's not blowing out anymore. I don't feel it. Look, the diaphragm stopped working!" She seemed so genuinely upset like she wasn't getting enough air. We switched tubes on her believing that would help. We even started thinking it was all in her head. It seemed too late to bother hospice, so we told her everything was okay. The ladies left after we got Mom in that bed for the first time. I sat in her recliner watching her, and once when Sean walked through to get some water, she noticed and held out her hands for him to come hug her. I don't think he saw. He merely grumbled goodnight again as she said, "I love you, Sean, it's so good to have you here!" And I sat silently letting the tears fall.

   She seemed to fall asleep all right, yet I awoke in the middle of the night hearing a bunch of banging around. I jumped up, groggy as ever, to find her saying, "Oh, gosh," over and over again, stumbling around by the fireplace! As I got closer, she seemed almost delirious, tangled up in her tube, trying to find the nosepiece end. "Where is it?" she asked me desperately, almost in tears. My heart softened like never before. "Here, Mom, come sit down. I'll untangle it. I'll fix it for you. It'll be ok Honey—I'm here," I assured her. She kept repeating how there was something wrong with it; it was blowing too much air and bothering her throat. I was so tired I thought she was half hallucinating. Thus, after giving her another round of drugs and getting her back in bed, I hugged her goodnight again. She didn't want to release me. Her grip tightened around my back as I tried to stand. "Please stay here with me awhile, Kathleen," she pleaded. Unfortunately, I was too exhausted after all the past nights of little sleep plus my back was hurting from leaning over her. "Mom, I've got to go to sleep now. I'm exhausted! You go back to sleep and we'll see you in just a few hours, ok?" And with that I forcefully pulled away.

   The next morning I was heart broken to realize she had bruises on her from banging around. She obviously was not used to all the furniture being in different places and was too foggy-headed to figure it out. When the hospice supply unit arrived, we discovered that her diaphragm was faulty, and the plain tube we'd put on created double the amount of airflow into her throat. *I gasped with horror as I thought about how right she had been and now how shameful I felt. All she wanted was restful sleep to snap out of it! Instead she had been helpless and disturbed all night with excess wind in her throat! How could I forgive myself for this one? And to realize I could have insisted that hospice come out that very night; they were on call for a reason. "I just didn't know, I really didn't! Oh God, help me with this awful feeling! Please, I'm doing my best . . . oh dear God!"*

   It seemed like such a crowded house all day. Carla and Alyssa were now taking turns assisting us, and Alyssa's husband stopped by to bring some necessities. Mom awoke to say, "Hey, Dave, what are you doin' here?" "Uh, just dropping off some toilet paper!" he answered, standing awkwardly at the front door. "Oh Dave, that's so funny!" she chuckled as they waved goodbye to each other. Edward was there, and Diana stayed in short little spurts, as baby James was too much to handle around Mom now. Ken went on a Boy Scout campout for the weekend, and wouldn't return until late afternoon the following day. Other friends visited delivering a huge deli tray for us to have as snacks. And several hospice staff came and went, including the on-call nurse who was to stop by later that afternoon.

Meanwhile, Edward pulled me aside and asked, "Do you think this is it?" "I don't know," I said, "I just can't tell!" "Well, do you think I should call the priest? I don't want Mom to wakeup and think we gave up on her when she sees a priest, but I don't want to be late with it either," his eyes grappled with me to help him make this decision. "Just wait a little while, we'll see," was all I could think of to say. Alyssa and I went to my bedroom and she sat beside me as I cried. Then she supported me while I called the list of people Mom cared about to say she wasn't doing well. When we came walking out into the living room, Mom was just beginning to awake again, and I could hear my brothers talking and eating in the kitchen. Alyssa and I sat down next to her, with me taking her hand after she held it out showing she wanted to talk.

"Am I Dying?" Her illumined green eyes bore through my Being as she desperately pleaded to comprehend what was happening. **I felt a serene energy wave cradle me with Divinity as my eyes so compassionately gazed through the windows of her Soul. "I don't know Mom, are you?" I heard an Angel softly speak through me. As our hearts connected like never before,** her deep confused eyes glassed over as she answered, "Well, I don't know! I just feel so different! I never felt like this before!" **"Well . . . if you are dying, that's okay,"** **I found myself explaining from a deep Spiritual guidance. "I'll be here to hold you with love like I promised. And if you're not, that's okay too. I'll still be right here for you!" After an intense reassuring gaze, I gently continued** as she more tightly gripped my hand, **"Tell ya' what—the next time you fall asleep, go into your heart and ask God. You'll know . . . Jesus will help you."** Tears of apprehension yet understanding rolled down her cheeks as she nodded with gratefulness and love. Then she slowly closed her eyes as her hand released it's grip, and she fell back to sleep. Sensing her heavy energy dissipate **I realized just how beautiful and intimate that moment was. That penetrating look, how she reached out and drew me towards her, and the peaceful Divine connection, etched a special message across my heart: I am truly blessed to have had this transformational experience!** And even though I was amazed at how wonderfully I handled my response, **I was in an extremely grateful and**

serene state. Then, when she awoke an hour later, and calmly asked Edward to call the Priest, **I knew I would forever be striving to feel that channeling energy again and to be open to receiving God's will for me in my life!! Humbled to my knees, I thank You, God!**

Later, when the hospice nurse was ready to leave, she pulled me outside to talk. I asked for my brothers to be included. We had never met before yet she was very nice. She looked at us and solemnly said, "There isn't much time left now. Your Mother is dying . . . she shows the signs of maybe a day or two." We stood there dumbfounded; not believing this was really the moment after all we'd been through. The nurse was still talking about sending over drops of morphine to keep Mom comfortable, among other things, to which we all nodded as tears choked our throats. The looks on both of my brothers' faces alone were enough to tear me apart. What a moment that was, all of us standing suspended in time, in that spot in the garage where I had stood so often, as the nurse drove away. We did a three-way group hug, both my brothers crying and me standing in shock, for a few minutes before getting the nerve to go back inside. I had encouraged both of them to tell Mom that they would be okay if it was time for her to go.

Events went quickly, yet time seemed to stand still. Mom continued awaking off and on, and talked fairly coherently with us, only she had refused to eat all day. I did manage to get her to drink a little water, and she even used that potty chair for us once, as she was getting drastically weaker. While the sun was setting low, the new priest from Mom's parish arrived to give her "last rights." We formed a circle around that old recliner, and he asked if we were all going to receive communion. I found myself without hesitation nodding my head yes along with my brothers. Mom was alert now and looking around with loving pride at all of us. As he said the prayers, she nodded and smiled, **seeming to have a luminescent quality about her, while Angelic love surrounded us.** He gave her a host first, and then she looked into each one of our eyes as he passed them around to us. When he held it to my mouth and said, "The body of Christ," her eyes grew huge with disbelief and gratitude for her long awaited prayer. **"Amen," I replied with love flowing out of my eyes and into hers. I took that host and for the first time in my life, really believed I was sharing Jesus Christ with her and my brothers. It was one of the most special moments in my life.** I may never do it again, however that moment meant the world to her and me— only in different ways.

An hour later, a second priest arrived because of a miscommunication. We welcomed the visit anyway and Mom really got a kick out of it, saying, "Well, I must be special in God's kingdom!" He did the rights of passage prayer again, but without communion. My brothers later shared with me that I was lucky the new priest didn't know I was not Catholic or he may not have given me communion. However, I was hardly able to ponder that deep issue at that time. And then to the surprise of us all, Mom's favorite priest in the whole world, Father Edmondson, showed up at about eleven o'clock that evening. Edward had left a message for him about Mom, however we assumed he wouldn't be able to make the long distance drive on such short notice. Mom awoke again then started laughing and crying at the same time when she saw him. It was worth the look on her face. Moreover, when he told her he was going to do her funeral, her expression was indescribable. She looked up to that man with so much love and surrender as he performed her last, last, last rights. And we all joked "three times a charm," then she fell peacefully back to sleep.

During the night Carla and Alyssa had arranged to stay up monitoring Mom to allow us kids to get a "good night's sleep." Around 4am they woke Sean and I to say she wasn't doing well. She was having another pain attack, but was being obstinate and refusing to take anything. She also kept trying to walk around, yet wouldn't go to the bathroom. She wasn't making any sense. Her mutterings were unclear and I was unable to fully wake her. **I found myself telling them not to call Edward, that she would be okay. I then held onto her, in a hug-like fashion, comforting and rocking her until she settled back down and fell asleep in her chair. I went back to bed somehow knowing we had time,** while leaving all of them standing there, unsure of whether to follow my lead or not. . . .

Now, it is Sunday morning and together we lift her and place her onto that bed. We cannot wake her, therefore she is "dead weight" and hard to move around. Alyssa and Carla leave just as the nurse is arriving to show me how to give Mom a sponge bath and oral meds. She also explains how I will soon need to start giving anal meds. *I try not to really watch the bath. I try not to feel a little grossed-out at these thoughts. "What the hell am I getting myself into?"* my head keeps saying, then, "Ok, God, get me through this, I'll do anything for her!" I know Mom is probably listening saying, "Lord, take me now. Do not put my daughter through this!"

Later, our two sets of aunts and uncles show up, for a very short time. **The interaction feels strangely uncomfortable** and *floods my memory with old feelings of rejection. (I need more of those feelings like I need a hole in the head—as Mom would say.) I am saddened that we all couldn't "bond" better, especially in light of the situation, because my heart yearned for it.* **Again I hear, "Be grateful for the gesture."** Most of Mom's friends also visit, yet she still remains asleep. Now, she only smiles in her sleep a lot; however, for the last two days she was "sleep-talking" up a storm to whoever was "hovering." This was very unusual behavior for her. I've watched this woman sleep daily for the last six weeks and she never talked or laughed out loud. A couple of times I tried to get her to talk about it, or even get in the dream with her, but she always awoke and then forgot whom she saw. I would've loved for her to talk about the Angels and Spirits waiting for her . . . And they tell me this is just another sign of impending death.

At one point I "freak-out" thinking I'm not turning her enough. I start crying, "I don't know what to do now! I think I should flip her again! I don't remember how long ago it last was!" only to have Mom's friend Mindy say, "I'll help you, Kathleen. You're doing fine Sweetie. Don't worry, she's ok!" I then catch Edward in her bedroom later and say privately to him, *"Oh my God, Edward, what will I do around here after she goes? I never thought about that! I can't be all alone in her house without her here!" The sheer terror of that thought shows intensely in my eyes* as he pulls me into him and hugs me tight. "You can come stay with us. I'll help you get through this. You have done so much. You'll never know how appreciative I am to have you here. I could've never done all this without you," and we both weep for several minutes.

Around 5pm Ken comes walking in holding a big stuffed penguin (Mom has collected them for years). His eyes show redness of recent tears, his face of fear and pain; Diana has been briefing him since she picked him up from his trip. "Why won't she wakeup?" he pleads to us. We keep explaining what is happening and how she has been waiting to say goodbye to him, only in her sleep. After several trips to the bed to say a few lines, then back to the kitchen for a moment to gather himself together again, he finally gets the nerve to say, "and here's the penguin I told you about that I was gonna give you, Grandma!" He lets himself cry now as he places it under her arm, then chokingly adds, "I love you, Grandma!" and runs to Diana for a hug. It breaks my heart seeing him like this. I also hug him goodbye and tell him how proud I am of him to do that for her. "I know it's hard to see her like this, Pumpkin. I know this is difficult to understand. I love you, Ken, and I promise I'll do what I can to help you through this." He nods and then Diana ushers him back home.

Carla left to go to an Illinois football game, so just Alyssa, my brothers and I take turns watching Mom peacefully sleep. It's now around 10pm, Alyssa and I are sitting at the kitchen table talking, *and I actually start griping about Mom.* Earlier, Mindy had made the comment that Mom was so sharp, she bet we could never pull one over on her! I point out how many of Mom's friends see her that way when it is *far from the truth. It amazes me that people can't see how insensitive or controlling she can really be. Albeit naive, she definitely doesn't have the street smarts or crude sense of humor like I do.* "And she never let me have any emotions," I complain to Alyssa, "especially tears! She would take *them on or invalidate us."* "That's funny," Alyssa comments back, "one time she told me how when your dad died, she told you not to cry, and what an idiotic thing that was to tell such a young girl!"

My mouth drops open in disbelief, my eyes grow wide as I struggle to comprehend what she has just shared with me. *"Why didn't she ever tell me that?"* *I demand* as Alyssa shrugs and empathetically says, "I don't know." *"We've had all this time together . . ."* **and then it hits me,** "She actually remembers saying that to me?" to which Alyssa nods, "I guess so." I continue, "Oh my God! That statement affected me so much! I tried to never cry around her again. I even wrote a paper on it back in college twenty years ago! I can't believe she said that to you!" Just then Sean asks us to take over watching Mom. He wants to lie down for a while. Also, hospice has arrived at the front door delivering wet swabs to keep her mouth moist, morphine drops to put under her tongue, and anxiety med patches for her skin to absorb. The pharmacist is explaining how to use them as I hear Alyssa call for me, several times. I keep trying to get away, however this guy wants to talk. Finally I say, "I'll figure it out—gotta go," and left Edward standing there thanking him for the umpteenth time.

As I approach the bed, Alyssa says softly, "I think this is it." So, I start trying to put drops in Mom's mouth and open a patch when she interrupts, "No, Kathleen, I think this is really it . . . her lips are turning blue, and her nails . . ." *I panic wanting to make sure she is comfortable,* and then **a gentle wave of "knowing" comes over me—I get it.** After calling in both brothers, we all stand around her watching her slightly labored breathing get shallower. With my hands on her shoulders, I lean across her chest and hold her like I promised, while

148

kissing her cheek. Suddenly Carla walks in, stethoscope around her neck, like she knows she'll need it. **This is the most serenely subtle state I have ever experienced. There is a shift in air pressure; there is a Spiritual comforting occurring as we watch our Mother's Spirit rise out of her body.** After several small gasps for air, her body somehow changes as we sense it being now lifeless. Carla nods the "death nod" to us, after detecting no more pulse. Sean cries out, "Tell Dad hello!" and Edward says, "We love you, Mom!" Suddenly, her mouth gasps one last time, surprising us all, and I say, "Oh, you just had to get the last word in now didn't you!" *For a split second I fear that everyone will disapprove of me for making an inappropriate comment,* yet when I instead hear everyone's tension-releasing laughter, I chuckle too. After all, it was so true!

After saying our goodbyes and waiting for the undertakers to arrive, **I suddenly find myself back at her side. Without thinking, I practically lie on top of her and start bawling my head off. I cry for all the times I couldn't in my life! I cry thirty-eight years worth of tears! I cry for all the times that I wished she would've just held me and let me cry! I swear I feel her arms wrap around me, finally holding me with unconditional love! I swear I feel Jesus come down and hug me too! I swear I can hear her heart beating plus feel the rise and fall of her chest as I sob! I know I feel someone start to approach to pull me off as if I've lost it, like I'll never let go. Then, it feels as though an Angel is gently pushing them away, to allow me this time, my time, to just cry . . . The most healing gift of my life . . . and one I would not have received had Mom's Spirit not prompted Alyssa and I to have had that conversation just moments before. Wow! Thank you, Mom!**

~~~~

Like the rain I sit and cry . . .
From the cloudburst deep with-in-side.

Like the sun I always rise . . .
After rest from under God's eyes.

~~~~

ANGELIC HARMONIES

6

"Autopilot"

*M*om had told every visitor to the house, every worker we encountered during errands and at her appointments, every friend and family member she talked to on the phone—that I was there to visit for six weeks, and how special that was to her. Meanwhile, I was always smiling in the background, saying I could stay longer if need be, or just quietly agreeing with her. However, she was right. The proverbial kind of right, which demonstrates the axiom: "Mothers are always right." **Six weeks from the day I arrived, was the exact amount of time we had together! Incredibly, she died six weeks after I got there. . . .**

Right now her condo is quiet. I'm walking around in autopilot feeling totally numb while my brothers are at the funeral home making arrangements. We each slept, as best we could anyway, for a couple of hours. When I first stumble out into the living room, I see that Sean has already opened the blinds so the sun is pouring in making last night seem all the more like a dream. My eyes instantly notice the bouquet of beautiful flowers, which Carla had given her on Friday. Mom absolutely loved this arrangement and commented on it more than any other nearly every time she awoke. The wonderful fragrance alone could wake anyone with a loving smile. **I feel my knees start to shake as I realize that every flower has closed up. The roses were just partially opening yesterday. Now they, and even the lilies, have brought their petals together in namaste' for my Mother. It seems as though her Spirit took the life of the flowers with her;** an omen I think must be preserved. Thus, I hang them upside down in the garage to dry out for possible safekeeping.

As I start packing all the hospice equipment in anticipation of the supply truck arriving soon, I am realizing how much I want this stuff out of here. Again, she was right. She only spent two nights (barely) and one day in that hospital bed, and she died before I even had to start washing her or using the adult diapers. I think about this as I pull the still fairly wet sheet off that bed, with a faint smell of urine, yet mostly damp from all the sweating her body had undergone yesterday—her last day. **I find myself putting my head on her slightly moist pillow, and for a moment I feel as if she is still here and I am holding her crying again.**

Two streams of tears slowly roll almost emotionlessly down my cheeks as I deeply inhale her smell on that pillow. It is amazing how that material captures her scent exactly from these last few days: a little fabric softener aroma mixed with slight shampoo and soap perfumes, plus her light-soft-damp-motherly-scent, all of which I hadn't noticed before. It's so hard to believe that I just showered her, cut her hair and put lotion all over her on Friday! That was only three days ago, and she was eating, walking around, and doing crossword puzzles. Two days ago she was joking around with everybody, saying how much she appreciated us all, and labeling her tears as those of great joy as she hugged visitors goodbye. Yesterday she slept; today she's gone . . .

I know she was glad that she was alert and with it up to the end—the cancer never progressed to her brain. She luckily never had a lengthy stay in the hospital, and never had to be put in a nursing home, which she had always said she would hate. Plus, out of all of her limiting beliefs, she never thought of herself as old, and disliked people that complained about every little physical ache and problem they had. Ironically, she did become obsessed with her disease progression, however she never whined about anything. Instead, she talked incessantly from more of a medical viewpoint. And she had to be relieved that she never got to the point of catheterization nor having to put her daughter through washing her and administering meds anally. I think about how **all her prayers were answered** as I throw away that old bed sheet. I'm glad I hadn't put a good set on the bed Friday night for her. Little did I know it at the time, but the undertakers rolled her up and took her away in the top sheet off the bed. She also had on a very old nightgown, one which grandma, dad's mom, had owned. (She died in 1973 at the age of 72 from a stroke just a couple years after dad.) So, we definitely didn't care about getting that back! Nobody ever warns you about these types of things.

I call hospice out of habit to schedule appointments with Nurse Evelyn and the wonderful social worker who has been counseling me weekly since I arrived, only to be told that since Mom had died, they would not be working with me any longer. I (we) will be turned over to the grief team now, and someone should be contacting us soon. I am *heart-broken*, and I know Mom would have been disappointed to know this. Of course it makes sense though, it just wasn't clearly spelled out. It never occurred to me that I would have to say goodbye to these people too. I never realized that I would get attached to the people who helped me with my Mother, so now I have to grieve these relationships as well. *I didn't expect to have this hurt on top of all the other.*

I find some morphine that got left behind by hospice after they destroyed her drugs, and *curiosity wins out. I have never taken it before. However, the amount left was so small, I feel confident I won't get addicted.* I take some but really don't feel much. Maybe it's the extreme grief and shock blocking my receptors. Perhaps my own brain endomorphins are providing extra natural pain relief, which prevents me from feeling the effects of this drug. The nurses had said that this was a weak dose. Boy, are they right! I can't believe how much pain Mom must've tolerated without using much medication. Now that's admirable!

Earlier, I chose a dress for her to wear inside the casket, which Sean took with him for their 10am appointment. It is a beautiful black dress covered with tiny bright teal-green ivy-like flowers; the very one I had helped her buy to wear to Edward's wedding three years prior. I also picked out her prettiest lacey pink bra (most were old and ratty looking), as well as her newest, nicest looking underwear, all the while remembering the saying: "always wear clean underwear, just in case . . ." Then, I sent along a pair of knee-high stockings with her favorite, not-so-nice-looking flat sandals that she wore everywhere when her feet weren't too swollen. (Like this stuff matters anyway!)

In a baggy we had put her glasses, and I included a small clear quartz crystal and an Angel card with a special message on it. Out of my little set of one-word Angel cards, I had asked Mom to help me pick the one message she most wanted me to get. "Humor" was the word, and on the card was a picture of two girls playing on a beach with the sun shining brightly. At first I thought, *"This doesn't apply!"* but then I let it sink in a little. Slowly, **I realized how I had lost my natural sense of humor lately, and my love of clowning around. I could feel my Guardian Angel giving me a message to lighten up and enjoy life more! I could sense Mom encouraging me to have more fun and to be**

happy! Moreover, a beach scene was one of my favorites in the world, and I always loved swimming and playing in the sun. So, I decided this would be the card to bury with Mom. Humor was my most crucial lifetime message— how apropos after all.

Later this afternoon Sean is preparing to drive back to Chicago. He has not brought any appropriate dress clothes with him for the weekend, as he never expected her to die. He has emotionally hugged me several times since she died, taking me by surprise, and saying things like "You're a good kid," and "Thank you for being here for Mom." Before he leaves her condo, I can hear him walking around, whimpering with a broken heart, looking in every room, and sobbing, "Oh, God," out loud. I listen to him beat himself up over things, saying, "I can't believe how much in denial I was! I just couldn't deal with her being sick! I should've come down more often. If I would've only known! Why didn't you tell me she was this bad?" **I look at him with such compassion, whilst a gentle Divine light shone forth around us, and softly reply,** "I did try to tell you. You didn't want to believe it, but that's ok, Sean!" **I feel that now-familiar Spirit speaking through me again,** "Don't you see—all three of us played different roles with Mom, and together we gave her exactly what she needed! She was so proud of you. What you did give her was a sense of family and history, which took her mind off her disease. How incredible! The rest of us only discussed her meds and taking care of herself. You provided much needed relief from that!" **I am amazed at my new strength of character around him. Something different is definitely happening to us and it feels so beautiful!**

He calms down momentarily upon hearing this, and defends himself a little better. "Yeah, I know how much Mom liked to discuss world events and I figured she had to be going through such a rough time with all that cancer-stuff being thrown in her face. I wanted to give her the sense that everything was fine, and all was back to normal. I wanted to look beyond the tubes and meds, and just have our little talks like 'old times.' I wanted her to know that I looked at her as the same ole Mom, not sickly with cancer like everyone else did. I figured she'd appreciate that!" I then interject, "And she did Sean! She looked so forward to your calls and visits because of just that! She was happy with what we all could give her—it was balanced. And since this was her time to die, she sure waited for your visit to be able to talk to you in person one last time! It's like she wanted us all together with her. She gave us such a gift! Can you imagine: peacefully leaving your body while your three kids are at your side with love? What a perfect way for Mom to die! She could've given up during that big pain attack Thursday night. Friday her oxygen was low enough for her to go, but she held on and stayed alert to have time with you!"

He nods, and starts crying harder as his remorse arises again, "I should've come sooner, then she wouldn't have had to wait!" **Again I keep validating and comforting, a role I never played with him before in my life.** "Look, I know you'll beat yourself as much as you feel you need to. I understand that, we all could! I could say I wasn't here enough for twenty years, whereas you were consistent every holiday, and took her on many vacations! What a gift you gave her when I couldn't! I could've been nicer to her, and more patient, many times, you know that. We tended to argue a lot in the past, yet it won't do me any good to beat myself up about it now. We all have our issues, including Mom. None of us are perfect and she knows that, especially now in Spirit form. She was so worried about you being ok after she died, Sean, the last thing she wants to see is you kicking yourself over anything!" Again he nods, but adds with a new rush of tears, "I'm just gonna miss our long morning talks, and endless hours of watching 'Golden Girls.' And I don't know where I'll go now for the holidays! She just died and I miss all this already!" As he walks away into Mom's room to get his luggage, all I can empathically say is, "I know."

My heart so aches watching him break down like this. I never really saw him cry before, and I can tell it is very hard for him to take care of the details of the funeral. However, I told both my brothers I can't be involved, that I need a break and for them to arrange everything. I could care less about her "death proceedings and formalities." I only cared about helping her while she was still alive.

As I watch Sean pull away from the condo, for the first time since we were very young I feel very close to him. This seems like Mom's Spirit at work! I choke up seeing his car disappear beyond the trees, realizing *I am now truly alone for the night.* Although I could crash at Edward's, their house is so tiny, crowded and noisy, I can't imagine fitting in there. Sean will return in the morning, yet for now I have the rest of the day and whole night to myself with nobody around. Even though I loved having personal time constantly at my own home, it feels strange being alone now after having gotten used to all those visitors for the past six weeks. It also seems eerie being at Mom's without her here. As I close the automatic garage door, it suddenly strikes me about **the Spiritually synchronistic timing of all the events surrounding Mom's death. I am**

especially in awe with how Mom "waited." She waited to have one last weekend with Sean, and for all of us to be together, as well as waiting to say goodbye to Ken, and Diana. She waited for all visitors to leave, and even for Alyssa and I to have that conversation. But that was it. She wasn't waiting, suffering, or putting us kids through anything else. **Bless her Soul!**

I try to keep busy cleaning and putting everything back where it belongs, especially after hospice hauled off their stuff. "Ha!" I laugh aloud realizing that it's not like anyone is going to be coming over here to visit anymore. Plus, we'll be donating almost everything to charity, so why bother straightening? Still, numbly, I find myself putting everything back the way she had it, and the way it had been for years. This condo really looks like a small version of the house we grew up in; therefore, to come here always felt like "going home" as if she never moved. I'm sure it felt that way even more to my brothers who visited her much more frequently than I. Over the past decade, I lived in Arizona thus it was logistically harder for me to go home. However, I actually had two decades of infrequent visits. I was not good at visiting even when I lived in the same hometown, making it home only for holidays as if I lived out-of-state! *Was this "grand finale" I just executed a way of compensating for lost time, a way to relinquish guilt for not coming around for so long?* Perhaps, yet another voice in my head defends that *I was just trying to be independent and not play along with her guilt games. I was just trying to figure things out in my young adult years. After all, she taught me how to be stubborn and self-sufficient, and she modeled how to not need anyone but your kids. Now, here I am with nobody—not even children.*

I notice how quiet and depressed my dogs seem, and it hits me what they have just witnessed. They have had very little attention lately except getting yelled at to get out of the way or quit barking. They were often locked in the spare bedroom to be out from underfoot, and because of everything else happening it was nearly impossible for me to love on them. I roll around on the floor with them now, telling them how proud and grateful I am to have them in my life. "Please don't leave me, my precious babies," I plead. "I love you guys and need you so much! Momma's so glad to have you in her life," I say in baby talk as they lick at me, snorting and groaning their love sounds.

After feeding them dinner, I realize I haven't eaten hardly anything in days. I've lost most of the extra twenty pounds I had gained since Mom's diagnosis only I know it wasn't in a healthy way. The medications I'm on plus the smoking and stress all inhibit appetite. Mom, as well as her guests, could even tell I'd dropped a lot of weight in just the six weeks I have been here. *However, I just don't care right now. I have more important things to tend.* I discover myself in Mom's bedroom, and suddenly on a mission to locate a letter she had left us. I almost forgot about it . . . One day shortly after I had arrived, I went into her bedroom and glanced down at her dresser. I saw this legal sized paper with a hand written note to all of us. My eyes could see that it started out with: Dear Sean, Kathleen, Edward, Diana, Ken and James. Quickly I had averted my attention elsewhere, and although I would have loved to read it, I just couldn't. It was obvious to me that she wanted us to read it after she died, and I wanted to respect her wishes. I also chose not to say anything to her, assuming that I just needed to **trust in the proper timing of things.**

Well, I search and search almost to *desperation*, but have no luck in finding that letter. I look through every drawer, every pile of papers, every business stack of documents, and still no letter. The hours are dragging, and slowly I find myself being transformed into a little girl again. I feel transported back to every age I had ever been as a child with her and every growing pain I went through as a teen with her. I see all the childhood art projects, love letters, and special cards we gave her, which she had saved for forty years! The baby books, the report cards, the vaccination records are all here. And these photographs, ones I remember as well as ones from her parents that I've never seen, all strike me down into a silent heap on the floor as I peruse them.

Hours go by, yet I have no concept of time as I continue to play in her room like a four-year-old. **I know her Spirit is here with me; I feel her giddiness fluttering around as I dance in front of the mirror.** It's the same mirror that I looked into when I used to play dress-up in our old-old house. The bedroom set in her room is the one our parents had bought after they got married. (In fact, most of the furniture throughout her condo was theirs.) I can still see a carving I had scratched into one dresser that reads "Sue"—the name of my favorite lifeguard when I was eight. With a smile I quickly recall how dad had yelled at me for that creative endeavor! I next find myself putting on some silky, sexy old nightgowns I didn't know Mom had, along with loads of costume jewelry. She never threw anything away it seems, so my inner child is taking a crazy trip down memory lane. 2am, 3am, and I'm still going strong, putting on nail polish and makeup from the seventies, just to see if it is still any good. I wish someone were here to take a picture. The circles of purple, green and blue eye shadows; the rouge and lipsticks; along with twenty different necklaces, bracelets and rings, many made out of shells or with antique charms, all looked outlandish together. In much more than Mardi gras or Halloween attire, I am something else!

All at once, I break down crying! It hits me as I fall on the bed in between the boxes, papers and junk: she never explained the jewelry to me! I pound at the pillow as I yell out, "Why, Mom, after all this time together, did you not tell me where all your jewelry came from?" *This really bothers me.* I don't know what is valuable or junk, which ones were special to her, what pieces had been her Mother's, how old they are, or from where they have originated. *Then my mind realizes that I haven't found that letter, and I sob even more. "Why didn't you leave it out for me to find? I've been curious for six weeks now! I need to know what you wanted to tell us! You wrote so little down! You shared so little of your deep thoughts and feelings! I wanted to read it, damn-it! Oh God, why did you let her tease me like this?"*

After awhile, I sit up wiping my eyes and nose, to glance around at the intense mess around me. The room looks like a tornado has hit! *Suddenly, I feel like I have invaded her private space and even feel a little guilty.* It also seems like dead-spirits are watching me look through her stuff like a *"scrounge,"* and prickly chills travel up my spine. **To switch this energy, I quickly go into the bathroom to clean up before I drag my exhausted body off to bed. Somehow I feel comforted by just knowing that with God's help I will take care of everything in the morning.**

Several hours later, I awake for the first time alone in my Mother's home. Before I can get up to walk the dogs, *I feel a dark shadow lowering itself over me, along with a stabbing pain in my solar plexus.* I pull the note pad and pen off the nightstand and very slowly write from a morose trance-like state: *"I don't feel needed anymore . . . Not only do I have to say goodbye to Mom, but also to her house and our family furnishings—still set up similarly as they have been for my whole life evoking a myriad of memories. Additionally, I must say goodbye to my hometown, which represents my childhood and young adult life. I also need to let go of my intense nursing role, as well as all of Mom's friends, plus hospice staff . . . even Edward's family."*

After calling a few more people with the news of Mom's death, as well as the visitation and funeral information, I keep busy organizing and boxing stuff to give away. *I can't sit still. I'm not yet ready to feel the full sting of Mom really being gone. I think the morphine is helping me, too. Even though I know most people would disapprove, it's almost gone so I decide to consume the rest. I also rationalize taking it due to the intense physical pain I have in my back from all the strain and work.* It actually seems more like cocaine than a depressant. I haven't slept hardly at all for the past week now, and am surprised at how much energy I have. I've spent hours constantly working up a sweat by moving as many things as I can into the garage. By the time Sean and then Edward arrive, they can't believe how much I have done. We then go through each room and Sean makes a list as we divvy up everything. It is wonderful how amiable we all are. Mom definitely raised us to be fair and share. Most items that mean something special to us, we are able to keep. Only a couple times have we needed to negotiate or compromise. The majority of her stuff, however, we are going to give away. None of us want to have a yard sale and watch strangers plow through our family history!

After a few hours, Edward has to go home, as it is time for us to prepare for the evening visitation. Unexpectedly, Becky and her husband stop by "to see how we are doing." I try to appreciate the attempt, yet **I feel leery**. She wants her poetry back that she had loaned Mom, so I hand it to her. Next, she walks around the condo checking everything out, and appears sad like she is taking it all in one last time. But, **as I study her it also seems like something else is going through her head**. Suddenly she asks, "So, I heard you might have a yard sale. Why not let us look through her stuff before you sell it to the public?" **"Here it is," I realize, "This is why I feel strange."**

I had told her sister Agnes right after I arrived that if Mom died while I was here, I would stay a while longer. This way I could settle the estate and maybe do a yard sale, so my brothers wouldn't get stuck with all the work. I tell Becky this and how we have decided against it. I refrain from saying that it's none of her business. Then she has the gall to ask, "What are you guys gonna do with this beautiful dining room furniture?" I feel my blood pressure rise as I answer, "My brothers and I will figure everything out. Don't you worry." "Well, I just wanted to point out that it's all antique and I'm sure worth a lot of money. I didn't know if you guys were aware of that or not. I'd hate to see you just give it away. Your Mother loved this set, you know." "Yes," I choke out, "we know. Now, thank you, but we need to get ready for the visitation tonight." "Ok, I'll see you there," she says as they leave. *"Oh great," I sarcastically whisper under my breath, then add, "We're doin' this for you, Mom!"*

As I walk into this funeral home, the very same one where my father's service had been held, I can't help but have a little flashback of that awful experience. This time, however, we are going through the front door. Yet, Mom is placed in the same room, same spot, as dad had been nearly twenty-nine years earlier! Sean informs me that because Mom looks so "good," they decided to have an open casket even though she probably would not have wanted it. We can hear her saying, "Oh, my God! Nobody needs to see my dead body lying here! Just close it!" However, she didn't talk much about her death plans or funeral arrangements. She just basically had said for us to make the decisions. And since she loved the "Footprints" poem, we had that printed on her funeral cards.

I slightly gasp at seeing her differently colored complexion glowing from that casket; it almost doesn't look like her. As I slowly approach, acknowledging a couple of family friends already sitting in prayer, *I am thinking, "You don't have to look. No one is making you this time,"* **yet I am being pulled forward anyway. I feel so much more mature this time, and somehow ready to say a special goodbye prayer to her physical body.** It really doesn't seem like her. I find myself staring for a while, trying to believe that this is the person whom I loved my whole life. This is the body that I just took care of and nursed to the best of my ability for the last six weeks. This is actually my Mother lying half-visible in that pretty dress. She wore that dress only twice before: Edward's wedding, then last May at Carla's daughter's wedding (where she got food poisoning). That event was also the only time all year that she felt good enough to go out with her friends. They captured her laughing face in a great photo from that party, and Alyssa's Mother surprised us with a blown-up framed version of it for these services. I smile thinking how this dress definitely seems to fit!

Her hair is styled differently than she would do it, all hair-sprayed nicely in place. Yet I admire the cut I had given her—perfectly layered feathering on each side of her face. Too bad we didn't get to enjoy it longer in real life. Then I guffaw out loud, half in horror/half in humor, when I see the red nail polish on her hands. I was always teasing Mom about painting her toenails while she was sleeping. She would adamantly talk against this as she thought it was silly, "Although it looks ok on you," she would add. Sometimes upon her waking in that recliner, I would say, "Don't her nails look beautiful?" to which she would quickly sit up and check her feet. "Oh Kathleen, you better not have!" Laughing along with anyone else in the room, I'd say, "Made ya look!" A couple of times other people played the same trick on her, but we never actually did it. I look around the room and then call Sean to come see this. He chuckles, shaking his head, and tells me that he and Edward had forgotten to include that little detail when they met with the undertakers. We didn't quite have the nerve to check out her toes, however.

One of her old-time-bridge-playing-good friends, Ellen, the one who moved back into town and had been checking in on her for the past year, approaches me at the casket just as I am starting to say my goodbye prayers to Mom. She starts rambling in the nervous manner that used to drive Mom crazy sometimes, even though I can be the same way so I understand. After listening to her tell me how she is sorry she hadn't made it over more during my visit, and how sick she'd been, I finally interrupt her. I just know Mom is hovering over us in disbelief saying, "Oh, my God, will you shut up and let Kathleen talk to me!" yet all the while getting a big kick out of it. This couldn't have been better timing. I put my hand on her shoulder and gently say, "I'd love to talk to you, only right now I'm praying over Mom and want to finish." "Of course!" she asserts then flits away. She really is a great woman, but Mom and I had a laugh at her expense.

I finally get up enough nerve to place that little crystal and my Angel humor card under her dress, directly over her heart. I don't care if anyone sees me, although it may look a little strange. **I then kneel at her side and lovingly whisper,** "Thank you so much for being my Mom, and for being such a good patient to take care of! I am very sorry for all the stress I ever caused you. Will you help me now in Spirit-form to forgive myself?" The tears stream down my face as I continue, "And please, show yourself to me, or at least give me signs when you are around. You know that I'll be open to that. I also pray for you to move on. Don't be earth-bound and afraid to leave us kids. Instead, follow God's will for your Soul now. Remember, you will still be our Guardian Angel whenever we call upon you, plus you can help us better if you are on your path." My hands cover my face as I think about how she could have served us better on earth by having served herself better, and I hope that she understands this now. **Again, comforted by a loving warm sensation of her Spirit affirming me, I hold my head up and finish.** "I promise that I will be truer to myself, and use all my God-given talents better like you told me. And thank you, Mom, for the gift your death has now afforded me. Goodbye body . . . I loved you."

After I wipe my eyes and stand, I mingle with some of the guests. Everyone is so sweet and supportive. And then, along come Becky and her husband again. My *stomach starts doing flip-flops as I think, "What's she gonna say this time?"* Sure enough if she doesn't remark, "You know, we should've come by more and forced you to leave that house. It would've been good for you to get out with your friends and do something, and we could've stayed with your Mom. You and your Mother had way too much time together in there. And those dogs— I'm sure they got on her nerves, being sick and all. She probably could've used a break from that . . ." *As she drones on, I stand in utter shock, as I really can't believe my ears. How the hell do I respond to this shit? Here I am at my Mother's visitation, with everyone else thanking me for my selfless work and devoted attention to my Mother in her dying days plus telling me how much they knew it meant to her to have me here, and here's this bitch talking to me again this way.* I find myself muttering something like, "Well, thank you for your concern, but we were fine. Now I gotta go," and I walk away while she's still talking! What is amazing is that **I know she really thinks she's just being helpful! Quickly, Spirit reminds me how Mom liked her and her help. I think of the needlepoint towels she had made for Mom, and suddenly decide I'll give her Mom's knitting supplies. I can tell Mom influenced that decision.**

The next morning for the funeral, I put on a dark gray skirt, black nylons and silky shirt with a vest full of fall-colored flowers in front. A friend had taken a picture of me in this very outfit back in 1996 and I gave it to Mom because she always wanted a photo of me "dressed-up." She carried that picture around in her purse and showed it to everyone. Since I didn't wear skirts all that often, it was still in great shape plus was my most funeral-looking attire. I also knew Mom would love it. Of course I had a bunch of Mom's jewelry on too, like her pearl necklace from her wedding, and her antique diamond studded sterling watch. I thought Mom had said it probably didn't work anymore, so for fun I set it to 11:04 figuring that was about the time she died. (The hospice nurse was the one to pronounce her at 11:40pm, and I know it took her a good half-hour to arrive. So, I switched the digits, liking both those numbers anyway!)

We met our Godfather, Paul, a man we love dearly and who drove in from Indianapolis, at the funeral home for prayers before the closing of the casket and the procession to "the" Catholic Church. There I got enough nerve to read the poem I had written Mom for Mother's Day just four months earlier: "To the Angels Among Us." My immediate family and Paul, the only ones there, all had tears in their eyes when I finished reading it. Paul was actually dad's best friend since grade school, and his wife, our Godmother, turned out to be Mom's best friend. As a child I remember them laughing, drinking, smoking, and playing bridge all night long whenever they would get together (several times a year). They always had such a great time. It was tough after dad died, and then our Godmother "followed suit" in 1984. And now here stood our wonderful Godfather, the last of the foursome. He was one of the few adults who I felt really liked me as a child. Of course, that's not surprising since he was such a big clown himself, plus his whole family was full of natural comedians.

I also have always felt close, in a distant kind of way, to my dad's brother and his wife, my uncle and aunt also from Indianapolis. A couple years ago their youngest daughter, and cousin of mine with whom I am closest, told me with tears in her eyes how I was always her dad's favorite. She wished he could've shown his own kids the kind of affection he'd shown me. I was surprised at hearing this, but a little part of me felt warm. After feeling like so many adults in my life didn't care for me, I was glad that a few did. Her dad was also very strict like mine; after all, they were raised together like that. They had similar body types too, and I remember how hugging him seemed like I was hugging my dad again.

This uncle has always loved to tell everyone the story of how when I was four, I left my Grandma's house at the crack of dawn. Not wanting to disturb anyone's sleep, I walked by myself the half-mile trek down the country road to his house. I was too excited about wanting to play with my two favorite cousins. When he finally answered the door in his pajamas, there I stood in the morning dew asking, "Can Kissy and Kawee come out to pway?" Boy, did everyone but him scold me! He recently told me that it was then he decided he could never be mad at me again. He figured I was always going to have plenty of other people doing enough of that in my life, and he was right. I thanked him and commented on how it was too bad others weren't that smart!

The funeral at my old grade school church was very small. This was a relief to me actually, *for a little part of me had irrationally feared this event for some time. (As if people from when I got kicked out, or ex-friends from the past would be hanging around to check us out!)* It was also mid-day middle of the week, and many people were at work. We only told Mom's short list of friends and our small family, plus some of the blood bank people showed. I am sure she loved all the wonderful things that Fr. Edmondson said about her. We each had given him tidbits about her life, and he integrated all of them very eloquently into the service.

He mentioned how she was well known throughout town for being very outspoken on her favorite talk radio program; she was a regular caller with a very distinct voice. (In fact one time, a childhood friend of mine who lived in Kansas called me in Phoenix. Her mom had just called her to say how my Mom had gotten really upset over the air on the topic of gay bashing! She was quoted as saying "They're people too, for God's sake!" . . . Hmmm.) He also described how in the early 1990's she loved volunteering to help "take back the streets" in the high-crime-poverty area of town. She found great joy in giving out nature pictures from magazines to the little children with whom she would meet and talk along the way. He then commented on what a great sense of humor she always had and how full of gratitude for her fellowman she was. His examples included how even right up to the end, she both joked with him and sincerely thanked him before closing her eyes for the last time. And of course he spoke of what a great Mother she was, and devout Catholic—fearless in the grips of terminal cancer because of her strong faith and belief in Jesus. Amen!

After the burial at the cemetery, almost everyone went back to a luncheon scheduled in a room next to "the" church. As usual I had trouble sitting still so instead I bopped around conversing with everyone there. Except, that is, my other uncle and aunt (dad's sister) who live in Chicago. Although I did like this uncle, I have never felt close to either of them. *It always seemed like they looked down on us. I don't know if it was because they were wealthier, and/or we were adopted and not "real" family, and/or they just didn't care for us. Especially my aunt acted this way. She has such thick walls surrounding her to keep her distance, it's really kind of sad.*

The day before Mom died, when they stopped by to visit, *I was actually hoping that she might have changed* since I had not seen her in twenty years. She called me to say they were coming to visit because she wanted to be there for us kids. I softened my heart and even pictured a warm embrace from someone who could appreciate what I had just been through with Mom. I really needed that kind of support and was open to it. Only, I soon learned that her interpretation of "to be there for us" meant: quick hugs, shallow catch-up talk *as if Mom weren't even lying there dying*, and then ready to leave fifteen minutes after arriving. *How disappointing!* I was *painfully* aware of just how much **I had changed instead, and tried to follow that voice— "Be grateful for the gesture."**

As I passed by where they were sitting at the table, she said to me, "Oh, Kathleen, I've been meaning to ask. I was wondering what you kids are planning to do with that good set of china that was your grandma's (her mother's)?" Again, I found myself standing in dismay. *I don't think she ever liked the fact that grandma had given it to our Mom* (who was her youngest son's wife). We thus thought it fitting that Mom's youngest son's wife (Diana) also inherit it. Something kept me from explaining our plans. Instead I replied, "My brothers and I will decide that." "Well, I was just wondering if you could look up the manufacturer on the back. I'd really like to order a set and believe it's a discontinued pattern. It's a rare antique you know, one your grandpa brought back from Japan during WWI. If you could be so kind as to let me know." Awkwardly I responded, "I'll put Sean on that task right away. He'll let you know!" and I moved on. *Incredibly, they soon left without saying goodbye to us.*

Afterwards back at the condo, only Alyssa and Carla, the "regulars," were able to stop by for a short visit. **I gave them special mementos by which to remember Mom. They never asked for anything, and gave so generously of themselves to all of us, therefore it was a pleasure handing them some of her things** (mostly stuff from her blood bank days or nursing related). **It touched my heart to see the gesture bring tears to their eyes. Now that's how giving and receiving was intended to be!** They commented on what a pretty watch I was wearing, so I thanked them as I explained how it was one of Mom's most prized treasures. When I glanced down at it, I saw that the hands read around 3 o'clock. "Huh?" I pondered aloud, "That's funny, I didn't think it worked . . . I must've accidentally wound it when I set it for 11:04. Oh, well . . ."

Now, several hours later, I am telling Edward about it. Only, as I look down again, **I realize that the watch had stopped and still remains at exactly 3:04. Chills run up my spine in huge waves as I am hit with what just happened.** "Oh my God! Edward, oh my God!" "What?" he asks, getting more curious by the second watching my reaction. "Holy shit! No! I don't believe this . . . **Yes! It's gotta be! How incredible!" I exclaim, trying to comprehend and pointing to my arms—"Look at these goose bumps! She's here, Edward! Mom's with us! This is my sign!"** "Ok, now you're scaring me, Kathleen! What the hell are you talking about? You're freaking me out," he keeps saying as I sit open-mouthed in awe for a moment, letting it all sink in.

"Ok," I slowly try to explain, "I set this watch at 11:04 as Sean and I left the house this morning at 9am." I inhale deeply as I tell him about how I derived at 11:04 and how I had asked Mom to give me signs. "Then, we get back at 1pm from the luncheon, right? I remember looking at the clock." I remind him of when Alyssa and Carla had asked me about the watch. "It read 3 o'clock so I assumed I had somehow wound it, and maybe I did. **Yet, we were gone exactly four hours! The watch stopped at exactly 3:04! It ran exactly four hours! My favorite number!** Mere coincidence? Perhaps, but what are the chances of me accidentally winding it for exactly four hours? And even if I did, what are the chances of it starting up the minute I left her condo, and stopping the minute I walked back inside?"

His jaw drops open. **His arms grow covered in goose bumps as he feels the same change in air pressure.** Tears start to well up in his eyes as he stares at me in disbelief. We both look around the room as if to see Mom, and then back at each other for an intense eye-locking moment. "Wow," is all he could finally mutter as he sits stunned. "Yeah!" I reinforce, "Wow is right!" "I wonder how she'll appear to me," he hoarsely asks. "Hard tellin'," I mysteriously reply!

≈≈≈

The next day *I started feeling depressed about not having received any cards, flowers or calls from Phoenix. It felt a little embarrassing. I've lived there for twelve years of my life, worked for the Agency for seven, and nobody showed much concern.* I called a couple of friends and coworkers to ask them to spread the word about my Mom. I also had talked to Angela on the phone. She actually called the day of the funeral to ask me if her daughter could stay at my house until I returned. I took a deep breath and said no, without explaining. I couldn't. Her daughter had house-sat for me when I flew out here in July. Only I didn't want Angela to know that I was upset with several things she had done. I just knew it would anger and embarrass her. Angela had promised me that she was a great kid and wouldn't do anything I had asked her not to do. Well, I should know how teens could schmooze their moms! Quite a few items were messed up when I returned home. However, I was just glad that my dogs were fine and that she hadn't thrown an all-night party (like I would have done at her age).

After I told Angela about some of the details of my Mom's death, *I felt a little disappointed when she seemed disinterested and got off the phone rather quickly. I assumed she was mad about my answer, especially in light of all that she was doing covering for me at work. She seemed upset that I hadn't called more frequently, too.* I hardly talked to anyone back home while I was taking

168

care of Mom, although I did check in a couple of times. Further, I had told them that I wanted to just be totally present for Mom. It wasn't that I didn't care; I just couldn't do anything anyway so why hear the drama. I was now ready to start getting caught up, but would have to call her back another day.

I never expected work to send anything; however, when both of my brothers received huge funeral bouquets to put beside the casket, *I felt left out. I couldn't believe how that added to my feelings of low self-worth.* And when we were sending out over thirty thank-you cards, and *not one went to Phoenix, it made me really wonder why the hell I live there anymore.* I had been away from work long enough; I finally felt "de-institutionalized." We jokingly say that about the youth, but it happens to the adults who work there as well. Additionally, I had been gone from Phoenix long enough to gain a clearer perspective: I'm done there. I guess I have nothing left to give or receive. All the energy that needed to be exchanged has happened. I started thinking that it was time to move. With another stab, **I also realized that I had created this situation.**

Two days after the funeral, Sean went back to Chicago saying he'd return the following weekend. That was when I was planning to return home. That was also the weekend that he and Edward were going to put the stuff that they wanted into a storage unit, while the rest of her things would be given away to organizations throughout the week. We put the condo on the market, too, and the realtor made plans to show it immediately. Both of my brothers returned to full workweeks. Meanwhile, I was still busy trying to clean amongst the sorting, reorganizing, and fixing of things for the showings. I discovered myself buckling under all the work, grief and upset.

The next morning I awoke with diarrhea and a cough. My lungs were rejecting all the smoking; my resistance was wearing down under the lack of sleep and food. A high fever ensued as I continued to push myself. I wanted to clear the estate, sell the house, and get my dogs and myself back home. I didn't want to stay there much longer. My job was just about done, so it was almost time to pack everything and go. As the condo became empty, and stuff for storage collected in the garage, my heart felt more vacant. It was strange being there now in this shell. It was hard watching people look at the place and talk about it, especially while I was getting sicker and sicker.

By Monday I couldn't move. The phone never rang anymore. Nobody stopped by either, except strangers to see the condo. I ached all over my body, had started my period again (I just had it two weeks prior) and had no energy to even walk the dogs. Shivering with chills, and bundled up like it was snowing, I would stand in front of her condo and plead, "Please babies, go potty right here for mama! I need to go back and lie down." I just couldn't walk without coughing and needing to go diarrhea again. They didn't listen to me, of course, and made me suffer, yanking my arms out of my weak sockets as they tried to chase every rabbit and squirrel they saw. The neighbors, with whom I had gotten fairly friendly, didn't help much by exclaiming how horrible I looked and sounded! Plus, the thought of that long drive back home with the way I felt loomed extra heavy over my head. Finally, Diana came over and walked the dogs a couple of times for me, as well Edward stopped by to keep me company a few evenings. However, I really needed to go to a doctor.

I called Alyssa the next day and asked her to take me to urgent care at the emergency room. I couldn't stop crying as the nice lady doctor asked me what else might be happening in my life. I shrugged and told her how my Mom had just died a week ago, but that I'm just really sick and need medicine to get better so I can drive home. She said that I had the beginnings of pneumonia and probably an intestinal bug. Therefore, I should not attempt that drive for at least two more weeks. She gave me an asthma treatment, which helped me breath easier, as well as heavy doses of Prednisone, antibiotics, cough medicine with codeine, and an inhaler.

As I was forced to become an invalid in my Mother's condo, the grief and depression hit like never before. It was so eerie to be taking the exact same drugs I had just administered to her. It was so weird to be stuck in time, forced to face the darkness in a space I wanted to hurry and leave. It felt cruel for God to ground me like this in such an empty, cold place with little help from anyone. It seemed like everything was being rubbed in my face. And to top that off, when I talked to Angela and Leonard back home, they seemed upset that I got myself sick and couldn't hurry back to the job. I never felt so far away from home and so alone in my life. I couldn't believe I needed a lesson like this after all the good I just did. **Through it all, though, for once I didn't want to die.** I very well could have felt that way, **yet miraculously, I no longer wished to leave this earth anymore. . . .**

~~~~

Crossword Puzzle Notes to Mom

Hi Mom! We love you!

I'm so proud of you! You are a strong and wonderful woman!

God is in control—you don't have to be!

My mommy is the best Mom in the whole world!

She's the Queen of our family!

Mom has 3 grateful children—because she adopted us and gave us love!

Good night Mom! Sleep tight and don't let the bedbugs bite! Sweet Dreams!

Time to close your little pee-pickers and get some shuteye, sweetheart!

I love you—you are special! God loves you very much and guides you!

Angels, please help Mom get through this stage of life with peace and grace!

You are my sunshine, my only sunshine! You make me happy!

Dream of dancing with Angels tonight!

Thank you for everything and every sacrifice you've ever made for me!

You are blessed!

Peace, Love and Happiness!

Remember: "The meek shall inherit the world!" It's yours!

"Know that I am always with you!" God gives us nothing we can't handle!

You must realize that your children will grow stronger with you entering heaven!

—For this you must pray!

And In Spirit, you will guide us always!

~~~~

7

"Dying so I may Live"

~present day~
May 2001

*I*n the past five months now since I quit my job, I feel that many old ways of thinking and behaving have been tested and are slowly being released, thank God. I have been doing daily rituals that honor myself. I have stuck to my goals and persevered through many frustrating situations. I have taken the time necessary to heal from my tremendous loss, both of my Mother and all of my past. I have never before been more serious about **devoting my life to me**, no matter what anyone else may think. I know if I didn't, I would literally be dead. I needed the time and space to do so; it was up to me, nobody else. I believe that by taking this time and doing these steps, I will change those patterns that attract unloving people and situations. There truly is only one way to find out. If I don't try, I'll never know. As long as I'm even doing the slightest thing that is dishonoring of myself, how can I be surprised when someone else in my world shows a dishonoring trait to me, albeit in a different form?

As I elaborated on before, I had to take a long, deep, brutally honest look at myself—how I treat myself in every aspect—and clean it up to as near perfection as possible. Don't I, after all, deserve that? **What is crucial is to treat myself the best way possible, like a queen, honoring all my God-given talents, appreciating all my gifts in life, and loving myself in a gentle sensitive way.** If I don't act like I'm an absolute treasure, something God created so special, and handle me with the utmost of care, then how can I expect anyone else to do so? I once heard Wayne Dyer (another Spiritual teacher) say that when we have a very expensive antique vase, for example, we want to protect it from damage and keep it clean to maintain it's value. Thus, we wouldn't want to put it in dangerous situations where it may get broken or not appreciated by another person. **We are God's most cherished and precious gifts. We deserve no less!**

I had to throw out all forms of self-abuse, from negative self-talk to putting any forms of toxins into my body. After excesses of caffeine, nicotine, codeine, and morphine—I was "eined" out! After high doses of anti-anxiety, anti-depression, anti-social phobia, and anti-insomnia drugs—I was "antied" out! After too many years of partying, including street drugs from the past to more recent and variable alcohol usage—I was "weekend warriored" out! After years of binge eating and junk food gorging—I was "grossed" out. And after years of cutting myself down—telling myself really horrible things sometimes, jabs I didn't even realize because they had been running through my head my whole life—it is no wonder I was left with suicidal ideology! Sadly, it also is no surprise that everyone in my world deserted me. I had deserted me. I just never really learned how to be there for me. **And this is the time now for me to learn.**

I quit smoking this time around by asking Spirit and the Archangels to take away my cravings. I had only a couple cigarettes left in a pack, and went to bed praying for a long time to awake without wanting to smoke. Well, that next morning I couldn't resist lighting up with my coffee. *"Yeah, that really works!"* I thought to myself. Then later that day when I ran out, I told myself to go to buy more, but I felt too tired. I just sat and watched TV all evening, and although I craved smoking, I was too lazy to run to the store. "I'll just go in the morning," I kept telling myself. Well, that second day upon awakening, I realized that I had no urge to smoke! I could have cared less about running out to buy some. I was very impressed, and grateful at the same time, thanking Spirit and the Angels over and over again, and apologizing for doubting the process. **"All in it's own time . . ." was the message they gave me, "We hear you!"**

I also reinforced this **gift from Spirit** by writing down all the health benefits I would receive by the day for one week, then weekly for a month, then monthly for a year. I included fitness goals as well as life wishes, and wrote for the next several years. I knew that not smoking combined along with everything else I was doing would help me accomplish all these heart's desires. This list included immediate benefits like a decrease of carbon monoxide in the blood stream, cilia awakening, toxins being cleared, and lungs showing an increase in aerobic capacity. It then had items such as increasing energy and passion, fine-tuning intuition, and swimming with the dolphins (my 6-month treat to myself).

As well it contained eventual goals of publishing my books, leading seminars, and helping heal institutions that serve children. In addition, just like the last time I had quit, every time the thought came up: *"I need a cigarette!"* I'd respond with "Where'd that thought come from?" Next I would affirm, "Why, I don't smoke! Never have, never will!" and made myself think about something else. I soon realized that I wasn't merely tricking my subconscious mind like I had thought; rather, **I was affirming a truth**. Just as the well-known Metaphysician, Louise L. Hay teaches: "We are perfect, whole and complete," then in light of that framework, **the totally perfect all-loving Spirit within me, truly is not a smoker.**

I also chose to quit taking all of the medications I was on "cold turkey," back in January when I ran out. I informed my doctors of this decision, who really didn't care one way or another. Instead, I loaded up on extra vitamins, minerals and some herbal supports. At first *I was worried I would not be strong enough on my own*, and again prayed for Spiritual assistance. *I had adopted the belief system that my brain was "wired differently" and I needed the meds to function.* In fact, I discovered that the opposite was true. (This is not to suggest that everyone should give up their psychotropic meds!) By cleaning out my system, I actually felt **clearer-headed and more able to hear the voice of my Soul and follow my intuition**. I realized just how far out-of-balance I had gotten and how blocked my creativity had become. Releasing the meds helped **unleash my natural artistic abilities**. Getting as healthy as possible has assisted me with **finding my own natural balance and inner wisdom**. So, now I'm better than ever.

The morning coffee habit took a little longer to break, but I wasn't pushing it. I slowly cut my overall amount down and mixed in more decaf over a couple months. However, after several months without caffeine, I realized I was often tired and taking a daily nap. I then learned that caffeine in moderation could help balance the metabolism of high-energy individuals. I found that just one cup each morning works perfect for me. I don't bounce off the walls, yet I also don't get so groggy midday. I also continually affirm that my **sunrise yoga and meditations will give me a healthy boost of energy**. Meanwhile, the daily exercise program of swimming laps, or dancing in my living room, or walking a couple miles, which I also started in January, has become a natural routine. I feel antsy and achy any day I happen to miss. I am very proud of myself for this habit. Along with occasional chiropractic visits and body massages, my work-outs have helped improve my back problems so I can even stay away from anti-inflammatory meds now, not to mention any pain killers or muscle relaxants which doctors seem to have thrown my way in the past. Even my dentist recently wanted to put me on relaxants to help my TMJ (jaw) problem. I pleased myself by saying, "No, thank you. I'm cleaning out my system. I'll take the herbs kava-kava and valerian root instead." Further yet, my "premenstrual syndrome" has diminished, as has my intense period cramping. I attribute this change to **honoring my cycle** now.

I also cleaned up my diet right away when I started my whole new regimen. It's still not exactly where I'd like it to be, but considering all the changes I've made, that's okay. In her book "The Lightworker's Way," Doreen Virtue talks about how Spirit will guide you when the time is right to help you shift your food preferences to a healthier variety. Her words are very comforting, saying you don't have to do it all at once. I've prayed for this along with everything else, and am seeing a subtle shift. Doreen also discusses in her book how animal products are heavy in our system and make it more difficult to "lighten up." Being a top clairvoyant and Angel therapist in this country, her Guides have communicated to her that by ingesting animal products, one also ingests any pain they went through, and this can block psychic ability. I do believe strongly in the correlations between health, lightness, fitness, higher frequencies, clearer intuition and the ability to heal.

Eating many more fruits and vegetables everyday has become second nature for me; I seldom crave the old junk foods, nor chicken like I used to. I never did eat cow, and hardly ever pig, yet now have little desire for it. However, I absolutely love seafood, and have no intentions of giving it up, and that's all right, too. I did switch to soy and rice milk right away and totally love it. Ice cream has been more difficult to stay away from, so I treat myself to it occasionally. I also love to eat cheese and do so almost daily, yet I'd eventually like to remove all milk products. And I still enjoy dark/amber malt beers now and then, but that's another one to turn over to Spirit. I'm sure all these cravings will pass as my carbohydrate addiction disappears.

Sonia Choquette (yet another Spiritual teacher) also emphasizes a wonderful point when it comes to food. She asserts that one of the most loving acts you can do for yourself is to only put "real" food into your body with love. Food after all, is an energy source for us. The purer and healthier it is, the more loving the act is to your system. The very least you can do, she further points out, is to say a prayer over it, even if you have to settle for fast food when away from home. However, it is best to eat organically grown nutritionally balanced foods, which you or someone you know has cooked with love, and to eat it with gratitude. How much better does a home-cooked meal taste and feel to your system when someone you love prepares it with joy on your behalf? If all food products can absorb energy, then they have the capability of taking in possible negative moods and thoughts of any cooks or servers around them, as well as then **positive prayers and grateful thoughts before consumption**. This is something I never used to think about.

With much more time in my control since I quit my job, I have learned to absolutely love cooking for myself, although sometimes I wish that there were people around with which to share. I do call my buddy Dick over occasionally, and have given him frozen portions when he couldn't get away. However, it has been a fun part of my new daily routine to cook healthy foods, as well as to sit and consciously eat with appreciation. This whole act is different for me. Plus, I love inventing things; it's another medium for my creative talents. Recently, for instance, I boiled mixed greens, garlic and bell peppers with organically grown crushed tomatoes, then added some organic whole wheat noodles and served it atop a bed of cottage cheese! Oh, was it delicious! I have also started making wonderful drinks with my juicer to get the benefits of mega-enzymes. I joyfully experiment, mixing whatever fruits and vegetables I have. And still another healthy liquid meal I enjoy concocting is fruit juice, rice milk, raw oatmeal, ground flaxseed, and banana in the blender. I feel so good about myself after drinking these juicer or blender drinks, too!

Speaking of creative talents, I started taking an oil painting class and cannot believe the latent artist awaking in me. **I feel like I was a painter in a past life**. I'm now painting a twilight scene on the ocean with a full moon rising and a translucent Angel hovering. Plus, I started drawing on my own, mostly Angels, yet it takes me a long time. I think that's why I didn't have the patience to develop the talent when I was a child. I worked many hours on the cover for this book, because I heard, **"What better way to cover your literary expression from the heart than with your very own reflection of such through a personalized drawing?"** Considering that I never drew much before, this picture makes me very proud. **I know Spirit flowed through me as I sketched, trance-like, for several days.** I think it is beautiful, and represents elements in life that I love. It further conveys many Spiritual messages. For example: There's an illusion of a woman alone on the beach. There's a subtle "dark day of the Soul," yet a clear rebirth. Plus, there's a connection to nature and the Angelic realm, which is how Spirit speaks. **I also know that my Higher Self made this artwork for me as a gift**, and I lovingly receive it with gratitude.

The artistic floodgates are open in another area, too. I've pulled out my guitar and started playing again. Even though "adults" tended to laugh at my singing and playing ("Don't give up your day job!") I have always loved doing it anyway. Playing guitar was another activity I stayed in the closet about. Well, I'm out now, and proud—especially knowing that I'm self-taught (as a teen, it was my refuge). Recently, **a song came to me from the Angelic realm** that I just love! It has inspired me to want to follow that path in my heart as well and eventually develop a CD of my songs. I now picture myself giving seminars or teaching classes that motivate people to develop their talents and pursue their dreams, all the while with my music playing in the air, my art hanging on the walls, and my books selling in the background. Of course, this will be integrated with others' works as well to create a richer tapestry. First, however, I must own and develop my talents before I collaborate.

Now, I may appear to be arrogant, self-centered, and/or egoistical. And that is partially true. If affirming aloud how wonderfully I am doing something seems conceited, then amen! If "not working" for people right now appears selfish, so be it! If focusing all my love and attention only on myself seems insensitive, then all right! If showing enthusiasm for creating my heart's desires and making my dreams come true appears to be self-absorbed, thank God! **For I believe that if we all did this, the world would be a much better place. And I believe for sure, that by doing this for myself now, I will have so much more to offer others down the line.** I trust that by following my Soul path, I will attract similar people who will honor my beautiful Spirit with all its gifts, and I will thus reflect those traits back to them! It's happening already . . . How wonderfully synchronistic this path is!

As I've formerly alluded, these last several months have been filled with me reading awesome metaphysical books, listening to inspirational audiocassettes, attending some phenomenal seminars and retreats, plus having some eye-opening discussions with "advisors" or "teachers" (both positively and negatively). Recently, I went to a four-day retreat in Sedona, AZ, called Womanheart, where 65 women gathered to change their lives and thus help heal the world. It was a great learning experience for me—training my body and mind to do hours of ancient Sanskrit chanting, Kundalini yoga, sunrise meditations, reiki healing circles, and prayer groups. I left thinking it was interesting but probably not totally for me, especially considering I'm not really a morning person. Surprisingly, however, **I now find my Angels lovingly waking me every morn at daybreak, in a state of awe and gratitude** (instead of grumpiness). I thank God and without thinking discover myself in the backyard playing recordings of the chants to beautiful music, and doing breathing exercises with yogic stretches. These practices help clear negativity and set a peaceful energy vibration for the body, besides being healthy at all levels—body, mind, emotions, and Spirit.

The staff that implemented this, work at a center located in Phoenix called: The Healing Source, run by Sangeet Khalsa. One lady there in particular, Diane, has been so helpful to me that **I am touched**. Several months ago when I was registering for the retreat, I told her about Charley's condition in case I had to rescind the commitment. Diane was the most supportive person I had encountered in my world for some time. She could see my inner beauty and potential, plus gave me many words of encouragement after hearing a little of my personal story. She said she would start sending Charley long distance healing through reiki prayer. At the time I didn't think much of it; however, as I watched Charley improve over the months, **I began to wonder about the power of reiki. I honestly believe that this lady has helped heal Charley.** If I were to take Charley to the vets, I know they'd be surprised at how well she's doing, and we'd probably see **a miraculous turn-around in her kidney sonogram**. However, I'm not putting her through any more medical procedures.

I feel blessed to have Diane in my life, and continue to feel honored at what this earth-Angel offers me. During Womanheart, she helped me through some heavy emotional processing. And afterwards, she called to partially gift me into Reiki I and II training classes. Now, I know how to better channel God's healing energy through hands-on techniques and certain prayers using special sounds and symbols. **Now, I can help heal Charley, as well as any other living thing including myself, in a way that is not even using my own energy. I am just a conduit for the natural Divine healing force,** and feel thankful for receiving this gift. I practice it daily along with my other habitual rituals—especially as part of my meditation.

While at Womanheart, I also made some great connections. One woman in particular, Trish, has quickly become a good friend. *I'm a little hesitant at trusting in new friendships because of my past,* yet am trying to be open to the flow. She has been so supportive of my endeavors in a gentle loving way, and we have fun together. We both have a similar life story in that she went through nearly the same death experience with her Mother three years ago, and thus is an empathetic Angel to me. She has a wonderful ability to heal others and is studying holistic health techniques. We've spent endless hours talking about everything; *thus far she loves my chatterbox ability and I pray it continues.* After my long haul, I deserve committed friends and I thank God daily for sending her. She is definitely a Soul sister!

In addition, I met another woman who lives in Hawaii and coordinates volunteers every year for the Maui Writer's Conference over Labor Day weekend. We hit it off, too, and when she told me I should attend, I got instant confirmation: **goose bumps tingling and butterflies fluttering.** She could get me in for free as a volunteer, all I had to do was work some shifts as a cashier, plus I'd have access to over 85 literary agents and publishers! **I am moved by this wonderful opportunity and the whole simple connection**! Trish is joining me and the plans are underway. We're going to have a great time! God keeps opening the doors along my path—I remain humbled . . .

During the couple of months prior to Womanheart, I had been slowly developing the friendship with Brenda. For the most part I enjoyed our "outings," yet was still **slightly uncomfortable** with some of the things she said and did. *I so longed to share time with a Spiritually minded friend that I ignored those little things that bothered me.* Further, because she is an avid dog-lover, and knew of my predicament in the past, she graciously offered to dog-sit for me during Womanheart and the upcoming Hawaii trips. However, she wanted to go with me to Sedona, only stay in a hotel with the dogs while I was at the retreat. As the date grew nearer, our arrangement **just didn't feel right to me.** I was also realizing that "the little things" were building-up; hence I needed to talk to her. **"Speak your Truth," I kept hearing, "True friendships will endure." I figured that more "Brenda's" would keep popping into my life if I didn't learn to shift this pattern.** She had always mentioned how strong her foundation was, so I felt confident that we could get through this. I told her that I felt she was not honoring my boundaries in a couple of areas. I explained the ways in which I felt like she was being "overly" generous to my dogs and I, as well as taking "unwelcome" liberties with some items I had loaned her. I also requested that she quit expressing her attraction for me because I knew I was not going to "fall in love." *I was getting concerned about having a friendship with someone who may possibly be doing things with an ulterior motive.*

She replied that she could honor my requests. Two days before the retreat, to my surprise I received a very hurt/angry email telling me that my words did upset her. She believed "boundaries" to be "walls" between friends, and she felt my requests were stifling her ability to just be herself. She canceled the trip, yet fortunately, she still dog-sat at my home during the retreat, which was really what I needed. I prayed for guidance on what to do next and Spirit advised me, **"Sometimes, your words come across harsher than you intend. Choose your words carefully, and feel them coming from your heart."** I then wrote her a loving letter, one I would've appreciated receiving had I been in her shoes. I also left her flowers and a thank-you card in my home. Since I have come back, things have definitely shifted: we hardly talk now even though we're still friends. She did tell me, however, that I have motivated her to follow her heart and write her books. She's such a sweetheart; I trust time will heal our friendship and pray for love to transcend it.

A month prior to Womanheart, I attended a wonderful weekend seminar in Mesa, AZ called: Celebration of Life. A local agency, Mishka Productions, brought in the following four great Spiritual presenters for this event: Clairvoyants Dr. Sonia Choquette and Dr. Judith Orloff, as well as established authors Shakti Gawain and Salle Redfield. Each had inspiring presentations, however I felt the most passion towards Sonia because I resonate with her work and the way she presents. I had started following her simple guidance tapes on "Creating Hearts' Desires" before I'd seen her in person, yet felt even more drawn to her teachings afterwards. I had all four women sign some pages of my book to put on my "manifesting" wall for good luck. However, when Sonia signed she wrote **messages that really touched my heart**, such as "Believe it will be, Many Blessings, and Absolute Success!" When I asked her at the break for advice about my book, she actually took the time to tell me I had an important message, which many people needed to hear. She also said she looked forward to reading my manuscript and assisting me!

She had an amazing way of looking at me like she could see the beauty of my Spirit. At the closing when I hugged her goodbye, I thanked her for that special look. She assured me that others would soon see it too; I just needed to keep believing and seeing it myself. Driving home, **I started crying with gratitude, shivering with enthusiasm, and committing to God that I will, from that day forward, open my heart and look at the Spiritual beauty in others the way she so graciously afforded me. Especially when I lead seminars** in the future, I will pass that gift on to others who may desperately need it! Just a simple look and a peaceful way of Being, resulted in me promising God to never forget that feeling I had in my healing heart.

I additionally got seduced by yet another Hawaii trip which Sonia and her sister, Cuky, are leading in October called, "Translucent You!" After talking to Cuky and meditating on it, **I know I am supposed to be there**. The timing is right in that I will have more life-path work done by then, and thus be ready for more Soul growth and heart-opening experiences. This retreat will involve daily bodywork and special Hawaiian massage (Lomi-Lomi). Plus, there will be creative, artistic expression classes, as well as multi-level Soul celebration and renewal sessions through private mentoring with Sonia. I look forward to being treated like a queen and becoming an even more energetically radiant Being.

This month, I've also had some very interesting appointments with various Spiritual counselors and psychics for help in healing, or just for the fun of it. One lady, Lea Blumberg, is a certified hypnotherapist whose wonderful session I actually won at a networking group. She spent so much time with me, it seemed as if we were old friends conversing freely. It was nice to relate to someone after so long, and even more impressive was how she treated me more like an equal than a client. After many years of varied "professional" help, this was a relief! She took me back in time through different negative emotions to understand when they originated and what the lesson was. Then, we worked on retaining the learning experiences while releasing all pent-up emotions.

It was amazing work. First, I had a flashback of being burned at the stake in a past life, with a crowd jeering and stoning me. When I asked what the lesson was, cold water was thrown on me. **I was told that I am capable of controlling it: put out the flames, cool off, it's all okay**. Next I was shown that I had been gay in many past lifetimes, while being ashamed of it, ridiculed for it, and hiding it. **I was told that this lifetime would be different; I have an opportunity now to change that pattern**. Another past visualization showed my natural mother crying as a baby with no bonding between her and her mother due to postpartum depression. This scene gave me more compassion and shifted my perspective on a deep level. **I learned that my situation is not so unique and there's nothing wrong with me just because we also did not bond**. Yet another view showed me feeling guilty right after my conception for causing my teenage mother so much anguish. **My Guides taught me that I have a right to be where I am and not to take other peoples' emotions personally**. When she was three months pregnant, I saw her yelling and hitting at me. **My lesson was to stop that pattern and quit hurting myself**. Later, during my birth process, it deeply hurt me how both my mother and the doctor were impatient with trying to "get me out." **This indicated that I need to learn to lovingly keep my own power, do things in my own time, stand up for myself, and set my boundaries**. These are definitely all Soul lessons in this lifetime!

I found that I was so ready to face these scenes and release them because of how my life had been going. As I've mentioned before, I want to do whatever I can to stop repeating patterns that aren't serving my Higher Good. Immediately prior to this session, I had been to a workshop with Debbie Ford who works at the Deepak Chopra Center for Well Being in California. She presented information on how to embrace your "shadow side." Since I had just read her book, "The Dark Side of the Light Chasers," as well as seen her on Oprah, I was ready to embrace all of my shadows. The timing was right for me, plus it makes total sense that **whatever you resist and don't like, you will attract until you accept and learn to love that same part within you**. I had too many recent painful examples in front of me for this not to be something that I needed to embrace. After all, I'm just following my Spirit's guidance these days.

There were times over these last few months of freedom that I tried contacting some of my past Spiritual counselors and found **we just didn't connect any longer**. Because I had clicked so strongly with them before, *it surprised and saddened me* temporarily. In light of all the new work I was doing, I let them go with the others from my past to make more room for my new future. I still appreciate all the gifts they gave me, however, **the comments they recently made no longer honored me and felt out of line with my Truth**. For example, one said, "I don't believe that your last job isn't where you still need to be. I don't feel that you're clear enough yet, on what the lessons were really about." Nonetheless, **I know that I did the right thing, made the best decision for my life, and deserve only those people around me who will support and respect my life path.**

I also recently talked to James Van Praagh, who is well known for his psychic connection with those who have passed-over. I called into my favorite radio station, KEZ 99.9 with Beth and Bill, and happened to get through, so **I figured it was Spiritually guided**. *However, I was disappointed because I thought he'd tell me more about my Mother "on the other side," plus he seemed to be reading my past energy not present. After working so hard on all these new steps* *that I'm taking, it was difficult to hear things like*: "You think of yourself at the lowest level in life; It feels like you're involved in an abusive relationship; You need to release a lot of anger and forgive others; You have to start moving your energy around more because it's stagnant; and, You must start eating better or you're about to get really sick." When I said, "I've already been changing these things for several months now," he replied, "Well, I'm supposed to reinforce that then." Although I do honor his work, *I feel his presentation of my information could have been more positive, especially over the air!* He did tell me though, that with a little more work, my book had great potential to touch many lives.

Even stranger was my experience with this palm-reader psychic with whom I scheduled a quick reading just for fun. She did tell me my Mom had passed-over and that I had two brothers, but then said I had a negative cloud around me. It was almost impossible to read anything else into my future because this negativity was blocking it, and had been holding me back from success most of my life. She also said that it came from my Mom who was now in purgatory and earth-bound because she couldn't let go of us kids. She indicated that it would take "extra" sessions, yet she could remove this for me. I told her nicely that I thought she was being a little extreme; besides, **I was already releasing negativity in my life, as well as sending Mom on her path. Moreover, I was sure my prayers were being answered and I didn't need her assistance.** Then she explained how it would lead to sickness, such as cancer, if it wasn't removed properly, and that she alone knew how to do it after some ceremony and lengthy meditation. I told her **I didn't appreciate her using fear tactics to hook people**. After I left I prayed to release the experience from my energy field as well as to "embrace the shadow." I handled it well, even though I didn't understand why I attracted such an extreme example of what I don't need. **An Angel whispered, "This is merely practice for following your Truth, and learning that you have all the answers within you!"**

On a "lighter" note, I get a tremendous amount of joy out of watching Oprah on television. I feel an Angelic love for her, and so appreciate the Spiritual light-work in her show. I am now grateful to have a schedule where I can see her almost every afternoon. Many of her shows make me cry; they touch my Soul and move my heart to sing. With all of the negative news-casting going on in the world today, plus all the dramas and violence on TV, her show is such a relief! She is truly an Angel and **I know that since I feel deeply affected and motivated by her many topics, I am hearing a calling for my Spirit too.** Debbie Ford teaches to embrace those "light" traits as well for they're merely unrecognized potential. I can do that! I can see myself possessing similar traits and contributing to this world in similar ways.

Another answer to a prayer has been a self-publisher's group, which I recently joined. I asked for a writer's support group, yet received even more than I expected. The owner/manager, Nick, has taught me much about the world of publishing and writing of books. Additionally, I have met many other writers in their monthly support meetings. Some of them are accomplished writers too, like Lynn V. Andrews, best-selling author of "Medicine Woman," and Dr. Gladys Taylor-McGarey who wrote "The PHYSICIAN Within YOU." Dr. Gladys currently runs the Scottsdale Clinic for Holistic Medicine and is having a screen play written of her life by actress Lindsay Wagner. Nick encourages writers to self-publish first using his connections in "the Valley" in order to make it the best book possible, and then submit that finished product to publishing companies. His website, along with his established community status and group networking philosophy, supports the marketing and promotion of the groups' products and services. It's a win-win situation to consider.

Recently, **Spirit has let me know that among others, Sonia Choquette and Doreen Virtue will be assisting me with my book in some capacity. I resonate with their work and get a sense of knowingness when I feel our connection. Fate would have it that I will study with both of them during seminars in Hawaii this year!** The first of my three Hawaii trips is a weeklong Spiritual retreat and dolphin swim with Doreen in July. I registered for this retreat back in January when I went to another Mishka sponsored workshop with Doreen on "Angel Readings; Communicating and Manifesting with Your Angels." I've always felt pulled to Hawaii, even though I have never been; **however as soon as I saw the flyer, I knew, without a doubt that this trip was for me! The excitement in my gut and passion soaring through my veins since registering has been constant validation that this event will be a crucial part of my life-path.** What a great gift this will be to myself after six months of hard work on getting healthy and writing my book. It further helps keep me motivated to swim those laps so I'll be able to keep up with the dolphins!

Back at the January workshop, Doreen's presentation was one of the best I've ever seen. She is so awe-inspiring and right-on with her readings in such a loving, positive, and sensitive way. She is truly about "healing in the light"—again something I gravitate towards. I felt my third eye, sixth chakra, open and my vibration level change to a point I had never before experienced in my life. **It gave me a taste of what I could have more of in my life if I continued to release, get healthy and practice.** That workshop truly marked the beginning of my freedom, and what a way to start!

I took with me, my long-time friend Linda. I wanted to treat her for having been so supportive of me this past year with the dying process of my Mother. I know she also had a wonderful time at this workshop. She was jazzed about having shared accurate readings with her paired-up partners for some of the aura readings and Angel guide exercises, as was I. However, for once, I was in a quiet mood. It had just been three and a half months since Mom passed and I was processing a lot of things.

During the workshop, **a little voice inside me had said to just be quiet and listen this whole weekend**. This felt especially important since Linda had told me earlier in the week during dinner that I talked so much, she didn't get to share her stories. I hadn't seen her since before I left for Mom's, plus we had barely talked on the phone. Therefore, I was excited about telling her everything: Mom's death, my job experiences leading up to my quitting, and my new life goals. Even though *her comments had hurt my feelings*, I know I hadn't been sensitive to her needs. I truly love her and want to be a good friend therefore I just let her talk throughout the whole workshop to make it up to her.

As I drove her home, tears rolled down my cheeks. She asked me twice what was wrong. Even though **my inner voice again told me not to share,** I heard myself telling her how *my last day of work, the previous day, left me feeling horrible.* I surprised myself with what feelings started to surface. I thought they'd be more about my Mom, which I'd been focused on during the workshop. Instead, *my pain turned to anger as I started cussing about how badly work treated me: no acknowledgement of my last day, or goodbye out of the ordinary.* Then, **I was thanking it as a blessing in disguise, because it led me to my new life now**. Suddenly, appearing very agitated, Linda started dramatically looking for her keys and cursing because she left them at the hotel. Realizing that she was also irritated with my emotional display, I told her not to take it on, "Just surround yourself with pink light like Doreen taught us." Well, that triggered her and she snapped, "Don't you tell me what to do! You're the one bouncing off the walls and yelling about everything! I just lost my keys!" *As I sat flabbergasted, I immediately shifted my emotions and wondered what just happened.* I drove back to the workshop site in silence, as she later tried to explain. "Look, I just don't like anger, ok? I can't handle being around it. My dad was a very angry man who took it out on all of us, so I do not do well hearing it." "Ok," I whispered, **realizing I should've been following that inner voice**.

Because of the workshop, the weekend was wonderful, even though this seemed like a bad ending. I went home trying to process what had transpired with my "best" friend. *I couldn't believe she used those very lines against me that she knew others had used to hurt me.* I prayed very deeply for clarity and guidance on this issue. It was not difficult because of the high Spiritual space in which the workshop had left me. **I knew this had to be Divinely guided to teach me a lesson. I had a feeling I wouldn't be connecting with her again for a long time; I could tell she needed space from our friendship**. More importantly, however, I did a meditation to apologize for dumping too much emotion on her as well as forgive her for her personal attack back towards me. It is now in God's hands . . .

Overall, I am extremely grateful for the experiences I received at Doreen's workshop, as well as the events around which it was centered. It took me a week to stop vibrating so intensely, and during that time I had wonderfully clairvoyant dreams and channeled some awesome poetry. The following literary works of art came flowing through me, while in a trance-like state, in the middle of the night:

∾∾∾∾

To those who befriend me:

I am not with you to hurt you, but to heal with you. My expressions of hurt and anger are not about you; they are those scabs from past trials and errors. As well they are about the tearing away of that which is not me so I may give you the gift of authenticity and love. I am not with you to frighten you, but to share life with you.

I desire to always feel safe in your presence, and only intend to show my friendship with truth and love. When you ask me to share—know that I will now answer my truth. It is not about you, so bitter words and aggressive actions toward me in reply only closes a part of me off towards you. I will no longer be fragments of that which I truly am. I am whole, complete, standing before you exposed and vulnerable. I am committed to only expressing my whole truth, so that I can be a better conduit of God's love.

I am an extension of God in your life, as you are in mine. Why do you throw salt at my healing wounds—attempting to stifle my genuineness, my passion, and my truth? I intend to not stand any less before you, nor anyone else, for that is cheating you, me, and God. I can no longer be just the parts of me you may like, for that is not really me. And I will no longer repeat those patterns.

So here are your grains of salt back—I refuse to rub them into my being any longer. I will also return any critical arrows, angry stones, controlling daggers, and judging rocks. I lovingly wrap them all in gold light with a bright indigo bow, which you may remove to use on others when you need to protect yourself from dying. Know that I understand your Soul also grows in it's own timing; and I am here, naked in my truth, willing to help you when you are ready to take my hand. For I have been dying for all of you, so that I may be living to heal you with Divine love and pure truth!

∾∾∾∾

Oh, Beloved One,

Don't you see that I am merely a reflection of you? I do not intend to add to your pain and fear; I desire to sparkle and shine for you. But sometimes we need to allow each other time to cleanse the Soul on the other side of the mirror.

Can't you see that your heart is my heart; your fears and pain are my own? Your love and humor are also mine. Why do you throw mud at your beautiful reflection? We've come so far assisting each other in Soul transformation—don't you understand that what you point out to me will reflect back? What is God trying to tell you—for am I not an extension of God, as are you? Our Soul intentions were to enable each other to clean our mirrors—allowing the pieces of dirt to fall away so that we may better reflect God's light in this lifetime.

Can't you understand that my truth is your truth—and expressing it through voice and emotions moves the energy through the glass and clears the chakras of lifetimes of hurt? Why are most emotions okay for you to see—and some cause you to lash out with red flares, shattering the glass and discounting an important part of you—an important part of me? For what really is the

187

difference between love and hate, joy and anger, peace and conflict? It is these very dichotomous circles of emotional energy vortexes that are really one in the same, in the spiraling sphere of life.

Please understand that if I hold back any part of me, any emotion, any feeling—I am also holding you back—for if I do not speak my truth, am I not also keeping you from speaking your truth? Yet my Soul understands and respectfully will shield those parts of me that discomfort you—if that is truly your desire, for I do not intent to show you that which causes you to recoil.

Please know that if there is a part of me you don't want yet to see, how can I truly reflect all that I am? Does that mean you don't really love all of me; all of you? Are you sure that's what you want to do right now? Is it from the soul, heart, ego? Please tell me when you're ready to look in the mirror again and I'll remove the cloak that prevents you from seeing all your beauty and light!

~~~~

I AM DYING.

That which has been me is speeding off into oblivion, as the layers are peeled off—ripping, tearing, stabbing, throbbing . . . as the thorns and stones are removed—bleeding, releasing, scabbing, healing . . .

I AM DYING.

For you, for truth, for love. All that I have learned is forgotten; societal norms—challenged; structure, order, conformity—nonexistent; all institutional being and thinking has dissipated. That which remains is your love and passion and light.

I AM DYING.

As relationships scatter; as materialism disappears; as competing, judging, and criticizing fades from existence . . . The voids are filling with your heavenly compassion, your endless love, as flickering lights of Angels dance in ecstasy.

I AM DYING.

Shaking off the dragging weights through the thick quick sand—as I fight to follow your path—to move to where you lead me. Trying to kick off the screaming bloody children clinging to my legs—begging and sobbing for me to stay and help them. Reaching out for you to help me out of the heavy mucky muck of attachment.

I AM DYING.

As my mental training is replaced with sentient guidance, my schooling receded by intuitive comprehension. My search for fulfillment, validation, approval and recognition from other people is being abandoned. My conformity fades as creativity takes over my life.

I AM DYING.

As I become one with you. I feel the excitement of your love, the intensity of your compassion. I breathe in the motivation to leave behind all that I know, believe, and understand. I look to you now for all the answers, and all the guidance for the direction of my life. I remain open to receiving you so that I may truly live, as I die away.

～～～～

I used to look for love
Through extensions of God,
Now I go directly to the source
And the extensions come to me.

I used to look to others
For assistance with my life,
Now I look within my heart
And God provides the directions.

～～～～

8

"Out of the Cocoon"

~back in time~
October 2000—January 2001

I left Mom's house as planned, one week after being at the emergency clinic. I really did feel okay. The steroids and antibiotics, of which I hadn't had any in over five years, helped within a couple of days. **I felt like a new woman, trusting God and my Angels to get me home safe and well**. I had to leave although I knew making a trip like this—twenty hours of driving, stopping at a hotel, then ten more hours—could easily bring my pneumonia back full-scale. Nonetheless, I was not waiting around there any longer. **It was time to get my dogs and myself home.**

Edward was there to see me off. He shook his head and smiled as he watched me load the last of things then put my dogs in what little space was left for them. Jamey was perched like a king atop four pillows (two I brought plus two of Mom's), which were over "his" seat as well as covering the dog food and cooler in front. Behind us, Charley was situated six inches higher and with a foot less length than before. A hanging clothes bag, four sets of sheets and two blankets stretched out over the back seat alongside boxes, paintings, suitcases and lawn chairs behind the seats. Above the rear dash I had spread out six sets of towels with the darkest color on top to prevent window glare. It was incredible how much of Mom's stuff I crammed into my car. I was very "anal" about it all indeed. I even measured under the car seats to see how much room I had to pack extra pictures, albums and papers. "I pray you don't get a flat, Kathleen," he laughed. "It'd take you an hour to unpack that trunk to find the spare!" **"The Angels will**

get me home ok," I replied with a smile. "Just picture a thousand of them keeping my tires inflated with this heavy load!"

Then we said "goodbye," and "I love you," and "I'll miss you," and "call regularly to check-in," many times in between hugs and looking around for the last time. The emptiness of the place was haunting. The absence of Mom and her belongings created a strange sense of hollow in our hearts. I watched him— red faced and teary eyed—searching her condo to make sure he didn't forget anything, to ensure he didn't forget everything. His lifeline was visibly ripped; his Soul ached for his sweet Mother to call out to him again. "I don't know what I'm gonna do without her, Kathleen," he hoarsely whispered. "She was the only person, the only one in this world who really loved me no matter what! There will never be anyone who is capable of loving me that deeply, that completely!" I just listened and hugged him as he expressed his sorrow. I understood what he was saying. I know how connected he felt before and how lost he must feel now. "You better get home, Edward. Diana's gonna wonder why it's taking us hours to say goodbye!" He nodded then added in his solemn state, "This is really it! It's really over, isn't it?" "Yeah," I softly replied, feeling more sadness towards my beautiful baby brother than towards Mom's condo. I always felt so close to him, yet this incident brought our hearts closer together than ever before. We both supported each other so complimentary. We both shared similar values and responses toward the care of our Mother lately: ones of utter love and selflessness. We were both very grateful for the help the other offered, it truly was the best partnership a brother-sister team could have within the context of a dying mother. I realized then just how much I was going to miss him. I remembered the poem I wrote to him when he got married, and how he cried as he read it at the wedding party:

On Angels' Wings

To my little brother, a blessing sent with love,
For through my heart the words are delivered from above.
I am so proud to have you in my family as my friend,
And as always I feel sure that we'll be close until the end.

I'll never forget our growing up together over the years,

Through all the turmoil, the grief, the fighting and the tears.
But most important of all is the laughter that we shared,
We always had a way to joke that showed each other we cared.

And now at this special time when you're getting married,
I give to you a little prayer, on Angels' wings it's carried:
May all your days be less of stress and more of joy and fun,
And may your family receive more love after each setting sun!

I choked up as I pulled away for the last time, driving around that cul-de-sac to the one clear spot between the trees where I knew he'd be watching to catch my eye for that last wave. Mom always did that to all of us. She'd stand in the garage doorway waiting for that moment when we'd glance back. Then she'd wave goodbye with a big teary smile full of love as we disappeared, before lowering the automatic door and going back into her humble little space. I can see her sitting in that old recliner, spacing out and missing us, all the while staring at that huge pine tree in her side yard that used to have "twin towers" until lightening struck one down. After that happened, she always said that the lone tower would make the most perfect little Christmas tree if you cut it off. She loved watching that tree over the years and telling us about which birds would come and go.

Now there I was, feeling like I had also been struck by lightening. I still felt numb as if I had fallen from the main tree. I shook my head to clear the cobwebs like I had been in "twilight zone" as I headed for the freeway. It was 9pm and I purposely wanted to drive through the night first and then into the next day to make those first twenty hours easier. It would be much harder to stay awake driving the second half of the trek in the dark. "Oh, no!" I exclaimed and turned on the wipers as it started to rain. I continued southbound while the rain became interspersed with layers of fog, ever-increasing in density. Visibility quickly reached zero, and I came upon amber glows of taillights where cars had pulled over to the side of the road. My heart pounded heavily for a while as I realized I had to get through this. I did not have time to slow down nor pull aside.

"Angels, Mom, get me home, please! Help me drive—take the wheel and guide the car! I need you now and turn this trip over to you!" I repeatedly said like a mantra as I began to get mesmerized by the tunnel vision. Hours go by, and either the rain pelted down like bullets with headlights bouncing off it like a laser show, or the fog engulfed my car creating the illusion that I was floating in a cloud. **I actually felt like I was an Angel flying around in heaven. I could feel Beings take over the steering wheel many times** as I was doing things in my car to stay awake. All the while, I managed to keep the cruise control set at 69mph, even though I could only see one yellow median stripe at a time next to my driver's side front corner of the car to judge where I was. **I let go of all fear and completely surrendered to my fate.** "Hey," I thought to myself, **"whatever may happen, then so be it!"** For the first time in my life, **I could literally feel just how out of control I was; yet how responsible I was for paying attention to the flow.**

It seemed like a tunnel of light was pulling me towards heaven as I drove on. I have never felt more serene, loved and strangely comforted in my whole life, and could actually see Angels dance with me through the night. I knew rationally that many people would think I was crazy. I also realized that I might be near delirium and having optic illusions. However I didn't care. **I was enjoying the peaceful ride of a lifetime knowing Mom would help me get home okay. This incredible amount of trust, I sensed, would get me through whatever else I may encounter in my life. I knew intuitively through this experience, especially when it kept dragging on all night, I was supposed to always remember this feeling to help me. I even had Soul memories of traveling like this before.** Amazingly, I continued on for eight hours with limited visibility until I finally saw relief with the rising sun in Missouri at daybreak.

My head was like a movie-screen playing back many of the scenes, which I had just witnessed over the last couple months. I felt a wave of empathy for Ken as I remembered how much he struggled with understanding his Grandma's death. I also felt proud of how I handled this—the way I wished I had been treated when my dad died. Just a few days after Mom died, he was helping me walk the dogs, like he often did, when he started crying. It was nighttime, and very quiet around this predominantly retired community interspersed with family units. As we strolled on the sidewalk that curved over decorative bridges and around deciduous trees and pines, he began wailing out his pain. He kept asking me, "Why'd my Grandma have to get sick? Why'd she have to die? Why was she so mean sometimes, like about my animals and stuff? This means we won't be coming over to her house anymore, huh?"

He became louder and louder as he cried out his anguish into the night. For just a moment, *I thought about how we might be disturbing the neighbors, or they might think I was doing something wrong to him,* but I quickly disregarded any thoughts of that nature to take care of this young boy next to me. I cared so deeply about helping him and letting him know that **whatever he felt—it was okay**. I wanted desperately to assist with his understanding of this life-stage and to know how special he was to his Grandma. From the bottom of my old broken heart I wanted to nurture his grief and allow him the freedom of expression without limits! **This was real! It was crucial for us to get through this together by sharing, talking, expressing and loving. That's what family was for.**

I could only think about how much I loved Ken and intended to give him what he needed from me. He seldom asked for any kind of emotional support. He tried to be tougher now especially since he was getting older. However, when I see him run up to me with excitement, and look forward to my visits, it makes me feel important on a certain level. He doesn't want to talk much about his problems, or hyperactivity related issues, or family concerns, which I can respect. It is just enough that I extend myself to him. I let him know that if he ever does want to talk, I am here and I understand. Someday he may need it; many days I wished that I had had that from somebody.

As I drove on, I recalled all of the times we related to each other, those moments we giggled and got crazy when the rest of the family just shook their head. I remembered how important it was to have adults with whom you could relate—ones to let you know it wasn't all serious and cold hearted to be "grown-up." I recalled the many times Ken helped me get in touch with my inner child by laughing, playing and being silly. **I remembered how important it was now for me to not get so serious with life and to be forgiving of those who are cross with me.** Just like his Grandma, I have a special relationship with him too, and I realized how lucky this young man was to have been adopted into our family after his beginnings. Someday, he'll realize it too.

I chuckled aloud remembering the time just a couple weeks earlier, when he had brought his scooter over to the condo. After showing me his flips, turns and high-speed maneuvers, he asked me if I was ready to try. I replied that I had never done it before. Well, this kid knew how to manipulate me—"But I thought you were naturally good at everything you did, Aunt Kathleen? I bet you'd be great at this too!" A huge smile broke out over my face as I accepted the challenge. After adjusting the height and learning how to brake, I was off scooting around the cul-de-sac. "Weeeeee!" I shrieked like a mouse. "Hey, this is fun!" I yelled as

I went flying by him. He started chasing me, saying, "Ok, it's my turn!" as I teasingly out-rolled him pretending to be unable to stop.

Eventually we wound all around the curvy sidewalks through Mom's neighborhood. One of us would take a turn walking while the other rode the scooter in search of the low-grade slopes. These would increase our speed to provide a greater thrill on this rather flat terrain landscape. At one point a thought occurred to me, and I paused all covered in sweat to ask him, "Hey, Ken? Ya think the neighbors are watching us saying, 'Look at that crazy middle-aged lady acting like a teenager on that scooter out there!'" He laughed and replied, "Yeah, but so what!?" as he grabbed the scooter from me and sailed off again. I stood there frozen momentarily as it hit me that I was no longer really a kid, although I knew I would always act like one as often as I could. It was just too much fun and life was too short!

It was sad to think how I probably wouldn't see Ken or baby James again for a long time. I had been out there for seven different trips within a year and a half, this recent one lasting over two months; hence, I had gotten very close to Edward's family. Watching both boys mature during these crucial ages was so rewarding for me, *however, I worried James would not even remember me the next time he saw me*. And Ken, with puberty just around the corner, was bound to be deep-voiced, taller and with who knows what kind of personality by the time I see him again, probably in several years.

As I continued driving home, I kept making phone calls to check-in with everyone and prevent boredom, in between my memory flashbacks. I was delighted with the beautiful autumn colors across the country as well as the great weather the rest of the way home. The air smelled so fresh, I kept the windows opened most of the trip, after the rain had stopped. The bouquet of flowers that I had hung in Mom's garage was directly behind me on top of a box, partially lined in cardboard for protection, plus tied to the clothes hook. **I watched with awe as bits and pieces of those flowers flew around inside the car and out the window. It surreally felt like Mother was with me, while little pieces of her were being spread-out along the countryside like ashes to the wind**. I figured the bouquet would be ruined by the time I got home, but having had no alternative, I shrugged and "let it go."

I then thought about all the **synchronicities** that had occurred surrounding Mom's death and shook my head with wonder of the whole process. Of course, Diana had pointed out several times how I was the only one who thought that way. She'd say, "What a different perspective you have on things!" Yet, I love seeing connections from different angles to get a bigger picture and explore possibilities. Sometimes that means *reading too much into things*, but other times **I'm right on target** even if nobody else can see it. There were some events, however, with which my family just couldn't argue. **And I knew these were Spirit-guided interventions**. For example, Edward bought Mom this beautiful, framed painting of the blessed Mother Mary. He had planned on giving it to her during our Sunday dinner, on that last weekend when Sean was visiting. Well, that Friday night prior, at Diana's **persistent urging**, he decided to bring it over early. Mom just loved it! We hung it next to the fireplace with the altar I had arranged. And that bouquet of flowers which was displayed in front of it, accented it radiantly. As Mom awoke each time, her face would light up seeing those items of beauty around her. Unbeknownst to us at the time, of course, she never woke again after that Saturday night.

Just as a memory would bring tears to my eyes, the next would make me laugh. I recalled the time soon after I arrived when Mom was looking all over the house for her hearing-aid brush. This was a tiny thing, the handle being about the size of a toothpick with perpendicular, quarter-inch black bristles running halfway down it. She was frustrated with not knowing what she had done with it, and we spent a couple of days searching the condo. One evening, when I had been in the garage for my usual break, I saw the snow-scraper for her car lying on a shelf and got a humorous idea. Now, this apparatus was about a foot and a half long with a plastic scraper on one end and on the other, a brush with three-inch black bristles sticking out half the way down. I walked into the living room exclaiming with a straight face, "Hey, Mom! Guess what? I found your hearing aid brush!" and held it up to her with all sincerity. After a gasp and a pause, she started giggling, and then laughing so hard tears rolled down her face. Those moments I hold so dear to my heart.

We never did find that letter she wrote either. It wasn't in the safety deposit box, or with her lawyer as we had hoped. Her talkative ole friend, Ellen, the one who babbled away at the funeral home, had given me hope when I told her about it. "I bet your Mother wrote that letter before you came out here, and at a time when she wasn't sure how she might die. But I know she felt like she was able to spend such valuable time with all you kids in the end, that she had nothing unsaid left to say. If she would have died without you near her, then she may not have gotten rid of it . . ."

On several occasions in the past, Mom had dreamt of Jesus placing his hand on her shoulder. Then she'd awake really sensing it, and not want to open her eyes for fear it might disappear. When I was visiting once during Christmas of 1997, I gave her a plaque inscribed with the "Footprints" prayer. She incredibly had never seen that prayer before, and the words deeply touched her heart. It hung in the kitchen until I moved it over her hospital bed, alongside a picture of Jesus, which I had shellacked and given to her when I was eighteen. One of the last things I reminded her about while she was awake was that **Jesus was carrying her now. I told her how there was only one set of footprints because her arms were wrapped around his shoulders this time.** She heard me and knew it was true.

I wiped the tears from my face and changed the music in my car as I continued on towards my home. I was still coughing a lot, and finishing up the meds, yet feeling great considering. "I'll be fine," I told myself, and then laughingly added, "My biorhythms wouldn't lie!" It was strange even to me to realize how in-line this trip was with my "biorhythms." The cell phone I bought specially for the drive had a featured capability of determining the dates when people are at their best to perform certain tasks. I looked at days over the months I'd be gone to find the optimal times, mentally, emotionally and physically, for me to do long distance travel. **These amazingly turned out to be around August 10 and October 16—the exact dates I ended up driving! Just another sign from the Angels of how meant-to-be all of this was, and further, indicating how I would be fine.**

I was starting to think about returning to work. Even though I had been through so much and was still a little sick, I was at the same time getting excited about returning to my Project. I knew I could concentrate better now. I was ready to learn about all that had happened during my absence. Plus, I was curious about the girls. When I called Angela a couple of times, however, she was too busy to talk. **I then knew I'd have to wait, deciding it was best to talk to her in person.**

When I finally arrived home, it felt so strange after everything I'd been through. One of my house-sitters had **left a few daisies** on the table, not even knowing they were Mom's actual favorite flower. Depressingly, they were already wilted because they had been there for a week. I sat down and cried. *It was the only thing anyone gave me for my Mom dying!* I went through all my mail, and found no sympathy cards. I called my bosses and very little was said except, "Sorry about your loss, now when are you returning to work?" When I answered,

"November first," I could sense their frustration. I explained how I needed to rest from the drive, unpack a million things, and recuperate from my illness so it didn't return. Plus, my yard needed much work after sitting untouched for so long. (It had been raining lately so the weeds and grasses were knee-high; little Jamey would just disappear in the backyard!) After being reminded that employees were only entitled to one week of bereavement, which I had already taken the week after Mom died, they conceded and I was allowed to use two more weeks of my sick-leave time.

One coworker, Tori, was absolutely livid to find out from me about my Mom's death. She, like Dick, was always sensitive to my issues, was one with whom I could be myself, and was fun to be around. I hadn't realized until she told me, that no one at work had written a memo nor did anyone announce it at any meeting. These were typical gestures our workplace did for any employee who underwent the loss of a family member. Somehow I slipped through the system. Dick was equally perturbed, and became very supportive of my situation. They seemed like the only two people who weren't afraid of me. It felt like everyone else was nervous not knowing how to deal with the issue of my Mom's death, *so they ignored me instead. Or maybe they kept distance out of fear that I'd freak out.*

I found it remarkable how every day I would call some friends from the past, trying to reach out to someone, with little response back. I was in the mood to give everyone a chance. I asked people very honestly for what I needed, saying my Mother had recently died and I just wanted a friend. I kept thinking someone over the years may have changed and would be willing to reconnect. *I kept hoping that someone would realize how sincere and deserving I was. I kept praying that God would align me with the right support system during my time of need. Nobody called,* but two cards finally came. One was from a past friend and the other from my therapist.

I had also been calling Angela and Rudy from work, trying to schedule a get-together and rather, becoming more frustrated by the day. I kept asking them about how they had been running things, what the girls were doing, what issues they had encountered, and how I would fit back into the schedule. They merely replied, "Gotta go—too busy! Will call ya later!" I felt in a humbled space, ready to have them tell me how I could best help with what was once my program. I was determined not to appear like the type who just wanted to take-over. But because they weren't answering my calls or giving me much feedback, *my head started racing*. Actually, the only information they did give me was how wonderful things had been while I was gone—there were no personality conflicts and everyone loved the program. *I imagined them talking badly about me*, yet I told myself not to personalize or emotionalize this. I could easily do that in light of what I had been through, so I was all the more determined to stop my mind-chatter.

I instead tried to keep focused on the tasks at hand. I was resting, loving my dogs, and unpacking. I was purging every room in my house, moving out the old to make room to integrate Mom's things where I felt guided to place them. I was straightening every drawer, cabinet and closet. I wanted to get it all over with as soon as possible so I could get on with my life. The smell of old smoke and mothballs hung heavily in my house for weeks. I cried several times a day as I uncovered more of her things, and read more of her notes or my notes to her. I collapsed in sorrow as I looked at photos of her, of us. Then I got up and kept going.

When I finally spoke with Angela, she told me, "We'll talk on your first day back, at the meeting," thus I surrendered. She seemed so nervous around me I assumed she was partially still mad about my response regarding her daughter, plus my taking of extra leave time. I could also tell she was very untrusting of how I may deal with my grief. Both she and Rudy knew of the many problems I had with various staff and how upset I was before I left. Additionally, I had confided with them on the "crazy" role that my ADHD played in this. They had said they'd be supportive, they said they understood—they were obviously changing their minds. *So, I became determined to prove to them just how "back to normal" I was. I was going to show everyone, including myself, how I had 200% to give to this project. Nothing would distract me now! After what I went through, and all this time off, nothing the Agency could do would bring me down.* I was ready to face all the challenges and make it the best program possible!

Even the next day when I sat in Leonard's office with Angela, and they finally showed me my new schedule, **I told myself I could handle it.** *Although my pulse pounded and my heart fell to the floor as they discussed my "separate" work hours and places,* **I knew God would help me through**. Then when I realized they were telling me, *with all my experience,* exactly what classes I was to teach, at exactly what time and with which girls, **I still figured I had something to learn and needed to be open.** *I tried not to feel hurt that they didn't ask for my input, nor let me decide which classes I'd like to teach. I tried not to feel* *angry that I was to start these classes in one week with little prep time, even though I had been asking for three weeks what my new plans were. Plus, I tried not to feel intimidated going back to an institution where I didn't know most of the girls, and wasn't being welcomed back nor introduced. I even tried not to be sad that I was on my own, whereas Angela and Rudy team-taught together.* I did ask about this and was told that the two of them got along so well together, they wanted to keep it that way. *And I restrained my tears when I walked back into the Club again after three months, and saw no "welcome back" sign or anything.*

As I kept processing my new life situation, **I began wondering if this was God's way of closing more doors to get me to find others**. I didn't know where to look yet, but kept that concept in mind. I remembered how *I did everything I could* to welcome these two co-workers into this *harsh* correctional environment. I spent hours explaining how everything operated, and trying to help ease them into difficult situations. *I worked hard at making us into a good team, only to now feel that my team was rejecting me.* I felt royally slapped in the face. And to top that, I wondered about the "show of teamwork" which this presented to the girls and other staff! Where was the continuity from me leaving to returning? Where was the demonstration of honest communication and professional respect? Where was the sense of community and example setting for the kids? We expected them to work through issues, tell their truths and do conflict resolutions to learn to get along. Was that what we adults were doing? Was this new arrangement really for the best needs of the girls? It certainly was not in-line with my values, or the goals on which I intended to base the program.

Still, I told myself to **"hang in there"** *and show them I could do it. Unfortunately, I would have to prove myself. I would have to earn their respect again. I obviously caused enough doubt in too many minds by being absent so much, and having "focusing" problems when I was there.* **I would get through this difficult time** *and then get my project back. I was still determined to show them!*

However, the next week when I was told that someone downtown in our personnel division accidentally terminated me, *I started to wear down.* Next, *when everyone seemed so rude and cranky with their explanations,* then expected me to fill out piles of paper work with no assistance, *I started buckling under.* The weeks dragged on and things still weren't being fixed in the system. Thus, I was kicked out of my insurance from the end of September on. This caused all my medical bills (medications, emergency room, and counseling services) to get sent back to me, *and I once again became drained. I felt worn out and beaten. I quickly lost my drive to be my best by spending so much energy dealing with these other issues, all of which should never have existed. And still, I received no apologies and little compassion.*

Somehow though, this time around, I didn't feel so victimized. *I was hurt, yet more angry and tired.* **I strangely felt more empowered than ever before, with a strong will arising to move onward and step into my own. I felt as if I was building up more self-esteem despite the setbacks, plus tuning into a new guided-like sensation: a wave and rush towards my future. I felt amazingly centered and focused. I decided I wanted to use this wonderful, creative energy for my own benefit with positive results only.** As the holiday approached, the first Thanksgiving without Mom, I stayed as busy at work as possible. I was getting very close to the girls and doing a great job with the new classes, however, **I had decided I was going to quit! I meditated and turned it over God. It felt right. Mom was telling me I deserved better.** I started praying this new affirmation:

"Thank you for the experiences. May I learn to forgive, release, thank the signs along the path, and move through this with love and grace. I am so excited, yet anxious and a little fearful. I want to turn my life over to Divine guidance—oh, help me follow it, know it, trust it—so that I may prosper within positive circles of creativity and love. It is time to explore new frontiers, and follow paths to my other creative dream forces. I am ready to tune in to the flow of Spirit, hear the pulse of Mother earth, and slowly breathe in the subtle serenity. It is time to know that I AM—wonderful and deserving of positive, loving, supportive, nurturing people in my life with whom I am respected and loved for just exactly who I AM—because I believe it! I am strong in my Spiritual power to guide me through this! I pray to you Lord, and call upon Mother, Father, and all of my Angels to help. And so it is!"

I had decided I would work through the Christmas vacation because it would help me stay busy. Plus, I was developing relationships with girls who desperately needed more activities during this time. I also wanted to let my coworkers take some time-off, since they hadn't had any yet. I figured I'd collect a couple more paychecks before starting my new life with the New Year, 2001. I told all the bosses and coworkers right away, even though this meant more weeks of possibly being treated badly for "jumping ship." I found I just couldn't lie and be part of future planning if I wasn't truly going to be there. It was a little surprising to some people, however most seemed unfazed.

In mid-December, after six weeks of doing excellent work, I finally was able to get Rudy and Angela to "open-up" with me. It turns out that they were mad. They had interpreted my "not-calling" as not caring. They were upset about my taking of extra time. Plus, they thought I was selfish for not letting Angela's daughter stay at my house. **I had intuited all this.** They had also believed that the personality conflicts were all about me, although I knew this often occurred with the beginning of any new program. They assumed they were doing great while I was away. Rudy even had the nerve to tell me that she didn't like me anymore, and no longer wished to work with me. Angela didn't go that far, nonetheless, I told both of them I was disappointed in them. I expressed hurt that while I was back home nursing my dying Mother through her death, and experiencing the single most transformational time of my life, *they were thinking these petty thoughts!*

What I didn't tell them was how I came back to a huge list of items that had been going "wrong" with the Club during my absence, and which our security department wanted me to "clean-up." What they didn't know was that the Agency felt uncomfortable about "redirecting" them because they were only contractual employees. I also came back to complications within our budgetary contracts due to some *poor* decisions made by my downtown boss, Louise. Further, I had to deal with purchasing problems because proper protocol had not been followed with regards to our Agency's procurement policies and procedures. To make matters worse, Rudy and Angela still had not received any of the training that I had been requesting for almost a year. Therefore, they had not been properly trained for what they were doing. For example, after I left, they were handed keys and a two-way radio with which to operate, and often had no staff assisting even though this was a technical liability. I had taught them the basics unofficially, and the girls even helped, but had an emergency ever occurred . . .

Additionally, I realized after being gone so long, they were even more set in their ways. Although they did do an awesome job, they were not open to feedback from me about their performance. I was viewed as an equal, not an authority, and therefore *felt I had to tiptoe carefully around certain topics.* I quickly noticed how lax things had gotten with security issues, and began to fear the day when I would be held personally responsible for something they allowed to happen. I knew it would only take one little piece of jewelry, or harmful chemical to get back in the housing units and hurt someone else, and it would be my ass, literally. I was not going to hang around for any potential "fall-out." I had had enough along the way. And I thought it was time for them to deal with the whole picture, not just the one painted for them.

As time went on, I had slowly been integrated back into the Club activities and working alongside them again. They both ended up apologizing and telling me I was better than they thought I'd be—more focused and joyful. They were also impressed with the quality of my classes as well as my healthy relationships with the girls. It was difficult for any of us to get close to these girls, only to see them being returned to their same home environment or community with lack of support.

We watched many girls being re-institutionalized time and time again. We heard of many runaways or transfers to adult systems. We were told of some being lost back into prostitution or drug trafficking or gang banging. We were helpless with a lack of resources to properly help mentor and support the girls. Our program appeared more unsuccessful because we had so many variables with which to deal. It broke our hearts to hear the girls' stories. We saw them so eagerly opening up to us about their years of abuse and/or neglect, and then how they got arrested. Many girls had records of runaway, incorrigibility, curfew violations and drug possession charges; some had weapons offenses, assault with intent, and theft charges. Most had homes worth running away from, and offenses incurred upon them without receiving proper help. This easily explains the self-abusive and low self-esteem cycles in which they were stuck. Many had babies already, some were pregnant, some delivered and had their babies separated from them while incarcerated, many had VD, and some were too damaged from abusive men in their lives to ever get pregnant. Many admitted wishing they were dead, or believed there was no hope for them. All of them, however, were capable of laughing, sharing and learning with us—and many of them did!

My leaving merely set the program goals back further. It meant more time before the Project could get a larger community support system in place to help the girls. We wanted to get them involved in the Kids Clubs along with schools and healthy activities. Yet, again because of my departure, we hadn't gotten "beyond the fence" like we had wanted with the project. Therefore, getting to know the girls but not being able to keep up with them upon release, created a losing situation. They needed help right away. Waiting months down the line was too long and broke the ties staff may have had with them. The girls can loose more trust in the system because staff can't be there for them as planned. What a frustrating situation to manage!

I honestly want to effect change at a higher level. I no longer feel like I can just help one-on-one. Those days are probably over, and it's time to find other like-minded adults to create systems that can sensitively address some of the issues upon which I just touched. The alternatives for the girls are death, lives of more misery and/or more incarceration into the adult system. I believe we could take the average $35,000/year we spend to send kids to jail, and put it to better use in preventative programs within the community. This prayer is in God's hands now, and I am open to guidance on how my role will manifest within this context.

My last day of employment, *not surprisingly, came with little attention.* I walked around the campus *feeling very empty.* I cleaned out my office and loaded up my car *without anybody really noticing.* I said goodbye to a few people, while many still didn't know I was going. I had announced it to all supervisors and managers at the last meeting, but the word didn't spread. I told the girls I was leaving during my last couple days, and they responded with the most emotion. All hugged me goodbye, some cried and begged for me to keep in touch, and a few got very distant as a defense mechanism because of their past losses. **Here were more signs** for me to consider: no goodbye party, no banner, and no cards once again. Only Tori expressed how much she would miss me. We had had a lot of fun leading training teams together in the past, plus we had done a few memorable "happy hours" after work! She was a good work ally—the only one at the girls' institution. I found myself sitting at my computer for the last time and writing her the following last memo:

"Sniff . . . sniff . . . I got tears in my eyes seeing my name off the schedule. But remember—please add me to your personal/social schedule! Thank you from my Mother for being one of my few support systems in my life this past year. You are really the only one that saw a lot of what was happening, heard the rest, and still hung in there with me when it seemed that nobody would (except Dick). Your timely tears and words of compassion for my situation touched my heart more than you will ever know . . . (Now the tears are really coming!) I am going to miss working with you! This is my last e-mail, on my last day, and I send it lovingly to you." Then, to use radio language with some of our institutional terms, I continued:

"I've been released—I'm on transition status, being Divinely guided in my life! This is not a code 200 nor code 3, so 10-22 any previous messages. I'm now 98 Corrections, 10-19 to freedom with a 10-14 from God; I'm 10-2 on receiving the messages with no 10-24's anymore; I'm becoming 10-6 with my own intuitive creative talents, and soon I'll be 97 at my personal 20 where you can give me a 21 anytime! This is Kathleen K'earns, signing out, with gratitude for what the Agency for Incarcerated Juveniles has contributed to my life . . ."

(Key: <ignore 10's> code 200-escape, code 3-emergency, 22-disregard, 98-leaving, 19-enroute, 14-escort, 2-clear, 24-problems needing assistance, 6-busy, 97-arriving, 20-location, and 21-phone call.)

After I got home, I received a call from my new boss who had taken the place of the one who quit earlier in the summer. We had barely worked together. She said she had brought in a cake for my "goodbye party" only to find that I already left for the day. It was clear she wanted me think she had something planned, and I appreciated the last minute effort. I had said goodbye to the other managers and obviously no one knew or they wouldn't have let me leave. I told her I was too busy to drive back there to share the cake later that afternoon. However, she talked me into coming the following week during another meeting. The cake was put in the fridge and pulled back out for my little goodbye. She attempted to tell the room about all the effort I had put into the Project, while many staff side-talked and acted rudely, not realizing what was really happening. Nobody redirected them, and few could really hear her. Yet I still was grateful for the gesture. It was something after all, plus she gave me a Deepak Chopra book, "7 Spiritual Laws of Success," which touched my heart (she knew how Spiritual I was).

A week later Angela dropped off a card and beautiful musical-Angel-crystal ball, which really moved me. Angela, Rudy and a third Club staff had pitched in for this gift; as well they signed the card in a loving, farewell manner. We also met for a happy hour right after I quit, and I actually had a glimmer of hope that we might continue growing and become better friends again.

Several months later, I heard from Angela. I was amazed to hear her being upset and crying about her new predicament. She said that after being told many times how all parties would renew our grant contract, they were told at the last minute it was being cancelled. She was given one week to finish classes, let girls know, then pack and move. Moreover, Leonard had told her she'd have to take a demotion because there was not a comparable position available in any Kids Club at that time. Money was already tight for her, especially since her relationship had become "rocky" and she just moved to a separate residence. Now, she had to cancel that lease and move in with her senior mother. She also said she was having some difficulties with her daughter, and was facing more unplanned expenses.

All this surprised me somewhat, and I just validated her feelings. She then spoke of all the hassles they had encountered at the institution. She never said I was right, or that she now understood what I had to endure. I don't know if she realized it yet or not. But, she talked about how so many people seemed to turn against them. The business office nitpicked about everything they bought. They had to follow "absurd" rules that were stifling them and hurting the Project in the long run. They kept getting in trouble for having contraband, and had to get rid of many supplies in the Club. They felt their freedom to teach was being encroached upon. Many staff stopped being so supportive and/or appeared too lazy to deliver girls to the classes. It became a major hassle to make things happen. New programs were cropping up and limiting their time and access for girls and classes. Pressures were mounting, as Leonard demanded more from them yet the institution provided less.

She also believed that if I hadn't quit, they might have renewed the contract. I don't know if that's accurate, and it doesn't really matter. Overall, the whole project seemed like a waste of hundreds of thousands of dollars! How sad! **I realized I was glad I finally listened to Spirit and left when I did**, because I would have had to quit anyway when the grant ended. This way, **I didn't have to experience the extra drama and stress at the end like she did. Plus, this gave me a head start on my future.** *I wondered if this was karmic justice* as I said goodbye to her and sincerely wished her luck.

Also that same month, I did not receive my retirement check as scheduled. I then learned that someone downtown had somehow misplaced the form so I needed to fill out another. I drove there, and *as usual, cold and impersonal was the treatment, with no apology*. I walked the paperwork through all the required routes to ensure I wouldn't have to hassle with them ever again. **I then found myself confidently marching up to the new Assistant Director's office,** a man with whom I used to work well at the boy's institution. **An obvious Spirit-directed synchronicity, he was available in his office, which was rare! Unexpectedly, he acted like an Angel as he allowed me to sit down and tell my story, the**

whole story, while listening empathetically to me. He was shocked by what I had encountered and told me he had heard I quit because of "personal problems." Next, he reminded me of how well I got along with everyone in the past, and of my fun-loving and creative Spirit that I brought to work (things I had long forgotten). My heart felt so grateful just to finally feel understood by someone who knew me before. How wonderful that this one conversation made up for all I went through in the last year! Then to top it off, he sent me the following email, which helped to make my seven years with the Agency worth every minute:

"Your dedication and commitment to this Agency did not go unnoticed. I know what our recreation department was like prior to your arrival and what it grew into under your leadership. You should be very proud of your accomplishments as I am. I've taken the liberty of sharing some of your concerns with the Director, and will take steps to ensure that no one else has the experiences that you had to endure.

"Kathleen, from our conversation, I could easily see that you were treated badly, but being the strong determined person you are, you have not let those experiences keep you down. You have a lot to give in whatever direction you choose to go in. I know this because I've seen you interact and work with others.

"I hope as time goes on that the last of your Mother and any other personal issues get resolved by you as you see fit. You know there is a saying in the Bible from God that goes something like this: 'God will not give you any more troubles, death, sickness, etc., etc., than you can handle.' He promised that he would help support us in our times of needs. God bless you."

9

"Over the rainbow"

~present day~
June 2001

*D*uring those last couple of months working for the Agency, *I felt extremely isolated and constricted.* After dealing with the many losses in my life both personally and socially, then to face the added *traumatic* work experiences— *I felt like my body was being ripped apart, my heart torn away, and my gut repeatedly stabbed. I was alone in a dark space accentuated by fear and depression,* **yet from some unknown source, a little light, a small streak of power shone forth**. Eventually, and timely with the New Year, I started tearing-off the confines of my encasement, allowing for an increased flow of light. With each layer that I removed, more strength of character came forth. I burst out of my cocoon only then to find my rightful place, my renewed body, my rebuilt heart, and my healed belly. I emerged from my incubation period a most beautiful butterfly ready to radiate all my colors and fly with gratitude over the rainbow of my Soul's newfound freedom.

When I first bought my home, Mom sent me a very special card with butterfly drawings from handicapped children. I had been worried about affording the home alone and expressed this to her. She wrote encouraging words to help get me through the "closing" without fear. "You can do it!" she had told me, "It will all work out ok—you'll see!" There again she was right. I got a raise at work one month later and have not needed a roommate nor had financial difficulties in the three years since I bought it. I decidedly placed that card in my front bathroom on the mirror, and then created a cheery butterfly motif throughout the rest of the room. They're on the shower curtain, wall pictures and stained glass in the window.

This decor lightened and brightened that room, greeting me everyday with a "good morning!" feeling.

Mom had loved butterflies, too. A month after she died I remember sitting in my backyard, and the most awesome little butterfly came gently soaring around me. I suddenly remembered a scene from the movie "Patch Adams" where he had believed the Spirit of his deceased loved one was flitting around in this butterfly, **and chills went up my spine. I felt like Spirit was bringing me a glimpse of Mom's Soul again through this insect-Angel. I watched with wonderment as it spoke of great love and understanding for me. After hovering longer than usual,** it finally disappeared beyond the neighbor's bushes. A poem I once read described how we are able to appreciate the beauty of a butterfly, and easily say goodbye as it flies away. How sad we can't do that with everything in life! **To just merely appreciate the beauty of a moment, a circumstance, or a person and then gratefully watch it/them go without attachment, without constricting, or without a feeling of great loss—is truly a Higher State of Being!**

I definitely believe that the more I learn to creatively express myself through my God-given talents, the more that the brilliant colors on my wings will shine forth for others to appreciate. I feel like I am really flying over my rainbow in life, seeing a much bigger and more beautiful picture than before. Reflections are still evident, only now it's like their colors resonate with hues from my rainbow. There is a favorite Native American proverb of mine which I have loved for years and thus share with others often: "The Soul would have no rainbow if the eyes had no tears." When someone I know has been crying a lot, I tell that person this proverb followed by, "So you must have a really beautiful rainbow now!" It always seems to bring comfort. And this gives me great joy, especially since tears, sadness and grief are often dishonored in our society/culture.

The analogy of rainbows has many connotations. As with butterflies, many people feel awe-struck by rainbows. How exciting it is to see those bright glowing colors after a sun-filled rain burst! Then as quickly as they appear in our life, they also fade, usually leaving us with a smile in our hearts or a skip in our walk. Yet, science tells us that rainbow prisms exist everywhere and in everything to some degree. Sometimes, it's just a matter of looking for them. Some people are blessed with clairvoyance and can see others' auras and the colors emanating from their energy fields. All energy waves have color frequencies associated with them, and we all have particular colors with which we resonate more. Being aware of these facets in life, I believe, can help one find their own rainbows and shine them brighter. There are also many great books/tapes on balancing the colorful chakras in our bodies in order to experience more balanced lives, which is crucial for happiness and contentment. (Sonia Choquette and Doreen Virtue both address wonderful techniques for balancing, in easy-to-follow formats.)

Rainbows also represent freedom for many people. They are a global symbol for acceptance and respect within the gay community, as well as a sign for peaceful relations and equality between peoples of all colors. Just as colors vibrate at different frequencies yet "band" together strong to create a brilliant display we call the rainbow, **so too should people shine forth their colorful Spirits and proudly connect together to reflect back the wonderful diversity God created here on earth. My mission is to be a part of this.**

I believe that by being on this path of following my heart's desires and Soul destiny, I am learning to trust that the "pot of gold" truly does lie on "either" side. **The rewards are coming. The riches are made evident by the ever-increasing density of colors, as well as the addition of more heartfelt love energy and support coming through to me. To totally trust that the benefits are arriving and the sacrifices are paying-off is a great lesson in surrender and patience.** *Yet, it is difficult to not have a monetary income presently. It has been pretty scary sometimes for me to use all of my savings in order to take this time for myself. I often think I'm being a little irrational, and sometimes downright crazy. I occasionally tell myself to find a part-time job to help me feel more secure.* But those are all states of my mind, and **when I go into a meditation, or talk to my Spiritual heart, I know I am okay. I trust that by completely surrendering myself to God right now—because I know without a doubt this is my time to do it—the payoff will be ten-fold. I also believe that this trust exercise will teach me how to follow the flow of my Soul path more intuitively. It helps to counteract the tendency towards mental control, which blocks out the voice of the Soul.**

Like I've described, I believe a thorough "housecleaning" is necessary in order to let our inner-lights shine the way God intended. Many people joke about having "skeletons" in the closet, and most know they are healthier when they can release these. Some use terms such as "coming out of the closet" to refer to embracing Self and speaking their Truth regardless of the consequences. Although typically used to describe gay people who have little fear in standing-up for their lifestyle, the term is also commonly used these days in Spiritual circles. People, who had been afraid to talk about their Spiritual belief systems because of possible ridicule or rejection, are now stepping out of that closet, and breaking free from those cocoons. Whether someone prefers to follow their heart intimately with a same-sex partner, or explore their Spirit through various metaphysical pathways, **the important thing is—they are doing that which brings them passion and joy in life! It is all an expression of the Soul, an act of self-love, and a means of creative destiny.**

By writing this book, not only am I following my Soul path and embracing my heart's desires, I am also clearing out "old skeletons" from my past. This will allow my future to be less a reflection of such, and more a clear showing of my true colors. I am a beautifully transformed butterfly busting out of that cocoon. As well, I am coming out of many closets on many levels. I am taking a deep breath and sharing my story as honestly as I can in the hopes that it will inspire others to do the same. I am standing up for what makes me passionate about life, and following those things that bring me joy. As time goes on, it really does get easier, even when things are difficult. **Learning to put my heart over my head is a process that is saving my life, and I know that my Mother is helping me in Spirit form to do this.**

When I think back now to all the people I worked with at the Agency, **I clearly realize how they were merely reflections of my inner-selves**. Hard as it was to see these shadows of myself outwardly, **I know that they were playing a part I needed to assist me with my Soul growth and help me find my heart**. The ways in which I describe them in this book, do not accurately describe who they are as people. I understand that everyone was doing their best, as was I. Another person may describe the same people in a totally different light. That is because **we see what we need to**. If there are parts of us that are not honoring, it is easy to project that onto others. At any point in time when we shift or change, miraculously other people seem to also. Further, **we always have choices along the way**, no matter what our heads may tell us, and no matter how our fears try to paralyze us. I have to take total responsibility for how I *thought* everyone was treating me, because I allowed it. I could have demanded more respect, I could have walked away, and I could have affected different changes. I didn't know how to or chose not to out of fear and low self-esteem.

Ignorance and fear are no longer running my life. As I embrace my shadows, they no longer show up to haunt me, although an occasional quick visit keeps me checked. It affords me an opportunity to get stronger in my new learning of not tolerating certain ways of being treated. Spirit has been sending me people lately with whom I can practice seeing potential shadows, and then by talking it over with them, I can watch my perspective totally change. If I think someone is speaking to me or treating me inappropriately, and I try to discuss it with them but have no success in resolving it, I simply walk away. Period. No excuses, no defenses. Often times, however, I discover a shift in how we relate to each other, which I believe is a gift. I am learning how to stand up for myself, and teaching others how to treat me in the process. I am also an example now for others who need to learn to do the same.

~~~

Over the last nine months since my Mother died, I have faced most of the major holidays without her. I really tried to personally "space-out" Thanksgiving and Christmas and just dove into work, since I was still at the institution with the girls. In fact, seeing their great need at this difficult time made it easier for me to take my mind off my own grief. For both of the holidays, I had the girls doing lots of arts, crafts, games, cooking and parties all with appropriate themes. For Thanksgiving, we made little decorative baskets full of special trinkets, for which the girls wrote a card describing what each item meant. I then passed these out at a senior center in town. At Christmas time, my coworkers and I held a talent show, a dance contest and a grand party full of festive activities and goodies that the cooking classes made. We were able to raffle off a bunch of presents to the girls. However, these gifts had to be secured for them until their release as very few items are allowed in their rooms.

During my free time at home in December, I was busy pulling my weeds, one by one, which were now knee-high. I know I could've sprayed or mowed, but I wanted to remove each and every one by hand. I told myself that every weed represented something from my past that no longer served me, and by grasping it near the foundation, making sure I got the main root, I would be eradicating it's effect on my life forever. I believed I was clearing out the old to make room for my new lush green landscape to grow. I literally stayed lost in this activity several hours everyday for weeks, and felt great when it finally was done.

For the first time in my life, I didn't really decorate my house for Christmas, although I did hang one strand of outside lights *to not appear like a "scrooge."* Then, I bought this beautiful four-foot Angel covered in white lights, and I placed it in my bedroom to guard me. Also, I didn't create a Southwest-gift-care-package for my family, like I always had in the past. Instead, I bought gift certificates for everyone and sent them with their cards. That was all I could muster of the Holiday Spirit during my first Christmas without Mom. I wrote the following poem after a long day of pulling those weeds, while staying grounded with bare feet and dirty hands, and actually leaving blood, sweat and tears behind:

CHRISTMAS ANGEL: MOM!

Caught, totally in creative flow,
Repeating mantra of random weed pulling;
Hypnotically, while letting myself go,
Listening to sounds of Christmas coming . . .

The air is quiet; the wind's so strong;
The children play while relatives gather;
Christmas eve, all alone with song—
To be with loved ones I would rather . . .

Three months ago today Mom passed,
Thus Christmas, the first without her cheer,
Nor cards, or gifts, or our talks that last,
Now in Spirit form, my new Angel is near!

The year is 2000; the moon is new;
This dark cold night how it stirs up magic;
For love's energy flows strongest and true;
I feel the connection; my life's so dynamic!

Peaceful, grounded with Divine awareness,
I continue, my hands methodically running,
Through Mother earth with total kindness,
As I make room for new growth that's coming!

When I was going through Mom's stack of unused cards to add to my pile, I found a Christmas card she had signed last year but never sent to anyone. It said, "May you remember the true meaning of Christmas, now and throughout the year," and of course there was a picture of baby Jesus on the front. Inside she wrote, "This is my wish too!" **When I read that it was as if this were her card to me this year. I got chills and started crying. "Thank you, God! Thank you Mom!" I wailed aloud, as I felt so touched to have received this, and on Christmas too!**

New Year's eve was not too difficult, but Valentine's Day hurt. I really missed Mom not sending me a card. I reread last year's card over and over, and *felt very lonely*. Just like for my birthday and Christmas, my buddy Dick showed-up with flowers, my favorite bottle of liquor, and a card. This meant the world to me! He knows I've been lonely for a while, and now to be missing my Mom on top of it, he sees how my heart aches even more. I was surprised because I never would have expected him to think of me on this day, so it meant more than the other occasions. He has such a good heart.

Easter was another tough one for me, which I never expected, and I found myself going to services at a Unity church. It was a very emotional time for me, for I knew Mom was crying tears of joy at seeing me there. I choked up a lot, and had trouble controlling my emotions. I felt so raw, and very vulnerable. I found it easy to relate to the Easter theme concerning "rebirth," because that is exactly how I see my life lately. The sermon included a motivational speech on **stepping beyond your limitations-of-mind to follow the path God has intended for you. "How apropos!" I again thought to myself. "Spirit sure is reinforcing my life decision!"**

Mother's Day brought some tears, but it was more difficult listening to all the advertising for two weeks prior. I never noticed this before, and didn't recall paying attention to the Father's Day ads in the past. However, for some reason, everywhere I looked, every TV show and radio station, zapped me with something about Mothers. I had enough already! I tried dodging them, turning them off, looking the other way, and changing the subject. Then finally, it was over. And life went on.

One of the most amazing shifts for me lately, is that my feelings toward Sean have totally transformed. Our relationship has been miraculously healed! There is no more tension or ill feeling. We've even apologized for any pain we may have caused each other in the past. Although he doesn't seem to realize just how much he really did hurt me, he is aware that I had a lot of resentment and respects the fact that I need to tell this story from my perspective. We call each other every holiday now since Mom died, and oftentimes in between "just because," plus, we regularly send each other cards, all of which is new behavior for us. I thank God daily for him and continue to hold him in my prayers, as I do love him very much and greatly appreciate his role in my life.

The next upcoming holiday, Labor Day, may be slightly tough because that was the last time our family was really together, just three weeks prior to Mom's death. This year, however, I will be in Hawaii with my two new friends from the Womanheart retreat, which will greatly help. The writer's conference will be so full of people to meet and information to gather, that it will help take my mind off "the anniversary." Not to mention that **just being in that environment—on the beach with full moon arising—will make my heart sing! I will be in heaven and the Angels will continue to assist with my healing work, per my intention.**

There are still times when *I wish there were more people in my life who care about me.* Deep down I know they will come and I truly do trust this process. I am also grateful for the new friends now standing by me. However, *sometimes I still want more from the people I do meet.* A couple weeks ago I was feeling some growing pains and I prayed to Archangel Michael during a meditation for guidance. The following words came through me while in a trance, and I was deeply moved:

"My Sweet Child, you are experiencing a rebirth of sorts; you are gaining strength of character—for it is time, your Soul is ready. You are being reborn into a world you so deserve. Do not be afraid for we are here to help guide you. Always just tune in to that light and ask, then you will feel my arms wrap around you and my wings take flight to elevate your heart. My Dear One, hear your Eternal Mother's heart beat in you, feel the comfort of that, and know through that we are all connected. You are traveling now through the womb of life. This is a necessary path, one we must all traverse alone. It can seem painful and constricting, especially if one resists. TRUST—trust the movement, feel the dancing of your Soul, see the light of God, and hear how that heartbeat of Eternal Mother guides you through. Just as your birth as an infant was painful, just as you felt so all alone with no connection to humans occurring then, be aware you are feeling those same feelings again, Precious One. Only this time, you are not helpless; you know what to do. You know we are here for you . . .

216

"You are growing up, my Dear Child. It's your beliefs that are hurting you—release them and know: time and distance truly do not matter in regards to the Spirit. Remember this! When someone you care about contacts you, rejoice! If they don't, know that their Soul is busy doing it's missions, working it's issues for growth with God. As in heaven, Angels flutter together and rejoice! Then they move on to help their loved ones as called upon. Your Soul understands this, for you do the same. TRUST—you will connect as needed. Believe—you are ever so deserving of all the love in this world. Finish your book, my Beautiful One, and your birth will be complete, and your bounty will fall. Then you shall understand."

Since these words flowed out of me, I have felt very serene. I feel comforted knowing **I'm where I am supposed to be.** The message felt too real to me, so Divinely directed, and very heart touching. Again, I sit humbled before God, in awe at what I see before me in my life. **I feel the presence of my Angel Guides much more than before—loving me, encouraging me, supporting me, and even making me giggle.** Slowly, my humor is coming back, and more people are finding me funny instead of looking at me strangely. And I recall the burial message from my Mother on that Angel card: Humor!

Recently, I have been reading and hearing about "indigo children." These are kids being born lately who are vibrating at a different Spiritual level. They are somehow gifted, extremely sensitive and know their Soul Path. I feel like I absolutely resonate with "indigo" descriptors. Not only have I seen the changes in children over the 25 years of my career, but also I believe **I am one of the few "older indigos" who have an important message to share.** I have witnessed and am a perfect example of what can happen when indigos are shut off from their feelings and their Truths—death of Spirit! I have always had an uncanny ability to relate to all children at all levels because they can tell I don't play games and I sincerely care about honesty and being "real." So many people deal with the same issues as mine for Soul growth, including abandonment and feeling "different," that I believe I can help shed light on the solutions. **We must follow our hearts and learn to serve in light and love, as we promised God before our birth!** Realizing this lately has helped to remove any old desires I had to die. Moreover, when I heard Doreen Virtue talk about how Souls are lined up in heaven just waiting for a body in order to advance, **something awoke inside of me. I'm now grateful to be here as I'm remembering my Soul agreement with God, which I strive to fulfill.**

I recently had a destiny reading done by Sangeet who runs the Healing Source and Womanheart retreats. She incorporated numerology from yet another perspective, which I found interesting. With knowing very little about me, she said the cycle I'd been in this past year, involved endings, letting go, and finishing up. Contrarily, this next year marks a new beginning, a different life cycle for me, involving endeavors which will carry me through the next decade. Beginning cycles can bring about worry, which she told me to avoid because miracles are right around the corner. The autumn months forward will bring a significant launching of my new goals, plus more fortunate opportunities for me as the last of the past is finally released.

She also told me I had some elevens in my chart, as well as fours, which indicate a very high Spiritual destiny. I found this interesting in light of the stories I told surrounding 11's and 4's in this book. She went on to say that my Spiritual calling has the potential of touching many people's lives. I have a tremendous amount of creativity and energy, which can be directed as a brilliant healing source for others. I just need to be walking the walk, and talking the talk for it to be genuine, effective and in line with my Soul path. I will be creating places for people to find God. I will be using my words and my voice, with charm, to help touch people's Souls. She then comforted me by saying to never doubt my "Path" because help will always be here for me.

I know I have a life-mission to write books and lead seminars that touch peoples' hearts while entertaining them. Additionally, these will motivate them to follow their Soul paths, and inspire them to team up to help affect changes in children's lives. I have a dream of being a successfully published author, and can see the momentum increase as the books flow. I visualize the calls coming as radio and television stations want me to talk about what I do. I can picture more people wanting private sessions with me as a life coach mentor, inspirational book writer, reiki healer, grief work processor, and heart passions explorer. I have a vision of institutions becoming more balanced with creativity, feminine energy and Spirit. I have a mission of seeing people connect and communicate better from the heart, holding hands together with pride as they celebrate their diversity and honor their uniqueness. I have goals to continue treating myself with love and respect, to listen and write about how Spirit speaks, and to reach out to as many people as Spirit so directs, all in Divine timing. And so it is!

This isn't really about ego anymore. In fact, the doubt and insecurities don't come up much anymore, as is evident in the last part of this book. It's not just for my ego that I want to be successful. **It's a burning passion in my heart to help people follow their Spiritual path and learn to live with more love in their lives that needs the success. It's an urge towards doing what I can towards social change that feels congruent to my Soul agreements with God. It's undoubtedly a matter of life or death with me!**

I know I chose all my experiences to help shape my life and give me the training and passion I need to follow my path. Being adopted, for example: I chose that mother to carry me, even though it left me with nightmares—in uterine memories that haunted me most of my life. That subject alone can touch many people's lives if they have any pregnancy issues whatsoever. I also chose to grow up in a relatively "heart-closed" family and social environment. Stories from my life experiences have the potential of helping to open other peoples' heart chakras, if they are so inclined. I have commonalities with recovering Catholics, drug addicts, Spiritually and emotionally sensitive people, hyperactive individuals, and low-esteem-victimized women. I also have years of hands-on experiences with child abuse, multicultural issues, as well as homosexual and female discrimination. I even have the ability to relate to men after years of working in the male institution and learning to become "one of the guys."

I now feel like I've resolved all the issues of my past, even though I'm left with some residual. Just a little reassurance helps me to continue trusting. My new friends are so supportive and aware of this; they are Angels showing me just that. What is beautiful is seeing how they believe in me, and in my work. Soon, I will no longer even question things anymore, **I will simply know as I get used to following my intuition.** It is nice to feel that transition coming on. This poem, and song which I wrote, speaks of Soul memories and Spiritual connectedness, and is dedicated to my new friends:

ANGEL EYES

I have seen your eyes in a thousand faces,
Shining with strength of Spirit, beauty and love,
Representing the wisdom of many fine ages,
And calling to my Soul from a gentle source above.

(Chorus)
And the Angels, put this twinkle in my eyes,
And the Angels, put this song in my heart,
And the Angels, made me tingle deep inside,
And the Angels, made my Soul feel this beat . . .
Soul feel this beat . . .
Soul feel this beat . . .

I have swam across oceans just to be with you,
Seduced by language and culture not my own,
Released from the grips of past beliefs and loves,
Made manifest you—to my heart be known.

(Chorus)
Oh! Angels so giddy and fluttering around,
They speak of great joy in our final recognition,
For many a full moon and splendored event did occur,
To lead our Souls to this lifetime's connection!

(Chorus)
I am that beautiful flower, you see against the wall,
Waiting and praying for you to embrace this chance,
Follow your heart and trust, just reach out your hand,
'Cause with you, my Angel, I'd like to share this dance!

(Chorus)

~~~

I can't believe my Charley is still alive! The vets didn't think she'd last a couple months, much less almost a year now. I have to believe she is a wonderful reflection of my life, like I've expressed before. It is remarkable to remember how I was preparing to deal with her death. I had the body bags. I had the plan of where to dig in my back yard. I had the vet ready to come give her a shot if she seemed to be suffering after she lost her appetite. I had told everyone she didn't have long, and *now I feel bad I had that perception.* We don't ever really know, even though it seemed like I did know with my Mom. Sometimes I think Mom is helping Charley live longer because she knows how much she means to me, plus she wasn't very supportive when Charley was sick at her condo.

She continues to act fine now; she isn't as slow and tired as she had been in the springtime. I even took her on some road trips, something I didn't think I'd ever do again, and she adapted great. No problem with going potty, for the first time in her life, and I was nicely surprised. My new friend Trisha is going to keep the dogs for me while I go to the Hawaiian Spiritual Retreat the end of July, so I've taken them to her place a few times. **Naturally, this is an answer to a prayer on many levels to have her doing this for me.** Charley and Jamey love her house, her little dog, and her backyard. I'm elated that they're comfortable around her! Her energy is so gentle and loving, they just adore her and she doesn't even have to "make over them," like some people try to do.

Trisha has also been amazing at helping me in other ways, too. She has been a main cheerleader through the writing of this book, and is affirming my life-path with me. We have been working on ways to collaborate and assist in each other's dreams, as she is a great healer and leader. I see her as the first of many like-minded adults who want to band together with me to help heal the world. I also am able to give her support in the areas she needs to follow her heart's desires, and she is equally grateful. **Thank you again, God, for yet another prayer has been answered. From the bottom of my heart, I listen to how Spirit speaks, and thus look forward to the rest of my life. . . .**

~~~~

Last Night I Cried

Last night I cried,
Tears of sorrow,
And there you stood,
Eyes filling up with pain,
As you remembered your own grief.

Last night I cried,
Tears of fear,
And there you stood,
Like a pillar of strength,
As you showed me how you believed in me.

Last night I cried,
Tears of joy,
And there you stood,
Laughing with gusto,
As you naturally enjoyed just being with me.

Last night I cried,
Tears of appreciation,
And there you stood,
Validating me again,
As you spoke of undying friendship . . .

And as you told me that you love me.

~~~~

EPILOGUE

July 2003

*T*wo years ago I wrote this story of my journey. That time period now seems so far away it feels surreal. So much has happened and yet so little. . . .

I went to Hawaii, all three times according to my plan. Each trip had many heart touching moments, however the first one, Doreen Virtue's Retreat, was absolutely the best vacation of my life. I could write another book on that alone. Suffice it to say that the miraculous day with the dolphins and whales, literally swimming amongst them off the Kona shore, was the life-altering highlight! After snorkeling through the turquoise surf with pods of spotted, spinner and bottlenose dolphins, we had the rare honor of a "false-killer" whale family-of-three floating with us for several long, breathtaking minutes. Then they slowly submerged lower into the cloudy green depths like submarines, all the while keeping one keen eye on us, until they disappeared from our sight.

Feeling totally satiated with those experiences and therefore expecting nothing more, we headed back to shore. A new friend and I sat on the bow, feet dangling over to feel the splashing water as we rode the waves full-throttle ahead. We were screeching with delight as the rocking ship tickled our tummies and the sea breeze refreshed our sun-scorched skin. The others even teased us about sounding like Meg Ryan in the café scene in "When Harry Met Sally," it was that fun! Suddenly, thousands of spinner dolphins joined us in our glee! They raced alongside the boat, jumping up and dancing in the air for us. I even felt one brush under my foot, and experienced the euphoria of a lifetime. "I get it!" I screamed with tears of ecstasy running down my face as the wind whipped them dry. "Thank you, Mom! Oh, thank you Spirit! I'm here because of you!" I turned to the others exclaiming, "I understand now! When I am totally in the moment and going with the flow, an abundance of joy and love will appear. Just like the dolphins! I need to Trust—that's all! Oh God, thank you!" And ever since that experience, I often reflect back on those <u>exact feelings</u> I had at that moment in my little Hawaiian heaven!

～～～

I actually did go home once more, sooner than expected because Sean and I became Godparents again for Edward and Diana's newest little addition, Sarah! It was after the Hawaii trips at Thanksgiving; it was also the first time I visited my family minus Mom. Sean and I stayed at a hotel, and we all got along beautifully. The atmosphere around our family was peaceful instead of chaotic for once, so I pondered this for a while. Remarkably, baby Sarah resembles our Mother, even though the adoptions would make that biologically impossible. All of us feel that a part of Mom's Spirit is in this child.

Now at a-year-and-a-half, she has a stubborn and headstrong personality, just like Mom! Little James, who just turned four, has reported several times that "Grandma loves me" as if she were just in the room telling him that. And he is the sweetest, most compassionate little boy, as well as extremely smart. Also, Ken, now sixteen, has recently seen an apparition glowing gold in the hallway of their new home, and emitting only love. He often saw Angels as a very young child, too. I told him the vision was one of his Guides, and to strike up a conversation! He has become quite the student of metaphysics and "other" philosophies, which expand his mind. I am touched to have him candidly share his newfound perspectives, and will enjoy watching him explore his gifts for years to come. He even called me for the first time recently to discuss some philosophies! According to Edward, he had told his counselor how I am the only adult with whom he can relate. Bless his heart! He's quite intuitive yet doesn't feel very understood by the people in his immediate world, which is common for many children. I know part of my work will involve helping youth develop their talents, and follow their Spiritual path without getting beaten down by out-dated systems in our society. As well I will help parents become aware of the Spiritual dynamic within their families, and how best to nurture and raise these precious enlightened children!

I have continued to stay close to both Edward's family and Sean. In fact, I absolutely love the relationship I have with Sean now, especially compared to the way it was. We talk often, I can tell him just about anything, and he gives me positive feedback! This is truly a miraculous healing as well! I have to shake my head remembering how I swore I'd never open up to this man.

∾∾∾

I still feel ready to leave Phoenix, however, I have really enjoyed the last couple years living here. My support system has grown tremendously, plus I've made some great networking contacts. The "mirrors" have been very pleasant, and often downright beautiful! I became a substitute teacher while working on my other talents, and have found it extremely rewarding. The principals like me, the teachers need me, and the kids love me. It unexpectedly has helped increase my self-esteem. After experimenting with all age groups, from preschool to eighth grade, I felt drawn to work with the "little ones." After my work with teens, it has been quite healing for me to connect with little hearts again. I'm being reminded why I need to work with youth and what a special skill I have. It's a challenge to step into a new school, classroom, group of kids and schedule almost daily, and have to quickly assess the structure of everything. My ADHD (Attention Divided for Higher Divinity) type personality flourishes in this multi-tasked dynamic! I take great pride in accomplishing all of the teacher's objectives with minimal disturbances within the classroom. I also am blessed to work on Sundays at a new age Science of the Mind Church. I run the nursery and assist the Sunday school while parents are in the service. We then walk the kids onto stage and the congregation sings, "Let there be Peace on Earth!" This just happened to be my favorite song when I was a child attending Catholic Church. All the children I work with now never cease to amaze me with how smart and "knowing" they are. Weekly, I have some child telling me how my hair is shiny like gold, or how my eyes are so blue. I see them seeing me through "other" eyes, and smile while Angels speak through me to respond to them accordingly. Many will often draw me pictures of Angels, or talk to me about seeing Angels, and I feel my heart open with love to these Divine little mirrors!

I have felt, like so many others right now, as though I was put on a "Spiritual-hold" of sorts. It seems like I am just waiting for further instructions and doors to open concerning my "career." Questions of where to be, what to do, and how to do it, all remain up to the Creator. There are possibilities I cannot even fathom yet, so I turn over my dreams to God, and Trust, like they keep reminding me to do. Meanwhile, I have had another Angel, JuliKaye, come into my life. I actually met her right after I quit my job in January of 2001; however, she was one of the people who "seemed to disappear" at that time. She later moved back into town, we ran into each other and quickly became good friends. One year later, we began dating and are currently sharing our lives together. She and her beautiful cat have turned my house into a home filled with love, just like I've been affirming. She has also been wonderfully supportive of my path, as I have been with hers. She painted the triad picture for this book based on my cover drawing, and we have plans to integrate more of our work together. Her vibrantly-colored-Divinely-abstract paintings and channeled-celestial-harmonies on her keyboards are just some examples of her gifts. As well, she is an herbalist and healer, and is assisting me with Charley . . . just as I had been moved once to ask her! And Charley is still my miracle! Almost three years have gone by, and she continues doing wonderfully. Although, she is slowing down a lot, her hips are bothering her, and this scorching hot summer is not easy on her. We have a very close relationship, and she knows it's okay to die whenever she is ready. I don't anticipate her lasting much longer, yet she keeps surprising me. . . .

This morning we were sitting in my backyard watching the hummingbirds dive bomb each other over our little feeder hanging in the mesquite tree. I chuckled aloud thinking how for years I would put out this feeder and attract no birds. Along comes JuliKaye making the "perfect" mixture, and suddenly this tree is full of life! It turns out I was only mixing a tablespoon of sugar instead of a cup with water. I then pictured the birds flying around the neighborhood telling all the other birds to stay away from my house. "There it is," I can hear one little bird chirp, "that's the house where the cheap lady lives! Don't go there!" Now they speak to me of gratitude for putting out more sweetness into the world, and I see how the beauty surrounding me has multiplied as a result!

~~~

The path my book has taken has been quite enlightening for me! I managed to give both Sonia Choquette and Doreen Virtue a copy of my manuscript. Sonia sent it on to her agent and editor, which is a very rare honor, and in turn these people provided valuable input for me! Doreen typically will not accept manuscripts before a publishing contract has been secured, however Angels kept me from learning this fact until I had already given her a copy. After all, I was following my intuition on this! One month later, she sent me a beautiful endorsement, and further advised me not to ever give up, though the times may be difficult on the path ahead. One year later, I met a beautiful Soul, Samone, who just knew she was Spiritually "contracted" to assist me also! Not only did she help me obtain a publishing contract, she spent extensive hours offering constructive editorial reviews. Moreover, she wrote the Foreword and some cover text, plus got her friend Sue to do the beautiful cover! What wonderful blessings I have been receiving in this process thus far, and I gratefully anticipate many more.

As for those tough times, there have been a few. Being patient was the hardest for me. I needed to wait for the right editors and publisher. I needed to wait until I had healed enough to be able to edit my own material; I was too close to it for too long. I had to deal with many people being not able to read it as intended, as well as some negative feedback. Thus, on the path of "going with the flow," I have been learning how to not take things so personally. One day, Archangel Michael comforted me: "My Dear Child, do not worry! Your heavy heart is merely reflecting your doubt. You are on the right track—stay strong! Do not allow others to judge you, pity you, nor conceal your truth. You have the answers; you know the direction. Your book is a special message many need to hear—do not forget this—for there will be those who reinforce that, soon they will thank you for your heart-touching lightwork. You sometimes need to describe the darkness to understand the light. Move forward and do not let others' fears backtrack your work! Know you are being led; your guides are already here. Look—you will recognize the Angels now in your life. More help is on the way, and will be made known to you, as you have requested. Move on with love in your heart, my Sweet Child, for you are being taken care of on another level! Know and Trust this . . ."

I have always requested through meditation that God guide my words from my heart and keep clear my intent to shine heavenly light through any darkness I describe or encounter. My Mother's Spirit was ever-present during this creation, and still is, with her constant blessings and words of encouragement to me: "Kathleen, you write exactly as you experienced things! Do not hold back, for your Truth is as precious as your love; the more you express the more you are blessed! I know that I restricted you when I was alive, and I know you understand that gift in disguise now, yet it is time for us all to speak from the heart and know how very much we are loved! Be a passionate example and use all your God-given talents to show others how to do the same! I know you can do it and I am so very proud of you!"

As time goes on, the wretched grief doesn't hit so hard or as often. Instead, a dull pang resounds in my heart, followed by a warming flow of love. Remarkably, when I think back on my childhood now, mostly good memories surface. I remember having a support system that loved me; as well I recall all the moments where our family laughed. Humor truly is a joyous feeling upon which I focus, thus my memories and current mirrors reflect such. I had to ride out the storm, in order to see the sun. I had to rise like the Phoenix out of the ashes of my past, and did this by listening to Spirit speak to me. And it was well worth the journey! The four greatest gifts I received through the death of my Mother were: a lifetime of healing in just one year's time, a more clearly opened Divine connection, a new will to live with a strong Soul purpose, and a support system to assist me in my Soul growth. And I am now well "On My Way!"

I know that my future also holds much more death with which to deal, as it does for us all. Yet along with this, also goes the gift of rebirth, on the wings of Angels. That which is taken by death, is merely being reborn into a different form of energy. And by allowing our Angels to guide us, we can get by with less fear and worry, and more love and grace. And by learning to tune in to how Spirit speaks, we discover how to truly live!

~~~~

FOOTPRINTS

One night I dreamed I was walking along the beach with the Lord.
Many scenes from my life flashed across the sky.
In each scene I noticed footprints in the sand.
Sometimes there were two sets of footprints.
Other times there was one set of footprints.
This bothered me because I noticed that during the low periods of my life,
When I was suffering from anguish, sorrow, or defeat,
I could see only one set of footprints.
So I said to the Lord,
"You promised me, Lord, that if I followed You,
You would walk with me always.
But I noticed that during the most trying periods of my life,
There has only been one set of prints in the sand.
Why, when I have needed You most, You have not been there for me?"
The Lord replied,
"The times when you have seen only one set of footprints,
is when I carried you."

(By Mary Stevenson)

~~~~

www.ingramcontent.com/pod-product-compliance
Lightning Source LLC
Chambersburg PA
CBHW031249090426
42742CB00007B/372